雅思考官口语

IELTS Speaking

（第三版）

编著：【英】John Burton 【美】Lontee Brinson　贾若寒
审订：【加】朱嘉玮

PROVEN TOOLS TO HELP YOU SCORE HIGHER!

一本全面提升
英文语言能力和口语表达能力的书

上海交通大学出版社
SHANGHAI JIAO TONG UNIVERSITY PRESS

内容提要

　　《雅思考官口语(第三版)》收录了雅思口语真题的常考话题并进行了分类。由于雅思口语考试是题库考,过去几年考过的题目在未来几年中会重复。因此,本书中的题目在之后的雅思考试中也会再次出现。考生在看过本书后会对雅思口语考试的整体框架、提问方式以及回答方式有完整和系统的了解。另外,本书中的所有真题都配备了考官原创答案。考生通过这些答案的学习,可以了解雅思口语考官所希望听到的雅思口语回答方式、风格以及语言特色。除了口语的回答范本之外,书中还对口语答案中的词组搭配和句型进行归纳整理,考生可以从中提升语言运用的能力。

　　本书中的雅思口语真题适用于全球考区,包括中国大陆、亚太、中东、欧洲以及北美等各大考区。

图书在版编目(CIP)数据

　　雅思考官口语／ (英) 约翰·伯顿(John Burton),
(美) 兰提·布林森(Lontee Brinson),贾若寒编著.
—3 版. —上海:上海交通大学出版社,2019(2023 重印)
　　ISBN 978 - 7 - 313 - 21037 - 1

　　Ⅰ. ①雅⋯　Ⅱ. ①约⋯ ②兰⋯ ③贾⋯　Ⅲ. ①
IELTS —口语—自学参考资料　Ⅳ. ①H319.9

　　中国版本图书馆 CIP 数据核字(2019)第 042288 号

雅思考官口语(第三版)

编　　著:［英］John Burton　［美］Lontee Brinson　贾若寒
出版发行:上海交通大学出版社　　　　地　　址:上海市番禺路 951 号
邮政编码:200030　　　　　　　　　　电　　话:021 - 64071208
印　　制:常熟市文化印刷有限公司　　经　　销:全国新华书店
开　　本:787 mm×1092 mm　1/16　　印　　张:20.25
字　　数:484 千字
版　　次:2013 年 8 月第 1 版 2019 年 3 月第 3 版　印　　次:2023 年 8 月第 6 次印刷
书　　号:ISBN 978 - 7 - 313 - 21037 - 1
定　　价:69.00 元

前　言

雅思考试每年在中国大陆有 48 次考试，而雅思口语考试天天都有。如此密集的考试频率导致雅思考试的出题形式为题库考。也就是说，不论是听说读写哪个科目，都有一个题库供每次考试出题选用。

雅思口语每四个月的题库相对稳定，即每年的 1—4 月、5—8 月以及 9—12 月的题库相对稳定。基本上固定是 60 个左右的话题，换季之后会更换其中的 30%。不过，总体而言，大多数话题的内容很相似。因此，备考雅思口语的时候，要充分熟悉雅思口语真题题库中的话题。

本书对雅思口语真题题库进行了分类整理，从中挑出有代表性的话题。先按照考试的流程分成 Part 1、Part 2 和 Part 3。然后每个部分中再按照话题进行分类，做到覆盖真题题库中的难点、重点和热点话题。

除了话题分类之外，书中所有的考试真题均配备考官原创的雅思口语答案。而且，口语答案之后，还附有答案中的好词好句的中英文对照。口语中的词组和句型学习是非常重要的。书中解析的词组和句型适用于各种话题。把这些词组和句型背出来可以使雅思口语答案的水准上升至少两个档次。

词组和句型学好之后，不仅对于雅思口语的分数提升有帮助，而且对雅思写作的语言分数提高也有作用。地道英文的学习绝不能背单个的单词，而是要通过上下文掌握词组搭配和句型。通过本书的学习，考生可以基本具备英文学习的词组搭配意识和句型掌控能力。

考生在学习本书中内容的时候，建议跟着书中的配套音频朗读，练习口语的发音和流利度。这两项在雅思口语评分中占到 50% 的比例。因此，每天不断提升发音和流利度对于雅思口语的分数提高非常有帮助。在跟读的时候，学习回答问题的扣题方式、展开逻辑、衔接手段以及词汇搭配和句型。这样的训练方式对于整体语言能力提高有显著效果。

雅思口语的评分重点是 Part 3。因此，考生对于书中 Part 3 的真题原题、范文以及词汇与句型的学习要投入比其他章节更多的时间。尤其是对于要冲击雅思口语 7.0 及以上的考生来说，Part 3 相关内容的学习是重中之重。

本书为考生从真题、范文、技巧、词汇搭配以及句型表达上提供高水准的学习素材。认真系统学习本书后，相信能达到雅思口语 7 分以上的水平。

目　录

·

第五章　IELTS Speaking Vocabulary

第一章　IELTS Speaking Analysis
雅思口语介绍

第一节　IELTS Speaking Description
雅思口语基本信息

Paper element	Description
Paper format	The Speaking test consists of an oral interview between the test takers and an examiner. All Speaking tests are recorded.
Timing	11 - 14 minutes
Task types	There are three parts to the test and each part fulfils a specific function in terms of interaction pattern, task input, and test takers' output.

第二节　IELTS Speaking in Detail
雅思口语测试流程

Part 1 - Introduction and interview

Task type and format	In this part, the examiner introduces him/herself and checks the test takers' identity. Then the examiner asks the test takers general questions on some familiar topics such as home, family, work, studies, and interests. To ensure consistency, questions are taken from a scripted examiner frame. 考官会向考生进行自我介绍,并核对考生的身份。之后,考官会就考生熟悉的话题(如家庭、工作学习与兴趣习惯)进行询问。为保证题目的一致性,这些问题都是从一个事先拟定的范围内抽取的。 **Part 1 lasts for 4 - 5 minutes.**
Task focus	This part of the test focuses on the test takers' ability to communicate opinions and information on everyday topics and common experiences or situations by answering a range of questions. 考生就日常性的观点和信息、常见的生活经历或情形以回答问题的形式进行交流的能力。
No. of questions	Variable 考官根据考生的能力,问题数量会有所不同

Part 2 - Long turn

Task type and format	Part 2 is the individual long turn. The examiner gives the test takers a task card which asks the test takers to talk about a particular topic，includes points to cover in their talk，and instructs the test takers to explain one aspect of the topic. Test takers are given 1 minute to prepare their talk and are given a pencil and paper to make notes. Using the points on the task card effectively and making notes during the preparation time will help the test takers think of appropriate things to say，structure their talk，and keep talking for 2 minutes. The examiner asks the test takers to talk for 1 to 2 minutes，stops the test takers after 2 minutes，and asks one or two questions on the same topic. 考官会交给考生一个答题任务卡、铅笔和草稿纸做笔记。答题任务卡上会给出一个话题和需要在个人陈述中包含的要点，并在最后提示考生解释这个话题的某一个方面。考生有一分钟的准备时间(如笔记)，然后需就此话题进行 1—2 分钟的陈述。考官会在 2 分钟后打断考生，并在最后提一两个问题作为结束语。 **Part 2 lasts 3 - 4 minutes，including the preparation time.**
Task focus	This part of the test focuses on the test takers' ability to speak at length on a given topic (without further prompts from the examiner)，using appropriate language and organising their ideas coherently. It is likely that the test takers will need to draw on their own experience to complete the long turn. 考生(在没有任何其他提示的情况下)就一个特定的话题进行较长时间陈述的能力，考查考生是否能恰当地运用语言、是否能连贯地组织自己的观点。考生有可能需要联系自己的经历来完成这部分内容。
No. of questions	Variable 考官会给一道 Part 2 考题和 1—2 个收尾问题

Part 3 - Discussion

Task type and format	In Part 3，the examiner and the test takers discuss issues related to the topic in Part 2 in a more general and abstract way and — where appropriate — in greater depth. 考官将与考生就第二部分中出现的话题较为抽象的部分进行双向讨论。 **Part 3 lasts 4 - 5 minutes.**
Task focus	This part of the test focuses on the test takers' ability to express and justify opinions and to analyse，discuss and speculate about issues. 考生表达和论述看法、分析、讨论以及深入思考问题的能力。
No. of questions	Variable 考官根据考生的能力，问题数量会有所不同

第三节　IELTS Speaking — How it's marked
雅思口语评分标准

Marking Criteria 评分标准

Fluency and Coherence（流利和连贯）

This criterion refers to the ability to talk with normal levels of continuity，rate，and effort and to link ideas and language together to form coherent，connected speech. The key indicators of fluency are speech rate and speech continuity. The key indicators of coherence are logical sequencing of sentences，clear marking of stages in a discussion，narration or argument，and the use of cohesive devices（e. g. connectors，pronouns and conjunctions）within and between sentences.

流利是指语速和语言连续性。连贯是指句子之间以及句子内部的逻辑顺序，讨论、叙述和论证的阶段层次递进以及连接手段（包含连词、代词和过渡词）的使用。

Lexical Resource（词汇资源）

This criterion refers to the range of vocabulary the test takers can use and the precision with which meanings and attitudes can be expressed. The key indicators are the variety of words used，the adequacy and appropriacy of the words used，and the ability to circumlocute（get around a vocabulary gap by using other words）with or without noticeable hesitation.

词汇测试学生使用词汇的广度和准确度，以及使用其他词汇解释他们所不知道的词汇的能力。

Grammatical Range and Accuracy（语法多样性和准确性）

This criterion refers to the range and the accurate and appropriate use of the test takers' grammatical resource. The key indicators of grammatical range are the length and complexity of the spoken sentences，the appropriate use of subordinate clauses，and the range of sentence structures，especially to move elements around for information focus. The key indicators of grammatical accuracy are the number of grammatical errors in a given amount of speech and the communicative effect of error.

语法主要测试考生语法的多样性和准确性，包括句子的长度和复杂度，使用从句的能力以及句子结构的多样性。考官最关键的是看考生一定语言量中的语法错误数量以及语法错误对沟通理解的影响程度。

Pronunciation（发音）

This criterion refers to the ability to produce comprehensible speech to fulfil the Speaking test requirements. The key indicators will be the amount of strain caused to the listener，the amount of the speech which is unintelligible，and the noticeability of L1 influence.

发音主要是看考生的发音对考官的理解造成的影响，有多少内容是考官无法听懂的以及母语对英文发音的影响程度。

雅思口语评分表(英文版)

Band	Fluency and coherence	Lexical resource	Grammatical range and accuracy	Pronunciation
9	• speaks fluently with only rare repetition or self-correction; • any hesitation is content-related rather than to find words or grammar • speaks coherently with fully appropriate cohesive features develops topics fully and appropriately	• uses vocabulary with full flexibility and precision in all topics • uses idiomatic language naturally and accurately	• uses a full range of structures naturally and appropriately • produces consistently accurate structures apart from "slips" characteristic of native speaker speech	• uses a full range of pronunciation features with precision and subtlety • sustains flexible use of features throughout • is effortless to understand
8	• speaks fluently with only occasional repetition or self-correction; hesitation is usually content-related and only rarely to search for language • develops topics coherently and appropriately	• uses a wide vocabulary resource readily and flexibly to convey precise meaning • uses less common and idiomatic vocabulary skilfully, with occasional inaccuracies • uses paraphrase effectively as required	• uses a wide range of structures flexibly • produces a majority of error-free sentences with only very occasional inappropriacies or basic/non-systematic errors	• uses a wide range of pronunciation features • sustains flexible use of features, with only occasional lapses • is easy to understand throughout; L1 accent has minimal effect on intelligibility
7	• speaks at length without noticeable effort or loss of coherence • may demonstrate language-related hesitation at times, or some repetition and/or self-correction • uses a range of connectives and discourse markers with some flexibility	• uses vocabulary resource flexibly to discuss a variety of topics • uses some less common and idiomatic vocabulary and shows some awareness of style and collocation, with some inappropriate choices • uses paraphrase effectively	• uses a range of complex structures with some flexibility • frequently produces error-free sentences, though some grammatical mistakes persist	• shows all the positive features of Band 6 and some, but not all, of the positive features of Band 8

（续表）

Band	Fluency and coherence	Lexical resource	Grammatical range and accuracy	Pronunciation
6	• is willing to speak at length，though may lose coherence at times duc to occasional repetition，self-correction or hesitation • uses a range of connectives and discourse markers but not always appropriately	• has a wide enough vocabulary to discuss topics at length and make meaning clear in spite of inappropriacies • generally paraphrases successfully	• uses a mix of simple and complex structures，but with limited flexibility • may make frequent mistakes with complex structures though these rarely cause comprehension problems	• uses a range of pronunciation features with mixed control • shows some effective usc of features but this is not sustained • can generally be understood throughout，though mispronunciation of individual words or sounds reduces clarity at times
5	• usually maintains flow of speech but uses repetition，self correction and/or slow speech to keep going • may over-use certain connectives and discourse markers • produces simple speech fluently，but more complex communication causes fluency problems	• manages to talk about familiar and unfamiliar topics but uses vocabulary with limited flexibility • attempts to use paraphrase but with mixed success	• produces basic sentence forms with reasonable accuracy • uses a limited range of more complex structures，but these usually contain errors and may cause some comprehension problems	• shows all the positive features of Band 4 and some，but not all，of the positive features of Band 6
4	• cannot respond without noticeable pauses and may speak slowly，with frequent repetition and self-correction • links basic sentences but with repetitious use of simple connectives and some breakdowns in coherence	• is able to talk about familiar topics but can only convey basic meaning on unfamiliar topics and makes frequent errors in word choice • rarely attempts paraphrase	• produces basic sentence forms and some correct simple sentences but subordinate structures are rare • errors are frequent and may lead to misunderstanding	• uses a limited range of pronunciation features • attempts to control features but lapses are frequent • mispronunciations are frequent and cause some difficulty for the listener

(续表)

Band	Fluency and coherence	Lexical resource	Grammatical range and accuracy	Pronunciation
3	• speaks with long pauses • has limited ability to link simple sentences • gives only simple responses and is frequently unable to convey basic message	• uses simple vocabulary to convey personal information • has insufficient vocabulary for less familiar topics	• attempts basic sentence forms but with limited success, or relies on apparently memorised utterances • makes numerous errors except in memorised expressions	shows some of the features of Band 2 and some, but not all, of the positive features of Band 4
2	• pauses lengthily before most words • little communication possible	only produces isolated words or memorised utterances	cannot produce basic sentence forms	Speech is often unintelligible
1	• no communication possible • no rateable language			
0	• does not attend			

雅思口语评分表(中文版)

得分	流利度与连贯性	词汇资源	语法结构的多样性和准确性	发音
9	说话时极少有重复或自我更正,偶尔的停顿也是由于在思考内容,而非搜寻合适的词汇和语法;发言连贯,语言中上下文流畅,联系自然而充分;全面而得体地围绕话题展开内容	面对任何话题都能灵活、准确地使用词汇;**自然、准确的地道英文**	自然、准确地使用**多样化的语法结构**;语法结构的使用**自始至终保持准确**,虽然偶尔犯一些英语为母语者也会犯的"口误"	灵活运用精确的语音交谈,很容易理解所表达的含义
8	说话时很少有重复或自我更正,偶尔的停顿也多是由于在思考内容,极少情况下是为了搜寻合适的语言;连贯而得体地围绕话题展开内容	能自然、灵活地使用多样词汇来准确表达思想,尽管偶尔有不准确;能按要求有效使用同一语言的其他表达方式	灵活使用多种结构;大部分语句无误,极偶尔情况下出现错误,或个别简单错误	易于理解,母语语音对英语的影响极小;使用多种语音手段来有效达意
7	能充分展开,且**不会有刻意思考的痕迹**,没有语言上的不连贯;能较灵活地使用**连接词**或语言中的信号词;有时出现由于语言水平而带来的重复或自我更正	能灵活使用词汇讨论多种话题;对**语体和搭配**有所了解,尽管有时不准确;能有效使用同一语言的其他表达方式	较灵活地使用多种复杂结构;多数语句无误,但有些错误一直存在	**发音自然**,偶尔出现发音错误,考官已经开始享受与你交谈的过程

(续表)

得分	流利度与连贯性	词汇资源	语法结构的多样性和准确性	发音
6	有充分交流的意识,但有时由于**重复、自我更正或停顿而导致说话不连贯**;能使用**连接词**或语言中的**信号词**,尽管有时不准确	有足够的词汇来充分讨论话题,清晰达意,尽管有不准确;**大致可使用同一语言的其他表达方式**	**能使用简单和复杂结构,但缺乏灵活性;复杂结构经常出现错误**,尽管这些错误很少导致交流障碍	自始至终可以被理解,尽管发音错误偶尔有一点费解
5	通常能维持语流,但需要通过重复、自我更正或放慢语速才能实现流畅;能流畅表达简单语言,复杂语言会导致语言不畅	能讨论相关话题,但词汇使用缺乏灵活性;尝试使用同一语言的其他表达方式,但未必都能成功	能使用基本的句子结构,且使用基本正确;复杂结构的使用有限,且通常包含错误,有时导致交流障碍	可听懂所说的内容,个别地方需要仔细分辨才能听懂
4	回答时有明显停顿,语速可能较慢,时常有重复、自我更正;能把基本句连接起来,但重复使用某些简单连接词,语意上多有不连贯之处	词汇的选择上时常犯错;很少尝试使用同一语言的其他表达方式	能使用基本的句子结构;错误频繁,可能导致误解;	可以发出某些语音,但总体较差,给听者带来严重理解困难
3	发言时停顿过长;连接简单句的能力有限;只给简单答复,时常难以表达基本想法	使用简单语言表达个人信息;词汇匮乏	明显背诵事先准备的语言;句子表达中错误很多(背过的表达除外)	能发出某些语音,语言经常无法识别
2	说大多数词前都要长时间地思考停顿;最简单基本的交流	只能说只言片语或事先背过的语言	不能使用基本的句子形式	语言经常无法识别
1	无法交流,语言无法评估			
0	缺席考试			

第四节 IELTS Speaking Tips
雅思口语应试技巧

IELTS Speaking Part 1 — Dos and Don'ts 雅思口语第一部分技巧

Do ♯ 1 - Know What to Expect 了解考官提问前的流程
You will probably be a little nervous and you don't want any surprises that will make you even more anxious，so you must be aware of exactly what will happen when you walk into the room.

Before Part 1 begins，four things will happen.

The examiners will introduce themselves and ask you what your name is. You can simply reply "My name's _____". Make sure that you use the contraction "name's" rather than "name is". This will remind you to use contractions (e. g. I'm, We'd, they'll) in the rest of the test.

The examiner will then ask you "What can I call you?". You can simply say "You can call me _____". If you have an English name, it is fine to use it, but make sure that you pronounce it correctly. If you can't say your own name properly, it does not create the best first impression. If unsure, just use your normal name.

They will then ask you where you are from. Simply state "I'm from _____". There is no need for you to give any extra information about your answers at this stage.

The examiner will finally ask to see your identification. Show it to them and then the test can begin.

By knowing these four things will happen, you will be more confident and start the exam well.

Do ♯ 2 - Create a Good First Impression 给考官良好的第一印象

My students often ask me, if they smile, are friendly, and give the examiner good eye contact, will they get a higher mark? The answer is no and yes.

There is nothing in the marking criteria which says that being nice, or looking the examiner in the eye will improve your grade. However, being confident helps you because it will have an effect on your answers.

If you look at the floor and give the impression that you would rather be anywhere in the world apart from in the room with the examiner, you will normally give very short monotone answers and this will lower your score.

However, if you are open and friendly with the examiner, you are more likely to give natural sounding answers.

Don't overdo the eye-contact thing. It feels really strange when someone looks at you straight in the eye for 15 minutes. Pretend that you are having a normal conversation with a friend. If you were looking at the floor the entire time, a friend would ask you if you were OK. If you were staring them dead in the eye, they would get a bit freaked out.

Pretend it is just a normal conversation and you will be fine.

Do ♯ 3 - Pretend You're Interested in the Questions 假装你对问题感兴趣

Let's face it. Most IELTS questions are really boring. If you listen to someone answer a boring question, you will notice one thing — their voice is monotone i. e. it does not go up or down in pitch at all; it sounds very flat. If you speak like this, you will get a lower mark for pronunciation because one of the crucial factors you will be tested on is intonation.

When native English speakers talk, their voice naturally falls and rises depending on how they feel about what they are saying.

Imagine you are late for class, you walk into the room, and the teacher says to you in a falling tone "Sit down, please." They are probably telling you, through their intonation, that they are not very happy with your lack of punctuality. However, if they said it with a rising tone at the start, they would probably be telling you they don't mind that you are late and are happy to see you.

Similarly, if you pretend that you are interested in what the examiner is saying, your intonation should become more varied. However, be careful not to overdo it and make your voice really high, or really low because you will sound like a crazy person.

Listening to native speakers talk and copying their intonation will give you a good idea of what natural intonation sounds like.

Do ♯ 4 - *Extend Your Answers* 扩展你的答案(给出更多细节)
There is no set amount of words or sentences that you should use in Part 1.

They shouldn't be too short because you want to show the examiner that you can actually use English, so "I'm a student." is not really long enough.

However, they should not be too long either, because Part 1 is about familiar topics (family, work, hobbies etc.) and you don't normally talk for 2 minutes when someone asks you where you are from. Also, you will have lots of opportunities to give longer answers in Parts 2 and 3.

As a general rule, if you only give a single sentence answer, with a single clause like "I'm from Ireland.", then your answer is too short. I also don't think Part 1 answers should ever have more than three sentences. Somewhere in between is just right.

Do ♯ 5 - *Practice* 不断练习(最好要录音并回听)
It is a very bad idea to prepare memorised answers before your speaking test, but because Part 1 is very predictable, you should practice the familiar topics mentioned above in number one.

Try recording yourself and then listen back and think about the following：

Don't # 1 - Give Yes/No Answers(不要只给出 Yes/No 的回答)
This might sound obvious，but you would be surprised how many people simply answer with "Yes" or "No." This is probably because many of the questions would naturally lead to a yes or no answer，but you must remember that you are in a test and you have to show the examiner how good your English is.

Giving yes or no answers does not allow the examiner to judge your ability and you will get a low mark no matter how good your English is.

Some people give yes or no answers because they are very nervous and they want the test to be over as soon as possible. The examiner is not there to trick you and most of them are nice people who want you to do your best，so don't be afraid to tell them you are a little nervous and this will normally relieve the tension.

Don't # 2 - Go Off Topic(不要跑题)
Some students try to tell you their life story or the entire history of their hometown when you ask about their name and where they are from. Remember that these are very simple questions and if you give more than 3 - 4 sentences，you are probably giving irrelevant details.

For example，I recently asked a girl what she did in her free time and she told me everything there was to know about badminton. However，I did not ask about the rules， history，great players，pros and cons of the sport. I only wanted to know just which sport she liked and why.

Don't # 3 - Give No Answer(不要冷场不说话)
You don't get to choose the question and if you don't know the answer to a question，or you simply don't like the question，you don't have a choice — you must answer it.

Remember that Part 1 is about YOU. There will be no question you don't understand because they will all be about you.

If you don't understand one word in a question，it is acceptable to ask the examiner to explain what that one word means. It is also acceptable to ask the examiner to repeat the question if you didn't quite understand what they said. However，do not abuse this privilege and use it for every question；only use it when absolutely necessary.

If you really have no idea，be honest with the examiner and tell them you don't really know and then have a guess. Since it is a test of your English and not an examination of your knowledge，it is perfectly acceptable to make something up when you are stuck.

Don't ♯ 4 - Speak Very Quietly（不要说话声音太轻）
This is one of the most annoying things for the examiner because no matter how good your English is，if we can't hear you，we can't give you a high score.

This has a lot to do with confidence and shyness. Make sure that you are not talking to the floor and speak a little louder than normally. The examiner will also be recording the test，so it has to be loud enough for the recording device to pick up your voice.

Try recording yourself and play it back. If you can't hear yourself clearly then you need to increase the volume of your voice a little more.

Don't ♯ 5 - Be a Perfectionist（不要完美主义）
The examiner knows that you are speaking in a non-native language and does not expect perfection. Even people who get a 9 make small mistakes，and people who get Band 7 and 8 make quite a few mistakes.

If you are constantly thinking about using the perfect grammar and vocabulary，it will reduce your fluency and pronunciation. Fluency and pronunciation make up 50% of your marks，so there is no point in trying to use perfect grammar and vocabulary，if you are losing half your marks in the process.

Speak as naturally as possible，with a focus on speaking at a natural speed and clear pronunciation，and the grammar and vocabulary will look after itself.

IELTS Speaking Part 2 雅思口语第二部分技巧

1. *You Don't Have to Talk About Every Bullet Point*（可以根据题卡上的四个小问题回答，也可以不完全回答所有的四个小问题，细节见下文）

In the Official Marking Criteria for the Speaking Test，there is nothing that states that you have to talk about every bullet point. Lots of IELTS examiners know this，but they don't tell students because they don't want to give them an unfair advantage.

You will always be given a general topic at the start of the test and then "You should say:" followed by 3 - 4 bullet points. The rule is that you must talk about the general topic at the top of the card，but you don't have to talk about all of the bullet points. Note that it says "You should say" and not "You must say".

The bullet points are there to help you, so if you want to talk about them, please do. However, if there are one or two that you don't like or you don't feel comfortable talking about, leave them out and talk about something else. Just make sure what you talk about is within the general topic and you will be fine.

2. *Preparation* (充分准备雅思口语第二部分的话题,但不要背答案)

They say practice makes perfect and this is very true for IELTS Speaking.

Don't memorise answers. There are too many topics for you to memorise and it is highly unlikely that you will get the same topic in the real test. It is a complete waste of time and leads to some very strange answers. If the examiner spots this, they are allowed to give you a Band 0!

Focus on fluency and pronunciation. Record yourself and listen to yourself. How could you improve your fluency and pronunciation?

Learn functional language used to describe common grammar functions, such as talking about the past, present or future, giving your opinion, evaluating someone's opinion, and talking hypothetically.

Time yourself so you know how much you have to speak in 2 minutes.

3. *Use 1 Minute Wisely* 充分利用雅思口语第二部分考试中 1 分钟准备时间

You will have one minute to prepare before you start talking. You will not have enough time to write full sentences. You will, however, be able to write down keywords. These keywords should guide you through your talk and will be helpful if you can't think of ideas.

Having a strategy will also help you because you will know exactly what to talk about and you will be able to make a clear plan using short notes and keywords.

4. *Personal Experiences are Best* (*but telling a lie is OK too*) (最好用真实的个人经历来回答,但是编个故事也可以)

The best answers are always about things you have actually experienced in your life. You will be able to describe these things in much more detail and you will also be able to talk more coherently about them. Students tend to be more confident talking about real experiences and this helps them with their fluency and pronunciation.

However，some of the cue cards will ask you to talk about things you might not have experienced at all in your entire life. It is fine to lie. The examiner will never check your answers or worry about whether they are the truth or not. However，they might ask you some follow-up questions，so be prepared for these.

In my experience，the best strategy is to use real experiences first and add in some lies to help you answer the question fully. Use your imagination and you will be fine.

5. *Expand Your Ideas*（利用 5Ws 扩展细节内容）

It is much better to fully expand each main idea than to simply state lots of main ideas and not develop them at all. This will help you give more impressive answers and it is also a better use of your time. It is much easier to think of a few relevant ideas and develop them than it is to think of lots of different ideas.

When you are practicing，a good way to expand your main ideas is to use "Who，what，why，where，how". This will help you develop your main ideas quickly and easily and you will also get used to the grammar structures needed to do this.

You can also use your senses to help you use a wide range of vocabulary. Think about how things looked，sounded，smelled，and tasted. You obviously won't be able to talk about all of these things for every topic（you would sound a little strange describing how a book tasted）but you will normally be able to use two or three of them. While practicing，you can use a dictionary to help you describe these sensations and expand your vocabulary.

6. *Mistakes are OK*（犯语法词汇错误不要紧张，继续往下说）

Everyone makes grammar and vocabulary mistakes. Every time I make a new video，it takes me longer to edit out the mistakes than it does to record the video. Even students who get a Band 8，or even 9，make small mistakes. This is totally understandable and you should therefore not panic when you make a mistake.

I have listened to students who were half way through their Part 2 question and then they made a small grammatical error and they completely lost their way and their score went from a very high one to an average one.

Being nervous and stressed affects your ideas，pronunciation，fluency and normally leads to further grammar mistakes. When you make a mistake，simply forget about it. There is nothing you can do. Don't panic and continue.

IELTS Speaking Part 3 雅思口语第三部分技巧

1. *Don't try to finish quickly* (不要期望速战速决,要给出丰富内容的回答)

Speaking for up to 15 minutes in a foreign language is tiring. You might not have slept the night before, you are stressed, and you might have also completed other tests that day. In short, you will be exhausted and your body will want you to take it home and tuck it into bed as quickly as possible.

Lots of students give very short answers because they simply want their test to be over as soon as possible. Know that the examiner will keep asking you questions (and the next ones will probably be more difficult), so it is much better to give a full answer and answer the question to the best of your ability, than to simply give a short answer and hope that it ends quickly.

2. *Know that the examiner is trying to stretch you* (了解考官在雅思口语第三部分会故意问一些你很难回答的问题)

Part 1 is really just a warm-up and Part 2 is a monologue, so Part 3 is the examiner's chance to really test you and stretch your language abilities to the very limit. The main thing to remember is that they will ask you questions you won't be able to answer as well as you hoped. They will often increase the difficulty until you can't answer the question. They are not trying to be cruel. This is just the best way for them to test your knowledge of grammatical structures and vocabulary.

Think about a personal trainer or athletics coach forcing an athlete to perform more and more strenuous exercises to judge their true ability.

If you know this is going to happen, you will not get stressed out and you will answer the questions more confidently and get higher scores.

3. *Don't be afraid to ask questions* (听不懂问题,可以问考官,但是只能让考官解释其中某个词的意思,而且这个特权只能使用一两次)

There will be words in some questions that you don't understand. The rule is that you can ask the examiner to explain what one word means, but you can't ask them to explain what a whole sentence means.

You can also ask them to repeat the question, if you didn't quite get what they said.

Please don't abuse this privilege and try to use it for every question.

4. *Always give an answer*（不要冷场，一定要回答问题）

There will be at least one question that you have no idea how to answer. Don't worry，this is normal — see point number one. The most important thing to do is to at least make an attempt to answer. You have been speaking for 15 minutes and one question is not going to lower your mark for the whole test. However，the worst thing you can do is to simply not attempt an answer. If you have this mindset，then you won't push yourself to the limit of your abilities.

It is also fine to admit that you have no idea. Simply say "I'm really not sure about this question，but if I had to answer，I would say . . ." The examiner will be much happier that you attempted an answer，rather than just saying "I don't know" or looking at them blankly（which happens more than you would think）.

You can also give yourself time to think about the question by saying "That is a difficult question，just give me a second to think about that." or "I've never thought about that，to be honest. Give me a moment." However，don't do this for every question，only use it for the ones you actually need to think about.

5. *Think about what structure the examiner is testing.*（注意语法结构多样性）

The examiner needs to know that you are capable of using a wide range of structures. Don't worry about inserting as many structures as possible into your answers because they will ask you specific questions to test specific grammar structures.

第二章　IELTS Speaking Part 1 Questions and Sample Answers 雅思口语 Part 1 真题和范文

第一节　雅思口语 Part 1 核心技巧

核心技巧 1

直接回答考官的问题,再说原因或者例子。如果没有直接回答问题而直接说例子会被认为逻辑混乱而失分。

核心技巧 2

举例法是雅思口语第一部分的重要应用技能。当你无话可说的时候记住要举例子,例子尽可能详细,但是记住例子要围绕话题,不能跑题,否则考官认为你逻辑混乱或者认为你背过答案在胡编乱造。

核心技巧 3

保持适当的紧张度,但是不能过于紧张而口齿不清造成失分。

核心技巧 4

一开始语速尽量保持正常,不能过快也不能过慢,口齿一定要清晰!

核心技巧 5

进考场之前把本书中的真题和相关的例子看熟,在候考室内脑子里再过一遍,对于考试的信息提升有极大帮助。

核心技巧 6

要注意和考官亲切自然地交流,语言一定要有节奏和语调!

核心技巧 7

回答考官的每个问题时候尽量多说,因为你多说了考官问题就少了。

核心技巧 8

当你什么都讲不出的时候运用"5Ws"原则，寻找 what，when，where，who，why 这些元素来回答问题。

第二节 雅思口语 Part 1 个人信息类 话题真题及范文

1. Names 名字

考试原题和范文

Do you like your name?

【Sample Answer】 Yeah，I'm perfectly happy with my name. I think it suits me，it sounds nice，and probably most importantly，it's got a good meaning. So yeah，I like it a lot.

Have you ever considered changing your name?

【Sample Answer】 No I haven't，and it's never even crossed my mind，mainly because I think it would be a bit disrespectful towards my parents，who put a lot of time and effort into choosing it for me.

How did your parents choose your name?

【Sample Answer】 To be honest，I'm not sure how they chose it；I've never asked them. I suppose it was just a name that they both liked，and maybe they thought it suited me.

Does your name have any special meaning?

【Sample Answer】 It might do，but I don't know what that meaning is；I've never looked it up. Maybe I'll google it later today；you've made me curious to find out.

Is your name common or unusual in your country?

【Sample Answer】 Yes，it's quite a common name. I remember that there were two other people with the same name as me in my class at school.

词汇和句型

I'm perfectly happy with my name 我对我的名字很满意
it suits me 这个名字很适合我
it sounds nice 这个名字听起来不错
it's never even crossed my mind 我从来没想过这个
mainly because 主要是因为
a bit disrespectful towards my parents 有点不尊敬我的父母

put a lot of time and effort into choosing it for me   花了很多时间为我起名字
To be honest   说实话
I'm not sure how they chose it   我不知道我的父母是怎么为我起名的
I suppose   我觉得
it was just a name that they both liked   这是一个他们都喜欢的名字
suited me   适合我
I don't know what that meaning is   我不知道具体的含义
I've never looked it up   我从来没有在词典中查过我名字的含义
I'll google it later today   我今天晚些时候会上网查一下

2. Major 专业

考试原题和范文

Is your major a very popular subject to study in your country?
【Sample Answer】
(*If yes*):
Yeah，I suppose it is quite a popular subject to study，and one of the reasons for this would probably be that a lot of students feel that this major will be useful in helping them find a good job after they graduate.
(*If no*):
I guess I probably wouldn't say so，no，mainly because it's a relatively new major in China，and as far as I know，there are not that many universities in China which offer this course.

Is your major very challenging (or difficult) to study?
【Sample Answer】
(*If yes*):
Yeah，I'd say it is quite challenging，mainly because of the huge workload we get. So for example，we're given a considerable amount of coursework to do，which always requires a ton of background reading.
(*If no*):
Actually，I wouldn't really say so，partly because we're not given that much work to do，and also because it's essentially not that complex (a major)，so everything's relatively easy to understand.

What do you do when you have a difficulty with your studies?
【Sample Answer】   I guess I normally either ask a coursemate for help or go on the Internet to try and solve the problem myself. And if I'm still stuck，then I'll go and ask my lecturer for help，but this would be as a last resort，as I don't really like to bother my lecturers unless I really need to.

How did you learn science at school?

【Sample Answer】　We mainly just went through the textbooks and took notes, so it was pretty similar to other subjects. Though saying that, we occasionally did some experiments, which were quite fun, but unfortunately those classes were pretty few and far between.

Why did you choose _____ as your major?

【Sample Answer】　Basically it was due to the fact that my parents thought it was a useful major which would stand me in good stead after I graduate. Personally, I'm not so sure, but seeing as I couldn't think of anything better, I went with my parents' decision.

What do you like about your major?

【Sample Answer】　That's a good question, and I guess basically the thing I find most enjoyable about my major is analyzing case studies of various international companies operating in China, because for me, stories are the best way to learn things. And as well as this, I also like the fact that our lectures are quite interactive, because we are encouraged to ask questions instead of just sitting and taking notes, and this tends to make the lectures much more interesting.

What's more important when studying — the student or teacher?

【Sample Answer】　It's really hard to say, because obviously both play an important role, but I guess I'd say the student is probably more important because generally speaking, most studying is done outside of the classroom — at least that's the way I see it.

词汇和句型

I suppose　我觉得

one of the reasons for this would probably be that ...　其中的一个原因可能是⋯⋯

a lot of students feel　很多学生觉得

find a good job after they graduate　他们毕业后找到好工作

I guess I probably wouldn't say so　我觉得我可能不这样认为

mainly because　主要是因为

it's a relatively new major　这是个相对比较新的专业

as far as I know　据我所知

there are not that many universities in China which offer this course　在中国并没有很多大学开设这个课程

it is quite challenging　这个专业非常有挑战性

mainly because of the huge workload we get　主要是因为我们的(课业)负担很重

a considerable amount of coursework　大量的课程作业

requires a ton of background reading　需要有巨大的背景阅读量

Actually, I wouldn't really say so　事实上,我并不这样认为

partly because ... and also because ...　其中一部分原因是,另一部分原因是……

we're not given that much work to do　老师并没有布置我们很多作业

it's essentially not that complex（a major）　这基本上不是一个复杂的专业

everything's relatively easy to understand　所有的东西都相对比较容易理解

I guess　我觉得

ask a coursemate for help　向学友寻求帮助

go on the Internet to try and solve the problem myself　上网尝试自己解决问题

if I'm still stuck　如果我还是不懂

I'll go and ask my lecturer for help　我会去向我的讲师(指大学老师)寻求帮助

a last resort　最后一着,最后的办法

I don't really like to bother my lecturers　我不太想要打扰我的老师

unless I really need to　除非我真的需要这样做

went through the textbooks　通读课本

it was pretty similar to other subjects　这和其他科目很相似

Though saying that　尽管这样说

we occasionally did some experiments　我们偶尔做一些实验

quite fun　非常有乐趣

those classes were pretty few and far between　那些课程很少而且间隔时间很长

Basically it was due to the fact that ...　主要是因为……

stand me in good stead　对我有利

seeing as I couldn't think of anything better，I went with my parents' decision　鉴于我想不到更好的专业,我就遵照我父母的决定了。

I guess basically the thing I find most enjoyable about my major is ...　我觉得基本上我最喜欢我专业的方面是……

and as well as this　除此之外

our lectures are quite interactive　我们的老师上课很有互动性

we are encouraged to ask questions instead of just sitting and taking notes　老师鼓励我们提问题而不是坐着记笔记

because obviously both play an important role　因为很明显两者都很重要

but I guess I'd say ...　但是我觉得……

because generally speaking　因为总体而言

at least that's the way I see it　最起码我是这样认为的

3. First Day at School/Work 第一天上学/工作

考试原题和范文

Could you tell me your first day at school?

【Sample Answer】　Yes. I remember that my first day at school was exciting. My teachers were nice and friendly；my classmates said hi to one another. One thing I remember clearly was that my math teacher taught us arithmetic，which was one plus one equals two. In addition，we had a PE lesson，in which I played football with my fellow students.

Could you tell me your first day at college?

【Sample Answer】　Yes. My first day at college impressed me a lot. That was the first day when I lived away from my parents. I had to be accustomed to the totally new campus environment. Fortunately，my college teachers were very helpful. They guided me on how to get to the lecture hall and assisted me to get rid of the nervousness.

Could you tell me your first day when you started to work?

【Sample Answer】　Yes. On the first day of work，I felt enthusiastic. In fact，the office atmosphere cheered me up. I had to be used to the challenging working demand and get along well with my colleagues.

词汇和句型

first day at school　第一天上学
One thing I remember clearly was that ...　我记得很清楚的一件事是······
my fellow students　我的同学们
impressed me a lot　让我印象很深刻
That was the first day when I lived away from my parents.　那是我离开父母生活的第一天
guided me how to get to the lecture hall　告诉我去听课的路线
assisted me to get rid of the nervousness　让我放松下来
cheered me up　让我振作起来
be used to the challenging working demand　习惯有挑战性的工作要求
get along well with my colleagues　和我的同事愉快共事

第三节　雅思口语 Part 1 兴趣爱好类话题真题及范文

1. Reading 看书

考试原题和范文

What kinds of books do you like to read?

【Sample Answer】　I'd say I like reading quite a variety of books，both fiction as well as nonfiction. So for example，I'm a big fan of detective novels，because I enjoy trying to solve the crimes while I'm reading，although I have to admit I'm pretty useless at it most of the time. And as for nonfiction stuff，I'd say I mostly like reading things like self-help books and biographies of people I admire，such as the book about Steve Jobs.

Are you reading any books at the moment?

【Sample Answer】 Yeah，I'm actually halfway through a couple of books right now. One of them's a novel which a friend of mine lent me，and the other is a book related to business，which I bought about a year ago，but didn't get round to reading until now.

词汇和句型

I'd say 我觉得

quite a variety of books 各种各样的书

fiction 小说

nonfiction 非小说

detective novel 侦探小说

self-help books 励志书籍

biographies 传记

I'm actually halfway through a couple of books 我正在同时看两本书

didn't get round to reading until now 到现在才开始看

2. Watching TV 看电视

考试原题和范文

Do you like watching TV?

【Sample Answer】 Yeah，I'd say I like watching TV quite a lot，and I'm actually a bit of a TV addict. There's just so much stuff on TV these days，a lot of which is surprisingly good，not like in the past when there was virtually nothing worth watching.

How much time do you spend watching TV?

【Sample Answer】 If I'm going to be totally honest，I spend a pretty ridiculous amount of time in front of the television，probably something like 3 or 4 hours a day or so. But then again，thinking about it，I guess that's actually quite normal.

What kinds of TV programs do you like watching?

【Sample Answer】 I'd say I like quite a variety of stuff，like TV series, chat shows, talent shows and dating shows. And actually I'd say dating shows are probably my favorite right now，because they're just really entertaining.

Do you prefer watching TV alone or with others?

【Sample Answer】 To be honest I don't really think there's that big a difference，but I guess I'd say my preference would probably be watching TV with others，because it's always nice to have some company，especially if there's a scary program on.

Do you prefer the TV or radio?

【Sample Answer】 Without a doubt, I much prefer watching TV, simply because TV programs on the whole are far more entertaining than radio programs. I also find that radio stations tend to play the same songs over and over again, which can be quite tiresome.

词汇和句型

I'd say 我觉得

quite a lot 非常

I'm actually a bit of a TV addict 我看电视真的有点上瘾

surprisingly good 非常好

virtually nothing 几乎没有东西

a pretty ridiculous amount of time 相当多的时间

something like 3 or 4 hours a day or so 差不多每天 3—4 小时左右

TV series 电视剧

chat shows 访谈节目

talent shows 才艺秀

dating shows 相亲节目

To be honest 说实话

I don't really think there's that big a difference 我不觉得有很大区别

have some company 有人陪伴

Without a doubt 毫无疑问

I much prefer 我很喜欢

simply because 主要是因为

on the whole 总的来说

over and over again 一次又一次

3. Dancing 跳舞

考试原题和范文

Do you like dancing?

【Sample Answer】 It's ok I suppose, but I wouldn't say I particularly like it, because I'm not very good at it, and I prefer to just listen to music instead of dancing to it.

Would you like to learn dancing in the future?

【Sample Answer】 I suppose it would be quite nice to learn dancing such as Latin dancing, which looks pretty cool when it's done well. And also if I took some classes, I wouldn't embarrass myself every time I got onto the dance floor. So yeah, I guess it is something that I'd quite like to do at some stage in the future, although I don't know if it will ever actually materialize.

Where do Chinese people like to go dancing?

【Sample Answer】　I suppose one of the most popular places to go is an outdoor square，where you'll often see people doing line-dancing there，especially in the early morning or evening.

Did you like dancing when you were a child?

【Sample Answer】　I did actually quite like dancing, and I think probably the reason was that I wasn't at all self-conscious when I danced，which I am now. So I mean，as a child，I wasn't really preoccupied with how I looked in front of others，so that made dancing a lot more enjoyable.

When was the last time you danced?

【Sample Answer】　It was ages ago. I honestly can't remember. I suppose it must have been，like，two or three years ago，but that's a complete guess，because it's just been such a long time.

词汇和句型

I wouldn't say I particularly like it　我觉得不是特别喜欢

dancing to it　随着音乐起舞

dance floor　舞池

actually materialize　真正实现

an outdoor square　一个户外的广场

be preoccupied with　一心想着······

4. Painting 绘画

考试原题和范文

Are you very interested in art?

【Sample Answer】　Yes，I am. I think art's great. I mean，I've always enjoyed looking at good drawings and paintings，and I've actually got a few up on my walls at home which I drew myself.

Have you ever painted before?

【Sample Answer】　Yeah，for sure I have. But the last time I painted anything was absolutely ages ago. I mean，I seem to remember doing quite a lot of painting when I was in kindergarten and primary school，but since then，I'd say I've done pretty much no painting at all.

Is painting（art）important for adults?

【Sample Answer】　No，I don't think it's important for them，quite simply because most adults don't have that much time on their hands，so they're probably better off doing something which is less time-consuming and more related to their work or study，like reading.

Is painting (art) important for children?

【Sample Answer】 I guess it is，yeah，because I mean，in a way，it helps develop children's creativity and imagination. And I think it's pretty safe to say that these two things are an important aspect of a child's education.

词汇和句型

I've actually got a few up on my walls at home which I drew myself 我把一些我自己画的画挂在家里的墙上

ages ago 很久以前

quite simply because 主要是因为

don't have that much time on their hands 手头上没有很多时间

better off doing ... 最好是做······

develop children's creativity and imagination 提升儿童的创造力和想象力

it's pretty safe to say that 可以这样说

5. Swimming 游泳

考试原题和范文

Do you like swimming?

【Sample Answer】 Yes，I do. Swimming is definitely my favorite sport. It brings me such a great sense of freedom that no other activity can allow me to have. I've found that swimming is the most effective way to take my mind off the things that are currently troubling me.

Is swimming good for children?

【Sample Answer】 Yes，it is. Children can benefit greatly from this activity. For one thing，swimming is one of the best ways for them to stay healthy and keep fit. For another，being able to swim from an early age can help save many lives from drowning accidents every year，which happen more frequently among children than adults.

Should swimming be a compulsory activity for children at school?

【Sample Answer】 I do think it's extremely useful for schools to include swimming in their curriculum so that drowning risks can be reduced. But whether or not it should be made mandatory is a different story. Some schools simply can't afford to provide proper swimming lessons for their students.

词汇和句型

definitely my favorite sport 绝对是我最喜欢的运动

a great sense of freedom 极大的自由感

take my mind off the things that are currently troubling me 使我思想上摆脱正让我烦恼的事情

stay healthy and keep fit 保持健康

drowning accidents 溺水事故

in their curriculum 在他们的课程安排中

drowning risks 溺水风险

mandatory 强制的,必修的

6. Sports 体育

考试原题和范文

What sports do you like?

【Sample Answer】 I like almost all kinds of sports, one of which is football. This sport is prevalent in every country. For example, England Premier League is so popular in China and other Asian countries that young people like me would watch every game broadcast live on TV. Another sport I prefer to play and watch is basketball. On weekends or after school, I would like to play basketball with my classmates because this game would not only relieve stress but also improve teamwork spirit. If there are NBA games broadcast on TV or on the Internet, I always watch those fantastic games because there are the best basketball players in NBA.

What sports would you like to learn?

【Sample Answer】 I would like to learn tennis if I had the chance. I have many tennis idols such as Serena Williams and Maria Sharapova. They are not only physically attractive but also mentally strong-willed. Although they are females, they are persistent in training. Sometimes they got injured, but they still participated in games. After watching them play the WTA tennis tour games, I have the incentive to learn the sport.

Do you like watching sports games live or on TV?

【Sample Answer】 I like watching sports on TV because I don't need to pay the admission fee and I could see the game in better detail on TV. The ticket price of sports games is quite high, especially some world-class games played by top athletes. In China, most sports games are broadcast live on TV, so if I stay at home to watch some live sports on TV, it would save me a lot of money. So that's the main reason why I prefer to watch games on TV. In addition, TV broadcast would use different cameras in a sports game, which means that I could see the specific actions or skills in a game clearly. That's why I like TV sports.

词汇和句型

prevalent in every country 在每个国家都很受欢迎

England Premier League 英超联赛

broadcast live on TV 在电视上直播

relieve stress 缓解压力

improve teamwork spirit 提升团队精神

have the incentive to learn the sport 有学这项运动的动力

the admission fee 入场费

world-class games 世界级的比赛

top athletes 顶尖运动员

7. Music 音乐

考试原题和范文

What music is suitable for children?

【Sample Answer】 I think it's probably fair to say that more or less all music is，even classical music，because although kids might not fully appreciate it，they can still enjoy it，and it's even been said that listening to composers like Mozart can make them smarter. So I would basically say that as long as a song's lyrics don't contain any inappropriate language，then it's suitable for children to listen to.

What's the difference between listening to a CD and going to a concert?

【Sample Answer】 I'd say it's huge. I mean，it's a completely different experience altogether，because listening to a CD is purely an audio experience，whereas in contrast，going to a concert，you get the visual side too.

What kinds of songs do children like listening to?

【Sample Answer】 Based on what I remember from my own childhood，I would say most kids tend to like listening to short，simple songs that have catchy tunes and memorable lyrics，and I suppose a lot of them are the theme songs to their favorite cartoons.

Do you often sing?

【Sample Answer】

（*If no*）:

No，I don't really sing that often，probably only something like once every two or three months，because I'm not that good at it. I find it quite hard to sing in tune.

（*If yes*）:

Yeah，I go singing quite a lot actually，probably about two or three times a month or so，because a lot of my friends like going to sing songs，and they often call me up and ask me to go with them.

Are your friends all good at singing?

【Sample Answer】 I'd say some of them aren't that bad at all，but most them are pretty average，and I'm glad they can't hear me say that.

词汇和句型

it's probably fair to say that 可以这样说

classical music 古典音乐

it's even been said that 据说

make them smarter 使他们更聪明

as long as 只要

a song's lyrics 一首歌的歌词

purely an audio experience 完全是声音的体验

whereas in contrast 但是相对比而言

I would say 我觉得

catchy tunes 容易记住的旋律

memorable lyrics 容易记住的歌词

theme songs 主题歌

sing in tune 唱歌不跑调

pretty average 很一般

8. Movies 电影

考试原题和范文

What kind of movie do you like?

【Sample Answer】 The kind of movie I like is action comedy. The reason I like action comedy movie is that it does not contain too much violence. Instead，it has some funny action scenes，from which I can relieve the stress from work and study，and feel totally relaxed.

How often do you watch a movie?

【Sample Answer】 I watch a movie almost once a week. Every weekend，I go to a cinema to watch a popular movie. If I am very tired and don't want to hang out，I would download a movie and see it on TV.

Is it easy for you to watch a movie?

【Sample Answer】 Yes. It is easy for me to watch a movie because there is a cinema close to where I live，and it is open from 9 in the morning to 11 in the evening so I can go there to watch a movie almost any time. Of course，in China，downloading a movie to watch is not illegal so I could do that without hesitation.

What are the differences between watching a movie on TV and watching a movie in the cinema?

【Sample Answer】　There are two differences. The first difference is the screen size，which is much bigger in the cinema. So the atmosphere is totally different. The second difference is that in the cinema，you can't talk to others，whereas you are free to talk about whatever you want if you watch a movie on TV at home.

词汇和句型

action comedy　动作喜剧

don't want to hang out　不想出去逛

without hesitation　毫不犹豫

9. Celebrities 名人

考试原题和范文

Who is your favorite celebrity in China?

【Sample Answer】　My favorite celebrity in China is，without a doubt，Jackie Chan，who is not only a world-famous movie superstar but also a person who always actively participates in charity work on a global scale. I like him because whenever he produces a movie，he devotes 100% of his energy to the movie production. That's why he has billions of fans all over the world. As a celebrity，he uses his influence to help the people in need. He went to a nursing home to see elderly people in Shanghai months ago，which is why many young people will follow his example. He is a role model for the young people because of his integrity，professionalism，and optimistic attitude. One more thing I would like to mention is that he was honored the Governors Award，which recognized his contributions to the movie industry. So Jackie Chan is my favorite celebrity in China

Do you like any foreign celebrities?

【Sample Answer】　Yes. There are many foreign famous people I like，one of whom is Matt Damon，who acted as Jason Bourne in the series movie. I have read the novel of The Bourne Identity. Matt Damon played the role to the full extent. I regard Matt Damon as Jason Bourne after watching the movie of Jason Bourne. Another celebrity I like is Adele，whose songs are extremely popular with people of all ages. Jackie Chan even sings the song "*Rolling in the Deep*" in the movie *Skiptrace*，which indicates the wide influence of Adele and her songs.

Would you want to be a celebrity in the future?

【Sample Answer】　Yes，I would love to be a famous person in the future because for one thing，being famous means social recognition. If what I do is accepted by the society，I would feel a sense of accomplishment even if I don't make much money. Another thing is that being a celebrity could bring me connections with other famous people so it's easier for me to do more projects.

Do you think we should protect famous people's privacy?

【Sample Answer】 Yes. The privacy of famous people should definitely be protected. In order to make money，the paparazzi of tabloid newspapers and magazines take photos of celebrities，which severely interferes with the lives of those people. So we should leave celebrities some private space. The journalists should not disturb the family of the famous people. Otherwise，conflicts may occur between famous people and journalists.

How do celebrities influence their fans in China?

【Sample Answer】 Celebrities influence their fans both in positive ways and in negative ways. On the positive side，celebrities could do some charity jobs to motivate their fans to follow their lead. As for the negative aspect，fans would do some undesirable things because their idols perform illegal or morally unacceptable actions. For example，some young people take drugs just because their idol has done the same thing.

词汇和句型
without a doubt　毫无疑问
Jackie Chan　成龙
charity work　慈善工作
a nursing home　养老院
a role model　榜样
integrity　正直
social recognition　社会认可
the paparazzi　狗仔队
severely interferes with the lives of those people　严重干扰那些人的生活
do some undesirable things　做一些不好的事情

第四节　雅思口语 Part 1 心理及行为类话题真题及范文

1. Time Management 时间管理

考试原题和范文

Are you good at organizing time?

【Sample Answer】

If yes:

Yeah，I'd say I'm actually not too bad at it actually. I mean，I always get my work done on time, and I always manage to set aside a bit of time each day to do exercise, like going for a jog or something. So I'd say I'm pretty organized in terms of my time.

If no:

No, to be honest with you, I'm pretty bad at it. I don't normally write much down, and I don't spend that much time organizing what I need to do. I just live each day as it comes. So I guess it's something I need to get better at.

How do you usually organize your time?

【Sample Answer】

I mainly organize it by using the calendar App on my phone, because I can put all my appointments and things onto it. And whenever I need to check something, I can just look at my phone. So I find it extremely helpful, and ever since I started using it, I've been a lot more organized.

Do you think planning is important for time management?

【Sample Answer】

Yeah, most certainly. I think planning is important for anything, and time management is no exception, because if you don't plan your time, how can you manage it? So I think they go hand-in-hand.

Why do you think some people pay to learn time management?

【Sample Answer】

I guess for some people, it's extremely important. For them, time is money, and if they don't manage their time efficiently, they won't be earning as much as they could. So they figure that if they pay an expert to help them manage their time well, then in the long run, they're gonna earn more money. So I guess you could say it's a kind of investment.

Do you think children should learn to manage time?

【Sample Answer】

Yeah, I actually think it's a really useful thing for them to learn, and in fact, a lot more useful than many other things they're taught at school. If they learn how to manage their time at an early age, then it's gonna help them throughout their life. So I think it's a very good idea to do this.

Why do some people find it hard to follow their plans?

【Sample Answer】

I guess there could be a number of reasons depending on the person. I mean, off the top of my head, one possible reason could be that some people make unrealistic plans, which are very hard to follow through on. For example, someone might plan to spend two hours a day at the gym, or practicing their English, but in reality, it might be quite difficult to do, especially for a long time. So this would be one reason, and I suppose another reason would be that people have bad habits which are difficult to break out of. Like for me, I spend a lot of time reading the sports news, which is not really a very productive thing to do. And that time could be better spent doing other things, which I'm very aware of, but I still do it. So I think these ingrained habits prevent many people from carrying out their plans.

How would you teach your children time management?
【Sample Answer】
Sample 1:
That's an interesting question, and I guess probably the way I would teach them would be to set a good example for them, in terms of how I manage my own time. So for example, I would show them my calendar and how I update it, so they can see how it's done, and then hopefully do something similar themselves.
Sample 2:
I would encourage them to get into the habit of doing something immediately, instead of putting it off to another time. For example, if they were given some homework with a one-week deadline, I would encourage them to do it straight away instead of leaving it to the last moment.

Do old people and young people manage their time in a similar way?
【Sample Answer】 It's really hard to generalize, I think, but on the whole, I'd say they don't really, no. I mean, young people mainly manage their time based on their studies and work. That's what their day revolves around — it's the focus of their day. So that could be managing their time based on their homework, on their class timetable and working hours. And for older people, it's basically just free time they're managing. So their plans, I guess, are more flexible, and not so detailed. I think it's probably fair to say that young people use technology to manage their time, such as using APPs on their mobile phone, whereas I guess the majority of old people just write down their plans in a calendar or something like that.

词汇和句型
I'd say I'm actually not too bad at it actually.　我觉得我在这方面还算不错。
get my work done on time　准时完成工作
set aside a bit of time　留出一些时间
like going for a jog or something　比如慢跑之类的
to be honest with you　跟你说实话
calendar App on my phone　手机上的日历应用
look at my phone　看手机
extremely helpful　很有帮助

be no exception　不例外

go hand-in-hand　密不可分，紧密相关

extremely important　非常重要

they won't be earning as much as they could　他们会赚不到他们本可以赚到的钱

in the long run　长期而言

really useful thing　非常有用的东西

at an early age　很小的时候

I guess　我觉得

off the top of my head　不假思索马上能想到的

make unrealistic plans　制定不切实际的计划

at the gym　在健身房健身

in reality　实际上

So this would be one reason　所以这可能是原因之一

I suppose another reason would be that ...　我觉得另外一个原因是……

ingrained habits　根深蒂固的习惯

set a good example for them　为他们树立个好榜样

do it straight away　立即就做

It's really hard to generalize.　真的很难概括

but on the whole　但是总体而言

the majority of old people　大多数老年人

2. Concentration 注意力

考试原题和范文

How do you concentrate on doing things?

【Sample Answer】 I have a variety of ways to concentrate on doing things. The first method is that I would stay in a quiet place where nobody could disturb me. Another way is that I would do one thing for a consecutive amount of time so that I can focus on it.

Is it difficult to concentrate on something?

【Sample Answer】 Yes. It is very difficult to pay attention to something because people would always distract me when I'm doing things and it is always noisy around in where I live. So it's not easy to focus on doing things.

What is the importance of concentration?

【Sample Answer】 Concentration is very important because if you want to be an expert，you have to be superior to others，which means that you have to focus on one thing for a long time. Otherwise，you could only know the superficial aspect of a matter.

词汇和句型

a variety of ways 各种方法

a consecutive amount of time 连续的一段时间

be superior to others 比别人优秀

3. Helping Others 帮助别人

考试原题和范文

Do you like helping people?

【Sample Answer】 Yes，I like helping people who are in need. For example，when my classmates have some trouble with solving math or physics problems，I would offer them a helping hand. When I saw them happy after we overcame the academic obstacles together，I felt happy as well. Also，if I find a stranger who needs assistance on the street，I would help him or her. I suppose people are anxious when they come across difficulties. I can gain a sense of satisfaction if I can help them deal with the trouble.

How did you help people?

【Sample Answer】 I helped people in many ways. In some cases，I gave people financial aid. For example，I donated money to charitable organizations to help the children in poverty-stricken areas. I also did some volunteer jobs in the local community to take care of the elderly and disabled people. The most common way is that I helped my classmates with their homework and helped strangers find their ways.

词汇和句型

offer them a helping hand 帮他们

come across difficulties 碰到困难

a sense of satisfaction 满足感

donated money to charitable organizations 把钱捐给慈善组织

help the children in poverty-stricken areas 帮助贫困地区的儿童

take care of the elderly and disabled people 照料老年人和残疾人

4. Being Polite 礼貌

考试原题和范文

Do you think people should be polite?

【Sample Answer】 Yes，sure. Politeness is a basic virtue that every person must acquire. Being well-mannered may not get you straight to the highest position at work within one day，but it will bring you respect，trust，and kindness from others，which are beneficial for you in the long run.

How do people in your culture show good manners towards others?

【Sample Answer】 Good manners can be shown through a wide range of acts in our culture. For example，when we run into people who are older than us like our parents，grandparents，or our university lecturers，we say hi and bow our head to show our respect towards them. Additionally，when we talk to them，we use certain pronouns and words to indicate the age gap between us.

Who taught you to be polite?

【Sample Answer】 I guess similar to most people，I was raised to be a polite person by my parents. As I spent most of my time around them，they tried to set good examples for me. They also gave me advice and told me moral stories about how being polite and kind to others can help me in my life.

词汇和句型

a basic virtue 基本的品德
Being well-mannered 有礼貌
in the long run 长期而言
a wide range of 各种各样的
run into 遇见，碰到
bow our head 低头，点头
show our respect towards them 对他们表示尊敬
age gap 年龄差
set good examples for me 为我树立榜样

5. Being Punctual 守时

考试原题和范文

Is it important to be punctual?

【Sample Answer】 I would say it is very important because people hate waiting. For example，if I am late to class，the professor will get annoyed and it can affect my grades.

Are you a punctual person?

【Sample Answer】 I would have to say I am punctual. I always show up 10 minutes early to class and I arrive early when I meet my friends too.

What do you think if your friends are always late?

【Sample Answer】 I really can't stand it when my friends arc always late. Sometimes it's ok，but when I have something planned and they are late，it drives me nuts.

How do you feel when you are late?

【Sample Answer】   I actually get upset. For example，if the bus is running late，I tend to get anxious and think of other ways to get to where I am going to.

词汇和句型

affect my grades   影响我的分数
show up 10 minutes early to class   提前十分钟去上课
can't stand it   不能忍受
it drives me nuts   这要把我逼疯了
get upset   感到心烦意乱
the bus is running late   公交车晚了
get anxious   开始焦虑,担心

6. Being in a Hurry 匆忙

考试原题和范文

When was the last time you did something in a hurry?

【Sample Answer】   I guess it was probably a few weeks ago，when I was on holiday，and I had booked a taxi to arrive at my hotel at around noon，but I still had some clearing up to do. I didn't want to leave the place in a mess，so I was basically in a hurry try to finish tidying everything up and packing before the taxi arrived.

What kinds of things do you never do in a hurry?

【Sample Answer】   I suppose things I would never do in a hurry would be important things，like coursework which counts towards my final grade，and getting to the airport to catch a flight. I'll always give myself lots of time to get there，even if it means I may arrive at the airport several hours in advance，because it gives me a peace of mind. I mean，if you miss a flight，then your holiday's probably gone down the drain，so it can be pretty disastrous.

词汇和句型

on holiday   度假
booked a taxi   预定了一辆出租车
I still had some clearing up to do   我还有一些打扫工作要做
leave the place in a mess   让这个地方很乱
coursework which counts towards my final grade   影响我最终分数的课程作业
several hours in advance   提前几小时
it gives me a peace of mind   这让我心情很放松
your holiday's probably gone down the drain   你的假期可能会泡汤了

第五节 雅思口语 Part 1 日常生活类 话题真题及范文

1. Clothes 衣服

考试原题和范文

What kind of clothes do you like wearing?

【Sample Answer】 On the whole，I usually like wearing casual clothing，most of which is pretty plain and simple，nothing too fancy. And I guess the main reason for this is that I find casual clothing a lot more comfortable to wear than formal clothes like suits.

Do you think it's a good idea to let students design their school uniforms?

【Sample Answer】 Yeah，I'd say it is，because young people are generally quite creative，and after all，they are the ones who have to wear the uniforms all day long. So yeah，I reckon it's a brilliant idea.

词汇和句型

On the whole 总的来说

casual clothing 休闲服饰

pretty plain and simple 非常朴素简单

too fancy 太花哨

I guess the main reason for this is that ... 我觉得主要原因是……

formal clothes 正装

quite creative 比较有创造力

after all 毕竟

all day long 一整天

I reckon 我觉得

it's a brilliant idea 这是个好主意

2. Shoes 鞋子

考试原题和范文

What kind of shoes do you like?

【Sample Answer】 The kind of shoes I like is sports shoes because I'm a super big fan of different kinds of sports. When I play basketball or football，I always wear sports shoes from Nike or Adidas because I think it is comfortable and it can help me avoid some injuries.

What is your favorite pair of shoes?

【Sample Answer】　My favorite pair of shoes is Nike Air. I bought that pair of shoes two years ago and I wore the shoes often to play sports. To my surprise, this pair of shoes has not been worn out and it still has good flexibility and durability. So I like this pair of shoes a lot.

Do you like shopping for shoes?

【Sample Answer】　It's ok I suppose, but it's not something I especially enjoy doing. For me it's just a matter of finding the right shoes and buying them, and the faster I can get it done, the better.

What kinds of shoes do you usually buy?

【Sample Answer】　The shoes I normally buy are just plain, simple walking shoes, because that's all I really need. Occasionally, I also buy trainers for running.

Do you prefer comfortable shoes or good-looking shoes?

【Sample Answer】

I like comfortable shoes because I walk a lot every day on campus, trying to get to different classrooms or labs. If I wear fashionable shoes, they look good but I can't bear the pain of walking long distances.

词汇和句型

sports shoes　运动鞋

avoid some injuries　避免受伤

good flexibility and durability　很柔韧和耐穿

It's ok I suppose　我觉得还行吧

but it's not something I especially enjoy doing　但这不是我特别喜欢做的事情

the faster I can get it done, the better　越快做完越好

trainers　（英式英语-运动鞋,美式英语为 sneakers）

3. Hats 帽子

考试原题和范文

Do you like wearing hats?

【Sample Answer】　No, definitely not. It is not comfortable to wear a hat when I'm in a subway train or walking on the street because the air flow is not smooth in the hat. Besides, my hair would be in an awkward shape when I take off the hat. Also, if I wear a hat in a public place, people around me would look at me, especially if I am in a crowded place. And it would be burning hot if I wear a hat in summer.

What kinds of hats do you like?

【Sample Answer】　While I don't like wearing hats，I prefer certain kinds of hats. One type of hats that I like are baseball caps because when a person wears a baseball cap，he or she looks energetic. It is suitable for young people to wear a baseball cap，a T-shirt，and a pair of jeans. That's the best fit. Another type of hats I like are motorcycle helmets，which look cool if a person wears one while riding a motorcycle.

Where do people buy hats?

【Sample Answer】　People purchase hats in department stores，online stores，and hats outlets. But these days most people shop hats online. Amazon and eBay are the most popular means for people to buy hats. After comparing the prices and reading the reviews，customers are free to make their decision about the style，color，and price that they want. So online stores are where most people choose to buy hats.

Is it popular for people to wear hats in your country?

【Sample Answer】　No，only a minority of people wear hats in China. Most people don't have the habit of wearing hats. But in the northern and southern parts of China，some people would choose to wear fur hats or sun hats in order to protect themselves from the extreme weather. Other people may wear hats for the purpose of showing fashionable styles. Overall，wearing hats is not popular in my country.

词汇和句型

when I'm in a subway train　当我在地铁车厢里

walking on the street　走在街上

air flow is not smooth　气流不通畅

in an awkward shape　造型很奇怪

take off the hat　脱掉帽子

burning hot　非常热

While I don't like wearing hats，I prefer certain kinds of hats.　尽管我不喜欢戴帽子，但我还是喜欢某些类型的帽子的。

baseball caps　棒球帽

looks energetic　看起来有活力

the best fit　最佳搭配

motorcycle helmets　摩托车头盔

online stores　在线商店

hats outlets　帽子专卖店

reading the reviews　看一下评论

only a minority of people　只有少部分人

fur hats　毛皮帽子

sun hats　阔边遮阳帽

4. Bags 包

词汇和句型

Do you carry a bag when you go out?

【Sample Answer】 Yes. In most cases, I carry a bag when I have some business to do because I have to bring a lot of things with me. My standard configuration when I leave the house is to have a smartphone, a wallet, a Kindle, or an iPad and most importantly, a Macbook Air. Without a bag, it's impossible for me to carry all these things to different places. One more thing I would mention is that a bag provides extra storage space. I mean if I want to buy some books or snacks, I would not need to worry about what I will use to take those things home. Additionally, a bag can be regarded as a stylish accessory. So I always carry a bag when I have something to do outside.

What kind of bags do you like?

【Sample Answer】 I really like handbags, and by handbags I mean the fashionable leather ones made in Italy or France. These bags are not only tools but also works of art. Gucci bags are a good example. Gucci handbags are made of full-grain leather, raw python skin and maybe even crocodile skin. So the texture is terrific. And the handles are made from bamboos, which will not be deformed after years of use. Prada bags are another example of these kinds of bags that combine the best design with high quality. These kinds of bag make me stand out whenever and wherever I use them. And they are able to withstand the test of time. That's why I like fashionable leather handbags.

Do you prefer the quality or the style of the bags?

【Sample Answer】 I prefer the style of the bags because if you use an ugly bag, you will not feel comfortable about it. Quality is a crucial factor as well. But if I had to choose one from these two factors, I would say style is more important because it is associated with a person's personality and preference.

Lots of people like to buy luxury bags. What do you think about it?

【Sample Answer】 If people don't have financial problems, it is reasonable for them to buy luxury bags. From my perspective, luxury bags indicate superior quality and refined design. They are indeed worth their prices. Most people would say luxury bags are too expensive and would not be willing to spend 1,000 or 2,000 Euros on a Louis Vuitton bag. But in the long run, they will realize that the bag is worth the money because it will not wear out soon and the style will not be out of fashion. So I always recommend my friends to buy luxury bags as long as they don't have budget problems.

词汇和句型

In most cases 在大多数情况下

carry a bag　拎着一个包
standard configuration　标准配置
One more thing I would mention is that ...　另外一个我要说的事情是……
stylish accessory　时髦的配饰
fashionable leather ones　时尚的真皮手袋
works of art　艺术品
full-grain leather　全粒面皮革
raw python skin　蟒蛇皮
crocodile skin　鳄鱼皮
the texture is terrific　质地很棒
handles　包把手
will not be deformed　不会变形
combine the best design with high quality　把最好的设计和高质量结合起来
withstand the test of time　经得起时间的考验
a crucial factor　重要因素
luxury bags　奢侈品包包
superior quality　优等的品质
refined design　精致的设计
worth their prices　物有所值
in the long run　长期而言
wear out　用坏
be out of fashion　过时
budget problems　预算问题

5. Watches 手表

考试原题和范文

Do you wear a watch?

【Sample Answer】

Yeah，I do. I always wear a watch，and I think it's the best way to keep track of time. I mean，it just saves you the trouble of always having to get your cell phone out to see the time，and if my phone's run out of battery，then having a watch is especially handy.

What was your first watch like?

【Sample Answer】 If I remember correctly，it was a Swatch. I think that was the brand，and it was an indestructible Swiss watch geared towards children，and there was nothing special about it，no bells and whistles. It just had a simple clock face with an hour hand and a minute hand.

Have you received a watch as a gift before?

【Sample Answer】

Yeah I have. Several times actually, usually as a birthday present, and they've all been really nice. So I guess I'm pretty lucky.

What kind of watches do you like to wear?

【Sample Answer】 I suppose basically just watches which look nice, because I mean, no one wants to wear something that they don't think looks good on them. So for me, I prefer wearing analogue watches. I think they generally look a bit classier than digital watches. I also like metal straps, as I think they're easier to put on and take off. I have had leather straps before and I found them a bit fiddly to use.

Why do you think some people like to wear expensive watches?

【Sample Answer】 Maybe it's to impress people, because it's a kind of reflection of your wealth and success. So that's a possible reason, and another one may simply be that wearing a nice watch makes them feel good and confident.

词汇和句型

keep track of the time　了解时间

it just saves you the trouble of always having to get your cell phone out to see the time　不用每次很麻烦地用手机查时间

run out of power / battery　没电了

especially handy　特别方便

indestructible Swiss watch　耐用的瑞士手表

geared towards　以……为用户群的,面向……市场的

bells and whistles　不必要的额外功能

simple clock face　简洁的表面

an hour hand and a minute hand　时针和分针

analogue watches　指针手表

digital watches　数码手表

metal straps　金属表带

they're easier to put on and take off　(金属表带)更容易带上和脱掉

leather straps　真皮表带

look a bit classier　看起来更有品位一点

a bit fiddly to use　用起来有点麻烦

it's a kind of reflection of your wealth and success　这可能会反应你的财富和成功吧

another one may simply be that ...　另外一个理由可能是……

6. Jewelry 珠宝

考试原题和范文

Do you like wearing jewelry?

【Sample Answer】

Sample 1:

Yes. I wear jewelry every day. I have two rings that I never take off，and I also wear other jewelry for special occasions. I think that jewelry can really enhance or compliment an outfit so I am all for wearing it.

Sample 2:

Actually I don't wear jewelry，because I am a male and it's not very socially accepted. I also have no desire to wear jewelry because I don't have much money and spending it on necklaces wouldn't be a good use of my cash.

Sample 3:

No. I don't ever use jewelry because I often forget to take them off when I'm going to take a bath（mostly bracelets）and break them. I also don't like those shiny accessories because they just make you stand out too much. I also think jewelry can make you look too extra if not used right. There is also a higher risk of being mugged or robbed，which is really dangerous.

Sample 4:

Yes，I particularly love jewelry. I always wear rings，earrings，bracelets，and necklaces. I like silver，gold，and also handmade jewelry. I wear earrings daily and I cannot leave the house without earrings. Lately I'm wearing small earrings，but sometimes I like to wear larger ones. Overall，I think that jewelry enhances our beauty.

How often do you wear jewelry?

【Sample Answer】

Sample 1:

Every day. I have nice earrings，so it is natural for me to wear them. I also wear my great aunt's ring，as she gave it to me just before she moved away，and it reminds me of her. However，I think my glasses are my best accessory,as they frame my face and make it look less square-ish.

Sample 2:

I wear jewelry on a regular basis，but it is not like I wear heavy jewelry everyday. For instance，I wear light weighted and elegant gemstones studs in the office，but for parties，I wear heavy jewelry such as gold，diamond necklace etc. As far as I am concerned，jewelry is important to enhance my look，and this is why I use it quite often.

On what occasion do you wear jewelry?

【Sample Answer】　There is no occasion where jewelry is more fitting than that of a wedding, particularly a winter wedding. Pearl earrings or a striking necklace are the perfect accompaniment to any wedding dress and will elevate your wedding outfit to a whole new level. Additionally, needless to say, you need to make a positive first impression when attending a job interview and nothing exudes more elegance and sophistication than jewelry. As the old saying goes, "you don't get a second chance to make a first impression" and you won't need any second chances if you turn up to your interview wearing a stylish bracelet or an understated and sophisticated necklace.

Which do you prefer to wear, a ring or a necklace?

【Sample Answer】

Sample 1:

I love rings, especially the chunky ones and I love collecting rings with colored gemstones. I have around eight of them and still want more.

Sample 2:

I'd have to say necklaces. Although I do like rings, I wash/moisturize my hands like twenty times a day so it'd be a hassle to take them off and put them back on.

Have you ever bought jewelry as gifts for others?

【Sample Answer】 Yes, I have. I have bought jewelry (usually earrings, pendants, and necklaces) to give as gifts to my family members including my mother and my wife. Personally, I think pendant necklaces will never go wrong because when I bought jewelries as gifts for other relatives, it's too hard to guess their ring or bracelet size. Necklaces allow a little more flexibility.

词汇和句型

take off 脱下

special occasions 特殊场合

enhance or compliment an outfit 弥补衣服的不足

shiny accessories 闪闪发光的配件

a higher risk of being mugged or robbed 更高的概率被打劫

rings, earrings, bracelets and necklaces 戒指、耳环、手镯和项链

lately 最近

frame my face 让我的脸型更好

look less square-ish 看起来不那么"方"。

gemstones studs 宝石耳钉

enhance my look 提升我的外貌

There is no occasion where jewelry is more fitting than that of a wedding. 没有比婚礼更适合戴首饰的场合了。

perfect accompaniment 完美的搭配

elevate your wedding outfit to a whole new level 把你的婚礼服装提升到一个全新的高度

make a positive first impression　留下积极的第一印象
nothing exudes more elegance and sophistication than jewelry　没有什么东西比珠宝首饰更能体现出优雅和成熟的了
a stylish bracelet　一个时尚的手镯
chunky　大块的
colored gemstones　彩色宝石
it'd be a hassle　这是件麻烦事
pendants　垂饰
pendant necklace　有挂坠的项链

7. Mirrors 镜子

考试原题和范文
Do you often look at yourself in the mirror?
【Sample Answer】
Sample 1:
Yes，I always look at myself in the mirror. Not just the mirror，but any kind of reflection. I guess you could say I'm a little vain. When I look into the mirror，I don't even realize time passing by. I can't say my beauty is perfect but I am happy with the way I am. I accept my appearance and I love myself.
Sample 2:
Sure，every time I pass one，and windows，and water，pretty much anything I can see my reflection in，I would look into it. I think I look pretty attractive. I'm not so sure if other people will agree.

Do you often buy mirrors?
【Sample Answer】　No，I don't frequently purchase mirrors because mirrors can be used for a long time，say five to ten years. So it's not necessary to buy a new one regularly.

Where do you put mirrors?
【Sample Answer】　The first place I think of a mirror is in a bathroom. Sure，it often gets clouded when I get out of the shower，but I cannot live without it — and shouldn't have to. Having a mirror mounted in a frame over the sink makes shaving and applying makeup much easier. If I have the space，I would also install a wall-hanging mirror with adjustable arms directly across from the mirror on the sink wall. I'd be able to look at the back of my head without having to juggle a hand-held mirror. But I currently have a really small bathroom，so I hang the framed mirror over the bathtub. It can really help to make a small bathroom look larger.

Do you think mirrors are a necessary decoration?

【Sample Answer】 Yes，if I hang a mirror in a room，I'll be adding a basic accessory and necessity. Whether it's a hallway，grand ballroom，baby's room，or bathroom，the addition of a mirror adds beauty to the space and makes the space feel more spacious. A mirror opposite a window will reflect a lovely outdoor setting and give the illusion of a second window. An interesting architectural feature can be reflected and give balance to a room.

词汇和句型

look at myself in the mirror 照镜子

I'm a little vain 我有一点自恋

frequently purchase mirrors 经常买镜子

buy a new one regularly 经常买新的

it often gets clouded （镜子)起雾

over the sink 在水槽上面

shaving and applying makeup 剃须和化妆

install a wall-hanging mirror with adjustable arms directly across from the mirror on the sink wall 安装一个直接在水槽上面、挂在墙上而且有可调节臂的镜子

juggle a hand-held mirror 很麻烦地操作手持的镜子

currently 目前

hang the framed mirror over the bathtub 在浴缸上装了一个带框的镜子

makes the space feel more open or spacious 使得空间感更大

8. Housework 家务

考试原题和范文

Do you like doing housework?

【Sample Answer】

Sample 1:

No. I can't stand doing housework to be honest with you. I mean，it's just a lot of work and I hate getting my hands dirty，so I avoid it whenever I can.

Sample 2:

No，I wouldn't say I do，because I find it tedious. But saying that，I feel quite accomplished when I'm finished and everything looks clean and tidy.

Did your parents ask you to do housework when you were a child?

【Sample Answer】

If yes:

Yeah they did. Mainly it was，like，tidying my room，because it was always quite messy. Yeah，that was the main thing. And uh，what else? Oh yeah，sometimes they would ask me to help with wash the dishes, but that was pretty much it. So I guess I'm lucky, as my mum did most of the housework.

If no:

No, on the whole, they didn't because they wanted me to focus on my homework. Occasionally, I did do a little bit to help, like sweeping or mopping the floor, if there was a lot to be done, but by and large, I escaped doing most of the household chores. I suppose I was pretty lucky.

Do you think children should do some housework?

【Sample Answer】 Yeah I think it's a good thing for children to do. I'd say it prevents them from taking things for granted, and it also helps them develop a good work ethic.

Which do you think is better for doing housework, a machine or a person?

【Sample Answer】 I think, on the whole, a person is better, because a machine might miss out a few bits. Just to give you an example, I've seen robots that suck up dust in some electrical appliance stores. They move in random motion, which is inefficient, as they might go over the same spots repeatedly whilst missing out other areas. And this is not something a person would do. Having said that, I think a combination of both — i. e. humans operating certain machines, like vacuum cleaners, is probably the most ideal way to do housework.

In the future, do you think machines will replace humans for doing housework?

【Sample Answer】 Not completely, no, because, as I mentioned just now, machines often need humans to operate them, so I think, in all likelihood, it will continue to be a combination of both machines and humans.

词汇和句型

I can't stand doing housework 我很不喜欢做家务
to be honest with you 和你说实话
it's just a lot of work 实在是有太多要做的了
I find it tedious 我觉得有点单调乏味
But saying that 但是话又说回来
everything looks clean and tidy 每样东西看起来干净整洁
tidying my room 整理我的房间
quite messy 很乱
Occasionally 偶尔
sweeping or mopping the floor 扫地或拖地
by and large 总体而言
taking things for granted 认为事情是理所当然的
develop a good work ethic 形成良好的职业品德

miss out a few bits　忽略一些东西
electrical appliance stores　家用电器商店
move in random motion　随机移动
suck up the dust　吸灰尘
vacuum cleaners　吸尘器
the most ideal way to do housework　做家务的最理想方式
in all likelihood　很可能

9. Emails & Letters 电邮和信件

考试原题和范文

Do you prefer writing letters or emails?

【Sample Answer】　I would rather write emails because it is more convenient. I don't need to sit at my desk and write things out on paper，or go to the post office and send the mail. Instead，I can use my cell phone to write emails and send them whenever and wherever I want.

Is writing letters popular now?

【Sample Answer】　No，it is not popular at all. People only write letters on some rare occasions. For example，for couples who are preparing to get married，they may prefer to handwrite wedding invitations. Apart from that，most people communicate with others through emails，because it is cheaper and much more convenient.

On what occasion do you often receive emails?

【Sample Answer】　I often receive emails at work. When we are doing projects for our clients，I usually receive tons of emails about the projects from my clients and my colleagues. My clients email me to tell me what they need and want，and my colleagues discuss with me through emails. My boss also sends me emails to check on our progress.

What do you feel when you receive emails?

【Sample Answer】　It depends on what the emails are about. If I get an email from an old friend，I would certainly be happy. When I am reading an email from the credit card company asking me to pay my debt，I feel sad and frustrated. When I receive emails from work，I just take it for granted because it is part of my job.

词汇和句型

go to the post office　去邮局
whenever and wherever I want　无论何时无论何地，只要我想，就能做到
on some rare occasions　在某些少数场合
handwrite wedding invitations　手写婚礼邀请函

pay my debt　还债

10. Mobile Phones 手机

考试原题和范文

Do you use a cell phone?

【Sample Answer】　Yes，I am constantly using my cell phone because it is more than a communication tool；it has become the entertainment hub for teenagers even the business center for business people. For me, I receive and send emails on my smart phone, which is crucial for my daily business. On the other hand, when I feel tired, I listen to music or watch a movie on my phone. I believe most people would do the same things as I do.

What do you use it for?

【Sample Answer】　In addition to the daily uses I have mentioned, I use my mobile phone to keep in touch with my friends. The Internet is so widely used that social networking system has become quite developed. I have downloaded Facebook and Twitter from the App Store, but these two Apps do not work well in China because of the firewall set by the government. So, in the majority of time, I use Wechat to communicate with my friends all over the world.

What do you think of the future development of cell phones?

【Sample Answer】　I think the future development of cell phones lies in the following aspects. The first development is that the screen size will be larger in the future so that the words and pictures can be seen clearly, even for the elderly people. The second development is that cell phones will be "smarter". Some cell phones could control cars or home appliances in the near future.

What are the differences between the cell phones now and the cell phones 10 years ago?

【Sample Answer】　There are two differences. The first difference is that cell phones now are implemented with computer functions, so those cell phones are actually small portable computers while the cell phone 10 years ago did not have the system so the functions were texting messages and calling others. The second difference is that the screen of modern cell phones is much larger than that of cell phones a decade ago.

What are the advantages and disadvantages of cell phones?

【Sample Answer】　The first advantage is that people can communicate with their friends with ease. In fact, as smart phones develop, people could make use of various Apps, such as Skype, Facebook, and Twitter to keep in contact with friends. The second benefit is that if there is an emergency, people can immediately call the police or ambulance for help. However, the disadvantage is that people are indifferent to each other as they are always using their smart phones in the subway，at dinner，or at home.

词汇和句型

constantly 一直

the entertainment hub 娱乐中心

social networking system 社交网络

in the majority of time 在大多数时间里

lies in 在于

the screen size 屏幕尺寸

the elderly people 老年人

are implemented with computer functions 被植入电脑功能

portable computers 便携电脑

texting messages 发送信息

with ease 方便地，轻松地

keep in contact with ... 和……保持联系

are indifferent to each other 互相冷漠

11. Gifts 礼物

考试原题和范文

What gift do people give in China?

【Sample Answer】 In China，people give a variety of things as gifts. The most common gift is flowers，which represent the best wishes people make to others. On some occasions，people give money in red envelopes to others as gifts，especially in wedding ceremonies and the Spring Festival.

When do people give gifts in your country?

【Sample Answer】 People give gifts in different cases. For example，when a baby is born，the relatives and friends of the parents would give gifts. Or when a person visits a friend's home，this person is supposed to bring gifts.

When was the last time someone gave you a gift?

【Sample Answer】 Last week，one of my colleagues gave me a portable hard drive as a gift for my birthday. I think that gift is very useful because I can store a lot of files in it.

Is it easy to choose gifts for others?

【Sample Answer】 No，it is not easy because it's hard for people to know what other people like. When choosing a gift，you need to know their personality，preference，family background，and so on，which is very difficult.

词汇和句型
On some occasions 在某些场合
wedding ceremonies 婚礼
in different cases 在不同的场合
a portable hard drive 一个移动硬盘

12. Maps 地图

考试原题和范文

Do you ever use a map?
【Sample Answer】 Yeah I do. I mean, I often use a GPS when I'm driving in an unfamiliar area, and I find it super helpful because I don't have a very good sense of direction.

When do you use a map?
【Sample Answer】 I use a map when I'm on holiday somewhere, because it gives me a better understanding of the place, and it also prevents me from getting lost.

Who taught you to use a map?
【Sample Answer】 I don't actually think anyone taught me how to use a map. I just figure it out myself. And I've never really had a problem understanding them because they tend to be pretty self-explanatory.

Do you prefer to use electronic maps or those made of paper?
【Sample Answer】 I'd say I prefer using electronic ones because they have more functions. For example, if you're not sure how to get somewhere, electronic maps will be able to highlight the best route to take, and not just that, they also give you detailed timings for each part of the journey, which is something that paper maps can't really do.

Have you ever asked others for directions?
【Sample Answer】 Yeah, sure I have, and I think it's fair to say most people have at some stage or other. Asking others for directions can save you from wandering around and getting hopelessly lost, and I've always found people to be very helpful whenever I've asked them how to get somewhere.

词汇和句型
I often use a GPS when I'm driving in an unfamiliar area. 当我在我不熟悉的地方开车的时候,我经常用 GPS 导航。
super helpful 非常有用
I don't have a very good sense of direction. 我的方向感不是太好。

on holiday 度假
prevents me from getting lost 防止我迷路
figured it out 搞清楚,弄明白
be pretty self-explanatory 非常明显的
electronic maps 电子地图
highlight the best route 突出最佳路线
detailed timings 具体的时间安排
paper maps 纸质地图
at some stage or other 在某些场合,在某个时间

13. Newspapers 报纸

考试原题和范文

Do you think it's important to read newspapers?

【Sample Answer】 Yes, of course. It's necessary for people to read newspapers, because they provide us with newly updated information, such as when a new traffic rule will be introduced or what price regulation policy will be adopted in the housing market. And news from newspapers is the most reliable. The second reason is that it is an era of globalization, so we need to learn about other countries through reading international news.

Why do people read newspapers?

【Sample Answer】 I think there are various reasons. The main reason would be to keep up with the fast-changing society. Newspapers always inform us of what's new. There are also some people who read newspapers for useful information, like job opportunities or where they can find reliable domestic help. Sports lovers would browse newspapers for upcoming games or game results, while old people may read for health tips.

What different types of newspaper are there in China?

【Sample Answer】 In terms of issuers, there are national and local newspapers. But if we look at the composition of content, I'd like to say there tends to be comprehensive papers and specialized ones like finance, sports, and job market.

Do you care about news?

【Sample Answer】 Yes, I care about most news, because news keeps us informed of latest happenings and sometimes helps us make the right decision. For example, if the news says there is unrest in Thailand, I would cancel my trip for safety reasons. However, the type of news I don't pay much attention to is the entertainment news, because most of it is gossip about celebrities. It does no good to our life and reading it is just a waste of time.

Do you like reading newspapers?

【Sample Answer】　Yes，I like reading newspapers，because newspapers provide a wide range of information，such as international and domestic news，local news，sports，health tips，finance，and columnists' comments on societal issues. Compared to Internet news which is more fragmented，newspapers are more reliable，and sometimes show detailed analysis and insight into some current issues.

What kinds of newspapers do people like reading in China?

【Sample Answer】　I think it is related to people's hobbies and professions. For people engaged in banking or stock deals，finance newspapers would be their first choice. Retired people may be interested in newspapers with a lot of healthcare information. But I think most people will read local newspapers which contain a lot of local news and government policies closely related to their life.

词汇和句型

price regulation policy　价格调控政策

the housing market　房地产市场

an era of globalization　全球化时代

the main reason　首要原因

inform us of what's new　让我了解到新东西

reliable domestic help　可以信赖的家政人员（佣人）

sports lovers　体育爱好者

upcoming games　即将到来的比赛

health tips　健康贴士

issuer　发行者

the composition of content　内容的组成

comprehensive papers　综合性报纸

news keeps us informed of latest happenings　新闻让我们了解到最新发生的事情

the type of news I don't pay much attention to is ...　我不关注的新闻类型是……

the entertainment news　娱乐新闻

the gossip about celebrities　关于名人的流言蜚语

It does no good to our life　这对我们的生活没什么好处

a wide range of information　各种信息

international and domestic news　国际和国内新闻

columnists' comments on societal issues　专栏作家评论社会时事

fragmented　不完整的，支离破碎的

detailed analysis and insight into some current issues　对一些热门话题的详细分析和洞察

people engaged in banking or stock deals　银行和证券交易的工作人员

finance newspapers　金融报纸

14. Magazines 杂志

考试原题和范文

Do people in your family read many magazines?

【Sample Answer】 I would say no. Some of us read magazines but not very frequently. My mother and I don't read anything apart from fashion magazines like *Vogue* and *Bazaar*. My husband doesn't read any magazines at all. My father used to read the Chinese version of *National Geographic*, but I don't know whether or not he still reads it.

What is your favorite magazine?

【Sample Answer】 As I mentioned，*Vogue*，a fashion magazine，is my favorite. The magazine is about woman's clothes and accessories. New issues are released monthly. In each issue，it introduces the latest trend which I try to keep up with. Also，the pages are well-designed. That's why I like it.

Where do you buy magazines?

【Sample Answer】 If I'm bored，I buy a copy of *Vogue* Magazine at the newspaper stand or 7-Eleven，which is a convenience store. When I was decorating my house，I booked 12 issues of an interior design magazine called *Space* on Amazon.com.

What type of magazines will be popular in the future do you think?

【Sample Answer】 Magazines with a bunch of pictures rather than a lot of words will be popular in the future. People don't like to read anymore. If they are given an article，they read a few lines and stop reading because their interest on the article lasts for only a few seconds. People prefer pictures now. So，I'd say magazines with more pictures and less words are going to sell well.

Is there a wide range of magazines available in your country?

【Sample Answer】 It is hard to say because I've never been to other places in China. So I'm just going to talk about the situation here. In Shanghai，you can get all kinds of magazines from fashion magazines to sports magazines to military magazines. There are also magazines about how to do business. So，yeah，there is a wide range of magazines.

词汇和句型

I would say no　我觉得不是
fashion magazines　时尚杂志
woman's clothes and accessories　女性的服饰和配件
In each issue　在每一期(杂志)中
the latest trend　最新的潮流
well-designed　设计精良的

buy a copy of Vogue Magazine 买一本 Vogue 杂志
at the newspaper stand 在报摊
an interior design magazine 一本室内设计杂志
a bunch of pictures 大量图片
sell well 卖得好
military magazines 军事杂志
a wide range of magazines 各种各样的杂志

15. Snacks 小吃

考试原题和范文

What kinds of snacks do you like to eat?

【Sample Answer】 I like eating quite a variety of snacks, such as nuts, and this includes cashew nuts, pistachios, peanuts, and also melon seeds, which you can find easily in the shops over here. And what else do I like eating? Oh yeah, dried beef, or beef jerky as I think it's also called. That's another snack I enjoy eating every now and then.

Is it healthy to eat snacks?

【Sample Answer】 I think it really depends on what snack it is, because a lot of snacks, like nuts, are actually pretty healthy. They're very nutritious, but other kinds of snacks like potato chips aren't so good for you, because they're basically processed food with a lot of additives and preservatives. So you should consume those snacks moderately.

Do your parents allow you to eat snacks?

【Sample Answer】 Yeah, they don't mind me eating snacks. They let me do what I want really. I'm old enough to decide for myself what I want to eat. So they don't really have a say in the matter. They used to, when I was younger, but now, I can pretty much do as I please.

What was the most popular snack when you were a child?

【Sample Answer】 Without a doubt, it was crisps, because I remember when I was a child, all my friends absolutely loved eating them, and we always had a bag of crisps in our lunch box to take to school. And they were popular among adults too, not just children. So yeah, I'd say crisps were definitely the number one snack when I was little.

词汇和句型
nuts 坚果
cashew nuts 腰果
pistachios 开心果
peanuts 花生

dried beef　牛肉干

beef jerky　牛肉干

every now and then　偶尔

very nutritious　非常有营养

processed food　加工食品

additives and preservatives　添加剂和防腐剂

consume those snacks moderately　适当地吃一些零食

have a say　有发言权

I can pretty much do as I please　我想做什么就做什么

without a doubt　毫无疑问

16. Chocolate 巧克力

考试原题和范文

Do you like eating chocolate?

【Sample Answer】 Yes, I love eating all kinds of chocolate. I remember that when I went to US two years ago, I shopped for chocolate in different stores. For example, I went to Walmart to purchase several bags of M&M's. These chocolates are like small buttons that have different colors and flavors. Those are my favorite ones. In addition to the M&M's, I also like the high-end chocolate such as Godiva. Its store was located in downtown LA and I bought many Godiva chocolate for my friends in China. Another brand of chocolate I like very much is See's Candies, whose chocolate was strongly recommended by the former US President Obama. I bought a lot of bags of See's Candies chocolate. But I gained weight from eating too much chocolate in recent years, so I am supposed to control the amount I consume.

Is it good to give chocolate as a gift?

【Sample Answer】 Yes. It's quite good to give others chocolate as a gift. Chocolate is more than a kind of food. Most people regard chocolate as love, care, and warmth. People could give chocolate as gifts on different occasions, such as a birthday party, wedding ceremony, graduation ceremony, and the like.

Why do you think people like chocolate?

【Sample Answer】 People like chocolate for a couple of reasons, one of which would be that the combination of sugar and cocoa is stimulating for most people, who feel motivated and excited after consumption. Also, eating chocolate is a form of relaxation. People enjoy lying in their sofa and eating chocolate on a sunny afternoon.

词汇和句型

I love eating all kinds of chocolate　我喜欢吃所有种类的巧克力

different colors and flavors　不同颜色和口味的
high-end chocolate　高端巧克力
in downtown LA　在洛杉矶市中心
gained weight　增肥了
control the amount I consume　控制摄入量
and the like　等等
for a couple of reasons　有几个原因
stimulating　刺激的

17. Color 色彩

考试原题和范文
What colors do you like?
【Sample Answer】　Since my taste always changes，my favorite color at the moment is black. I just bought some black items recently and black surprisingly suits me. I look more mature and more mysterious when I'm wearing my little black dresses. And because it's one of the basic colors，it's easy to be mixed and matched with other items of different colors and styles.

Do you like to wear dark or bright colors?
【Sample Answer】　I'm actually flexible between dark and bright colors. But bright colors give me a younger，more positive，and more cheerful look. They also match my skin tone better than dark colors. So I guess I prefer wearing bright colors.

Is color important when you buy things? Why?
【Sample Answer】
Sample 1: Male
Yes，color is very important when I buy something. For example，if I am buying a cell phone，I won't buy a pink cell phone because I'm a man and men don't carry pink phones. Also when I buy clothes，I will buy dark color clothes because those colors are more suitable for me in China.
Sample 2: Female
Yes，colors are very important to me when I buy something. For example，I'm a girl and I think girls should have pink things such as a pink phone，a pink laptop etc. Also when I buy clothes，I stick to buying light color clothes because I want to attract more attention.

Do you like dark or light colors?
【Sample Answer】
Sample 1:
Since I am student and I have to wash my clothes by hand，I really like dark colors for

two reasons. First，dark color clothes don't get dirty easily and I can usually brush the dirt off the clothes. Another reason is that if anything falls on my clothes while I'm eating，it is harder to stain the clothes.

Sample 2：

Since I'm a girl，I like light color clothes. I love to wear light color clothes because they make me seem outgoing and friendly. Also I love to decorate my room with light colors. For instance，my bed sheets are pink and so are my pillow covers.

How important were colors to you when you were a child?

【Sample Answer】

Sample 1：Boy

Colors were very important when I was a child especially when I was seven. I liked to dress like Superman，so everything I wore had to be blue and red. Even my bedroom had to be decorated with Superman colors.

Sample 2：Girl

Colors were very important when I was a child especially when I was seven. I liked to dress like Barbie，so everything I wore had to be pink and white. Even my bedroom had to be decorated with Barbie colors.

What is the significance of colors?

【Sample Answer】　Colors are a form of non-verbal expression. For example，red means love. So if I give somebody a red flower，that means love. Yellow means friendship. So if I give somebody a yellow rose，I want to be friends with that person. And white means purity. So during a wedding，the bride wears white to express that she is pure.

Do you like to wear colors that suit your personality?

【Sample Answer】　Of course I do. There are a couple of colors I can think of that fit my personality and mood. For example，if I want to be serious and taken seriously，I would wear black. And if I want to be outgoing and vibrant，I will wear red because this means I'm full of energy and I want people to look at me and talk to me.

Which color would you like to paint the walls in your room?

【Sample Answer】　I would have to say I would not paint my walls white because white walls remind me of hospitals and I can't stand sleeping in a room with white walls. I prefer to have blue walls because blue reminds me of the sky and it is also easier to decorate the walls with pictures because of the blue background.

What colors do you like?

【Sample Answer】　If we're talking about clothes I like light blue because I feel this color goes with a lot of other colors. When it comes to cars，I like yellow. I once saw a yellow Lamborghini and I really liked it. If I can't have a Lamborghini, I would still prefer black，because this color looks nice on a lot of cars.

What colors in your country have special meanings?

【Sample Answer】　In China the most important color is red. Red has been used in ancient China and new China and it represents good luck. This color is used in weddings and even holiday money is given in red envelopes. Yellow is important as well because it represents wisdom and in ancient China only the emperor was allowed to wear yellow.

词汇和句型

at the moment　现在

black surprisingly suits me　黑色非常适合我

it's easy to be mixed and matched with other items of different colors and styles　很容易和其他颜色和款式的衣服混搭。

I stick to buying light color clothes　我一直买浅色的衣服

wash my clothes by hand　手洗衣服

brush the dirt off the clothes　把污垢从衣服上刷掉

stain the clothes　弄脏衣服

pillow covers　枕头套

Barbie　芭比娃娃

a form of non-verbal expression　一种非言语的表达方式

There are a couple of colors I can think of that fit my personality and mood.　我觉得有两种颜色适合我的性格和情绪。

be outgoing and vibrant　外向有活力的

white walls remind me hospitals　白色的墙会让我想到医院

blue reminds me of the sky　蓝色让我想到天空

decorate the walls with pictures　用照片（图片）装饰墙

this colors goes with a lot of other colors　这个颜色容易和其他很多颜色搭配

When it comes to car color　说到汽车的颜色

a yellow Lamborghini　一辆黄色兰博基尼

this color looks nice on a lot of cars　很多这个颜色的车看起来都不错

represents good luck　代表好运

18. Handwriting 手写字迹

考试原题和范文

Do you usually write by hand or write using the computer?

【Sample Answer】　I prefer handwriting to writing using the computer. Even though writing by the computer is more efficient，I stick to writing by hand because it helps me memorize some important things.

How can children today improve their handwriting?

【Sample Answer】 Actually，there are a wide range of ways for children to improve their handwriting. For instance，children can improve their handwriting by imitating nice examples of handwriting before they develop their own style. As well as this，parents and teachers can teach their children by holding their hands and showing them how to write properly.

Do you think computers might one day replace handwriting?

【Sample Answer】 To be honest，I guess computers cannot fully replace handwriting. Even though computers enjoy obvious advantages，like convenience and fast speed，writing by computers drives children's attention to other things，like games. So handwriting has its own advantages as people's handwriting reveals a lot about their personality and conveys their feelings more effectively.

When do children begin to write in your country?

【Sample Answer】 I guess in China kids start to write when they are four or five years old，which is a golden time. They can learn better and quickly at that time before they develop their own style of handwriting.

What impression does a person's handwriting have on other people?

【Sample Answer】 If a person's handwriting is neat，people guess the person is probably thoughtful and patient. If a person's handwriting is pretty messy，they might think the person is careless.

词汇和句型

stick to writing by hand 坚持手写
a wide range of ways 各种方法
develop their own style 形成自己的风格
As well as this 除此之外
enjoy obvious advantages 有明显的好处
conveys their feelings 表达他们的感情
if a person's handwriting is neat 如果一个人的字迹很整洁
pretty messy 很乱

19. Handwork 手工作品

考试原题和范文

Did you do any handwork when you were a child?

【Sample Answer】 Yes，I did a variety of handwork in my childhood. I used to draw pictures in primary school and I won a couple of awards in the city. Also I enjoyed doing some wood work, by which I mean carving different shapes on wood. Although it was hard and time-consuming, I felt accomplished when I saw the finished work. I still keep those pieces of handwork in my home and regard those things as the best memory of my childhood.

What are the advantages of doing handwork?

【Sample Answer】　There are several benefits of doing handwork. The first advantage is that creativity could be inspired in the process. By continuously producing handwork, people could be more imaginative and use this in doing other things. Another benefit is that people's hands could be more flexible if they do handwork regularly. For the senior citizens, doing handwork can prevent them from some diseases such as Alzheimer's disease.

Do you like making things by hand?

【Sample Answer】

Sample 1:

Yeah I do. I find it quite fun making stuff by hand. It brings a certain amount of satisfaction once you've finished it, and you think "Wow! I made that!" So yeah, I enjoy making things.

Sample 2:

No, not particularly, because I've actually always found it to be a pretty frustrating experience. Something invariably goes wrong whenever I try to make something, and I gave up trying.

Do you like collecting things made by hand?

【Sample Answer】　No, I can't say I do. I mean, I've never really made the effort to collect anything made by hand. So it's not that I dislike it, it's just never been something that I've had the urge to do.

Did you ever take handicraft lessons at school?

【Sample Answer】　No, I never did, which I suppose is a bit of a pity, because I imagine they would have been quite fun. But my classes were unfortunately limited to just the typical subjects that most schools offer, like Math, Physics, and Geography, those kinds of things.

Are handicrafts popular in China?

【Sample Answer】　Yeah, I'd say they are, because we have certain handicrafts which are closely tied with our culture, such as paper cutting, which goes back hundreds of years in China. But I suppose it's also fair to say that handicrafts have become less popular in modern times, simply because of all the technology that's crept into our lives.

Do you think children should learn more about handicrafts?

【Sample Answer】 Yeah，I'd say they definitely should，because first of all it's fun，and children tend to learn more when they're having fun. And I think it would also make them appreciate things more. When you realize all the effort that goes into making something，you would appreciate it more. So yeah，I think it's beneficial for children to learn more about handicrafts.

词汇和句型

a variety of handwork   各种各样的手工作品

a couple of awards   几个奖项

wood work   木工

carving different shapes on wood   在一块木头上雕刻不同的形状

time-consuming   耗时的

I felt accomplished   我觉得很有满足感

the best memory of my childhood   童年的最好记忆

hands could be more flexible   手会更灵活

the senior citizens   老年人

Alzheimer's disease   阿尔茨海默病(早老痴呆症)

a certain amount of satisfaction   一些满足感

something invariably goes wrong   总是出错

I gave up trying   我放弃尝试了

it's not that I dislike it   这并不是说我不喜欢

had the urge to do   有动力去做

those kinds of things   诸如此类

handicrafts   手工艺品

are closely tied with our culture   和文化紧密相关

paper cutting   剪纸

in modern times   现在

the technology that's crept into our lives   渗透进我们生活的技术

20. Museums 博物馆

考试原题和范文

Do you like going to museums?

【Sample Answer】 Yes，I do. I like going to museums quite a lot. On weekends，I often choose to go to a museum near where I live，which is actually a history museum. I love everything about history，especially the things that are related to Second World War. So I like going to that museum to see what happened in that period and have some ideas about the relics from the war. Another reason I like going to museums is that I can learn about the cultural and historic development of the city I live in. For example，in

Shanghai Museum，I could see more about the history of Shanghai and its culture.

Who do you like going to museums with?

【Sample Answer】 I like going to museums with my family members，especially with my father. My father is a person who has a lot of life and work experience. So he gives me background information about the exhibits in different museums. And my father is a very patient and kind person. Whenever I ask him something I cannot totally understand about the objects exhibited in the museums，he always explains those things step by step till I catch the point completely. That's why I like to go to museums with my father.

Would you like working in a museum?

【Sample Answer】 Yes，I would because I have seen a movie about museums，which is called *Night At The Museum*. I suppose that I would probably come across the same things in a museum if I worked there. But I guess the most important reason for me to want to work in a museum is that I can meet many visitors and I could make friends with them. I am an extroverted person，so I think it is an advantage for me to guide the visitors in the museum.

词汇和句型

a museum near where I live 靠近我家的博物馆

Another reason I like going to museums is that ... 我喜欢去博物馆的另外一个原因是······

ask him something I cannot totally understand about the objects exhibited 问他一些关于展品的我不能理解的问题

Night At The Museum 博物馆奇妙夜

an extroverted person 一个外向的人

21. Camping 露营

考试原题和范文

Do you like camping?

【Sample Answer】 Yes. I like camping very much. During weekends，I always call my friends to go camping with me. Usually we drive to the local forest areas or mountain areas to camp. Sometimes I go camping by the sea to enjoy some seafood.

Do you have the experience of camping?

【Sample Answer】 Yes，I do. I have the experience of camping. During the process of camping，I can come close to nature，which relieves the stress of a whole week's work. I can also breathe the fresh air and enjoy fresh food. That is why it is a fantastic experience.

If you could pick a camping place, where would it be?

【Sample Answer】 I guess it would be in a natural environment of some sort，like a nature reserve，somewhere like that，which is peaceful and scenic. And I would also choose to be in a designated camping spot，where there are other people camping too，because that would make me feel a bit safer.

What kinds of problems might you have while camping?

【Sample Answer】 I imagine one problem might be insects，especially mosquitos，which I really can't stand. And another problem，I guess，would be security，because a tent doesn't provide that much protection. So there's a certain element of risk attached to it.

What kinds of preparation do people need to do for camping?

【Sample Answer】 I suppose，most importantly，you'd need to have the basic essentials，like water，food，sleeping bags，and tents. And then after that，I guess you'd need things like insect repellent，to keep the mosquitos and bugs away.

Should parents take their children camping?

【Sample Answer】 I don't think it's absolutely necessary for parents to do this，but I think it would be a good experience for children，and I'm sure they would find sleeping in a tent to be exciting. So if parents have the chance to do it，and they know a safe place to go，then I think it's a good thing to do.

词汇和句型

go camping   去露营

relieves the stress   缓解压力

of some sort   ……之类的

nature reserve   自然保护区

somewhere like that   类似于这样的地方

peaceful and scenic   安宁且风景优美的

a designated camping spot   一个指定的露营点

make me feel a bit safer   使我感到稍微安全一点

mosquitos   蚊子

I really can't stand ...   我真的不能忍受……

there's a certain element of risk attached to it   随之会有一定的风险

basic essentials   基本的必需品

sleeping bag and tent   睡袋和帐篷

insect repellent   杀虫剂

22. Nature 自然

考试原题和范文

Do you like nature?

【Sample Answer】 Yes. I like nature very much. If I have a holiday, I would like to go to some mountain areas to enjoy the natural view or go to the seaside to enjoy the sea view. If I don't have time to go on vacation, I would go to local parks to breathe fresh air. I like nature a lot.

What do you do to be close to nature?

【Sample Answer】 On weekends, I usually drop all my work and go to a small park, about 10-minute walking distance, to jog alone or with my family members. I often stay in the park for 2 to 3 hours after jogging to appreciate the flowers and trees. When I'm on summer vacation, my friends and I would go to some forests to go hiking. That is a challenge but I think it is the best way to be close to nature.

词汇和句型

natural view 自然风景

sea view 海景

go on vacation 去度假

drop all my work 放下手上的工作

go hiking 去徒步旅行

23. Outdoor Activities 户外活动

考试原题和范文

Do you like outdoor activities?

【Sample Answer】 I like outdoor activities when the air is fresh. When the air is clean, I like jogging and cycling in the countryside. I feel relaxed when I am doing those sports. I enjoy seeing the beautiful idyllic scenery. And the fresh air is good for my health. But I won't do any outside activities when there is haze, because it is harmful to inhale haze.

How often do you do that?

【Sample Answer】 On average I went two or three times a month. However, it was difficult to stick to the plan. I mean, sometimes I had to do other things and sometimes it rained on weekends. If I failed to do some outside activities on the weekend, I would go jogging around the garden in the neighborhood the next Monday. However, in some cases, I was busy the whole week and didn't have any time to exercise. So generally speaking, I try to do outdoor activities two to three times every month.

What outdoor activities do you like to do?

【Sample Answer】 When I have enough time，such as a whole morning or a whole evening，I like to ride the bike to the countryside to see the beautiful landscapes. If I only have one to two hours，I would go jogging around the neighborhood. Flying kites is also one of my favorite outside activities. When I look up to the sky，my eyes have a chance to relax.

Do people in your country prefer to spend time indoors or outdoors?

【Sample Answer】 It depends on their gender. Women prefer staying indoors because they don't want to be exposed to sunlight and get tanned. Men，however，don't care about their skin color. So I suppose they spend equal amounts of time indoors and outdoors.

词汇和句型

jogging and cycling 慢跑和骑车

idyllic scenery 田园风景

inhale haze 吸入雾霾

on average 平均

stick to the plan 坚持这个计划

the garden in the neighborhood 社区里的花园

ride the bike 骑自行车

Flying kites 放风筝

be exposed to sunlight 暴露于阳光下

get tanned 把皮肤晒黑

24. Park 公园

考试原题和范文

Do you like going to parks and/or public gardens?

【Sample Answer】

（*If yes:*）

Yeah，on the whole I do，as long as the weather's nice of course. I think they're nice places to go to get some fresh air and enjoy the natural environment. And I always tend to feel a bit less stressed out when I'm in a garden or park.

（*If no:*）

No I don't，because I think there's not really that much to do in parks. I mean，most of the ones near where I live have nothing in them. All you can really do is wander around，and after you've been there a few times，they get a bit boring.

When was the last time you went to a park?

【Sample Answer】 I suppose it must have been about two or three months ago，a bit before Christmas，because I remember that day the sky was really clear. And so I thought it would be nice to go out for a walk somewhere.

Do you think the parks and gardens where you live could be improved in any ways?
【Sample Answer】 Yeah，I do. I think they could be improved quite a bit. As I mentioned just now，there's not really that much you can do there，so I think some facilities could be added. For example，it would be nice if there was a café or something where you could sit and enjoy the scenery with a cup of coffee. Another thing that I think is missing is children's playing areas，like climbing frames，swings，and slides，because I've noticed that most parks have exercise equipment for adults，but nothing really for children. So this is another aspect in which I think parks could really improve on.

Would you like to see more parks and gardens in your hometown?
【Sample Answer】 Yeah，I would，because we only have a very small number at the moment，and considering there are several million people living here，I think it would definitely be good to have a few more.

Do you prefer to relax with your friends in a park or an indoor place?
【Sample Answer】 I'd say I generally prefer to relax with my friends somewhere indoors，because I mean，if I'm meeting up with them in a park，then everything could be ruined by the weather. So it's a bit easier arranging to meet somewhere indoors. Having said that though，if it's a really nice day out，then I suppose I would prefer to be outside with them somewhere，like a park.

词汇和句型
as long as the weather's nice 只要天气好
feel less stressed out 感觉放松一点
wander around 闲逛
another thing that I think is missing 另外一个我认为正缺乏的东西是……
children's playing areas 儿童乐园
climbing frames （儿童玩的）攀登架
swings and slides 秋千和滑梯
this is another aspect in which I think parks could really improve on 这是另外一个我认为公园真正要提高的方面
at the moment 现在，目前

25. Public Holidays 公共假日

考试原题和范文
What public holidays do you have in your country?
【Sample Answer】 We've got loads of them. For example，the one that's just passed was

the National Day holiday, and then we've got the Spring Festival of course — that's probably the most important one, which is at the beginning of the year, sometime around, like, late January or the beginning of February. Other important ones are the Dragon Boat Festival and Mid-Autumn Festival.

Do people in your country celebrate Christmas?
【Sample Answer】 It's hard to generalize, but I would say, to an extent, yeah. I mean, by and large, it's the younger generation that tends to celebrate Christmas, but they don't celebrate it in the way Westerners would. In the West, people go to church, open presents, whereas over here, it's more of a "let's get together for a party" sort of thing. So it is celebrated, but in a slightly different way.

Do you like public holidays?
【Sample Answer】 Yeah, I do. It gives me the opportunity to be together with my family, take some time off, so yeah, I always tend to look forward to them.

Which public holidays do you like the most?
【Sample Answer】 I guess I would have to say the Spring Festival, which I'm sure is most people's favorite. The main reason is that it's by far the most important festival in our culture. And everything feels just a bit different during that time. Everyone seems happier, the streets are livelier, and it's basically one long party which goes on for a week or two. And, it's also probably the only time of the year when you can eat and drink to your heart's content without feeling guilty about it.

What do other people in your country usually do on public holidays?
【Sample Answer】 I can't speak for everyone, but I guess most people either stay at home or go travelling. And if you've ever stayed in China during a public holiday, you'll have seen for yourself the hordes of people that flock to all the tourist spots across the country.

What would you like to do during the next public holiday?
【Sample Answer】 I haven't really given it much thought actually. But seeing as I went travelling during the last one, I'll probably just take it easy and spend the time chilling out at home.

Do you think public holidays are important?
【Sample Answer】 Yeah, I think they really are, because I mean, here in China, the public holidays are always on a certain festival, so it's one way of maintaining all the various customs and traditions we have. Just to give you an example. If you took away the Dragon Boat Festival holiday, it probably wouldn't get the attention it deserves, and

over time，people might simply stop bothering with all the customs that are associated with the festival，like dragon-boat racing. So yeah，I think it's pretty important that we continue to have them.

Do you think there should be more public holidays in your country?

【Sample Answer】 No，not really. I mean，I think we have enough as it is. Almost every month there seems to be a public holiday of some sort，and I think that's more or less enough. Otherwise，I guess these holidays would ruin the momentum of our daily lives.

词汇和句型
the National Day holiday 国庆节
the Dragon Boat Festival 端午节
Mid-Autumn Festival 中秋节
by and large 总的来说
they don't celebrate it in the way Westerners would 他们不像西方人那样庆祝（圣诞节）
whereas over here 但是在这里
take some time off 休息一段时间
look forward to them 期待（这些假日）
by far 目前
You can eat and drink to your heart's content without feeling guilty about it. 你可以想吃什么就吃什么而不用感到内疚。
hordes of people 很多人
flock to all the tourist spots 涌向所有的旅游景点
take it easy 放轻松
spend the time chilling out at home 在家放松一下
maintain all the various customs and traditions 保持所有的风俗和传统
Just to give you an example 给你举个例子
stop bothering with all the customs that are associated with the festival 不去管和这个节日相关的风俗活动
dragon-boat racing 赛龙舟
ruin the momentum of our daily lives 破坏我们日常生活的节奏

26. Boat 小船

考试原题和范文
Do you like boating?

【Sample Answer】 I'm afraid not. When I get on a boat，I always get a little bit scared because I don't know how to swim. I plan to learn how to swim in the next school holidays. Also if the boat is traveling too fast，I get sea sick，so I prefer to stay on land.

What have you ever done by boat?

【Sample Answer】　When I was a child, I used to go fishing with my dad on a boat. To be honest, it was boring but the fish didn't taste too bad. I have also crossed a river on a row boat once.

Do Chinese people travel by boat?

【Sample Answer】　No. In the past many people used to travel around by boat. However, currently people tend to travel by car and if the distance is long, they may choose to travel by plane.

词汇和句型

get a little bit scared　觉得有点害怕
get sea sick　晕船
stay on land　待在陆地上
row boat　划桨船

27. Trains 火车

考试原题和范文

Do you often travel by train?

【Sample Answer】　Yes, I do. I mean, I'd say I travel by train at least once a month. Because I have a brother living in Shanghai, and there's a high-speed train running from here to there, so I always take it whenever I go to see him.

What do you usually do when (you are) traveling by train?

【Sample Answer】　Most of the time, I bring a book with me to read on the train, because I'm a bookworm. And I also listen to music on my iPhone as well, especially if I'm traveling on my own. So yeah, that's pretty much all I do, and I know it's not a lot, but I'm not usually on the train for that long, probably only about an hour or so.

What do you think are the benefits of traveling by train?

【Sample Answer】　For me, I'd say one of the biggest benefits is that, with trains, you pretty much know exactly what time you'll arrive somewhere. Because I mean, unlike cars and buses, you won't get stuck in traffic if you go by train. So unless your train is delayed, which doesn't happen a lot here, you should be able to get to your destination on time. So that's one thing, and another good thing about traveling by train is that you can get up and move around during the journey, which isn't really possible if you're in a car. So I think this makes traveling by train a bit more comfortable and enjoyable than a lot of other forms of transportation. It's often very convenient traveling by train because the stations are usually quite central, as opposed to airports, which tend to be quite far out. So I think taking a train is a good alternative to flying.

Do you ever travel by subway?

【Sample Answer】

If yes:

Yeah，I do — quite a lot actually. Because we have a subway in our hometown，and there's a station not that far from where I live，it's a really convenient way to get around the city for me.

If no:

No，I don't，because unfortunately we don't yet have a subway in my hometown. So I have to make do with buses and taxis.

词汇和句型

high-speed train 高速火车

bookworm 书虫，喜欢看书的人（自嘲用法）

listen to some music on my iPhone 用手机听音乐

you pretty much know exactly what time you'll arrive somewhere 你可以准确知道你到那个地方的时间

get stuck in traffic 堵车

you should be able to get to your destination on time 你可以准时达到你的目的地

another good thing about traveling by train is that ... 坐火车旅行的另外一个好处是……

you can get up and move around during the journey 你可以在旅行途中站起来走一走

other forms of transportation 其他的交通方式

the stations are usually quite central 火车站通常是在市中心

taking a train is a good alternative to flying 坐火车是代替坐飞机的一个好选择

there's a station not that far from where I live 在我住的地方不远处有一个车站

make do with ... 将就着用……

28. Friends 朋友

考试原题和范文

How often do you hang out with friends?

【Sample Answer】

If not often:

I guess probably something like once or twice a week. Mainly on weekends，simply because that's the only time I am free. I would like to hang out with them more，but I'm just too busy during weekdays with studying. So yeah，by and large，I only get to do stuff with my friends on weekends.

If often:

Quite a lot actually. I mean，I'd say I hang out with them pretty much every day，because I go to class with them，and when class is over，we often chill out and do stuff together before heading back to our dormitory.

Who do you usually like to hang out with?

【Sample Answer】 I'd say it's mainly my classmates, because I get on with them really well, at least most of them anyway. And that's probably due to the fact that we've got a lot in common, such as the same class or similar interests. And we're quite a close-knit group, so I always tend to have a good time when I'm out with them.

Where do you like to go when you hang out with your friends?

【Sample Answer】 All sorts of places really, nowhere in particular. I mean, we just go where our mood takes us. So for example, if we want to just go somewhere to relax, then one place we like going to is Starbucks, because it's just a very chilled-out place and we all like coffee. And as well as that, other places we like to hang out at are shopping malls, because there's quite a lot to do there. So yeah, these would be the main places.

Do you like to go out with a big group or just a few friends?

【Sample Answer】

If you prefer being with just a few friends:

On the whole I'd say I prefer going out with just a few friends, because I find I enjoy myself more when I'm just chatting with a few friends. It just feels like we can have deeper conversations when there are just a few of us, as opposed to a big group. In a big group, it's difficult to have a meaningful conversation with anyone. Plus, it's also more effort to organize and do things in a large group, like getting a table in a restaurant. So I find it's not really as relaxing or enjoyable as being with just a few friends.

If you prefer being out with a big group:

I'd say I actually prefer going out with a big group of friends, because the more the merrier. A big group has more of a party feel to it, so for me it's a lot more fun. I mean, I don't mind going out with a small group, but when there's a big group of us, it just feels a bit more exciting.

How do people in your country meet others and make friends?

【Sample Answer】 I suppose for young people, they'll generally make friends with the other students around them at school. And it's the same thing for adults. They'll make friends with the people around them at work, whether it be the office or the factory. So I'd say these are probably the two main ways in which people make friends here.

Is it important for people to have good relationships with their colleagues at work?

【Sample Answer】 Yeah, I think it is, because I'm sure a lot of work involves doing stuff together with others, and if you get on well with your colleagues, then I think it's much more likely that you'll work better with them.

Would you say students at your school have a good relationship with each other?

【Sample Answer】 Yeah I'd say, on the whole, they do. And I mean, just to give you an example. In my class，we're all pretty close with each other，and it seems to be the same with all the other classes too. At least that's the feeling I get anyway.

How would you describe a good relationship?

【Sample Answer】 I guess I'd say that a good relationship is one in which there is mutual support and respect for each other. So in other words，each person treats the other well，and if their friend helps them out in some way，then they also reciprocate when they have thc chance to do so.

词汇和句型

hang out with them 跟他们一起出去玩

during weekdays 从周一到周五

by and large 总的来说

chill out 放松

heading back to our dormitory 回宿舍

that's probably due to the fact that 这可能是因为……

we've got a lot in common 有很多共同点

we're quite a close-knit group 我们的关系很好

have a good time 很开心

nowhere in particular 没有什么特别的地方

we just go where our mood takes us 我们去什么地方只是跟着感觉走

it's just a very chilled-out place 这是一个非常让人放松的地方

And as well as that 除此之外

It just feels like ... 只是觉得……

as opposed to ... 和……相比

the more the merrier 人越多,越开心

these are probably the two main ways in which people make friends here 这边的人们交朋友主要是这两种可能的方法。

get on well with your colleagues 和同事关系好

At least that's the feeling I get anyway 最起码我是这样感觉的

there is mutual support and respect for each other 朋友间互相支持和尊敬

reciprocate 报答

29．Neighbours 邻居

考试原题和范文

Are there many people living near you?

【Sample Answer】

If yes:

Yeah，there are，because I live in a residential area，so most of the buildings around my home are apartment blocks.

If no:

No，I wouldn't say there are，because I mean，a lot of the flats where I live are empty，which is probably due to the fact that most of the people who bought them didn't actually plan on moving in，but instead bought them simply as an investment. So yeah，it's a pretty quiet neighborhood.

Do you know all your neighbors?

【Sample Answer】

Sample 1:

I wouldn't say I know all of them，but I know quite a few，and that's mainly because I spend quite a lot of time in the gardens of my apartment complex，which is how I got to know them.

Sample 2:

No，not really，because my neighbors tend to keep pretty much to themselves. I mean，if I happen to see them，we might say hi to each other，but that's about it，and then they'll just continue with doing whatever it is they're doing.

When do you see your neighbors?

【Sample Answer】　I guess the time when I mostly see them is when I'm in the elevator. That's pretty much the only time I come into contact with them，because I don't really know them all that well，so I've never been to any of their homes.

How often do you see your neighbors?

【Sample Answer】　I guess it depends，because I mean，during the term，I don't see them at all，as I'm away at university，but during the holidays，when I'm back home，I probably see them about three or four times a week，because I'm quite good friends with a few of them.

Do you think it's important to know your neighbors?

【Sample Answer】

If yes:

Yeah，I suppose it is，because I think it helps create a good community spirit if we know our neighbors. In other words，it gives the neighborhood a nice，friendly feel，instead of a cold，unwelcoming one.

If no:

No，I wouldn't really say it is，because for me I think friends and family are enough. And I mean，in my case I don't spend nearly enough time with my family as it is，so I don't really see the need to get to know my neighbors. And this probably goes for a lot of people，not just me.

What do you think of your neighbors?

【Sample Answer】 They're all really nice people. They're always very pleasant to me whenever I see them. And I can't think of a single instance when I've had problems with any of them. So yeah，I feel pretty lucky to have such good neighbors.

What sorts of problems can people have with their neighbors?

【Sample Answer】 I guess one of the main ones would be noise，like putting on loud music or having the TV on full volume. So that's probably the biggest complaint that people have with their neighbors. And as well as this，I suppose another problematic issue could be pets，because a lot of neighbors who have them don't put their dogs on a leash when they're walking them，which I think is quite inconsiderate，seeing as a lot of people are quite scared of dogs.

In what ways can neighbors help each other?

【Sample Answer】 I'd say they can help each other in a variety of ways，such as babysitting，looking after a pet while you're away，and keeping a spare house key for emergencies，stuff like that.

How has the relationship between neighbors changed between now and the past?

【Sample Answer】 I'd say it's changed a lot，and probably the main change has been that now people don't really see their neighbors all that often，whereas in the past，they used to do quite a lot of things together. For example，people would often have their neighbors over for lunch or dinner，which doesn't really happen that much anymore.

词汇和句型

residential area 居民区

apartment blocks 公寓楼

simply as an investment 只是作为一种投资

apartment complex 公寓楼

my neighbors tend to keep pretty much to themselves 我的邻居们不太爱互相交流

come into contact with them 和他们接触

during the term 在上学期间

good community spirit 良好的团体(集体)精神

it gives the neighborhood a nice，friendly feel 这会给你居住的社区一种良好和友好的感觉

putting on loud music 放很响的音乐

having the TV on full volume 电视音量开足

problematic issue 有问题的方面

don't put their dogs on a leash 没有把狗拴上链子

when they're walking them 当他们遛(狗)的时候

quite inconsiderate 非常不体谅别人的
a lot of people are quite scared of dogs 很多人很害怕狗
in a variety of ways 通过各种方式
babysitting 做临时保姆
looking after a pet 照看宠物
keeping a spare house key for emergencies 保留一把房子的备用钥匙,以备不时之需
have their neighbors over for lunch or dinner 请他们的邻居来吃午餐或晚餐

30. Birthdays 生日

考试原题和范文

How do children celebrate birthdays in your country?

【Sample Answer】 For most children, their birthday is their biggest celebration, by which they have a birthday cake and a lot of friends and presents. Children in China are no exception. The birthday party can take place at home or even in class.

How did you celebrate your last birthday?

【Sample Answer】 Since I was in the middle of my final exam week, I had no time to think about my birthday. I celebrated it once the exam was over. My friends cooked dinner for me and bought me some cakes. And friends from my hometown also sent me lots of wishes.

What kinds of birthday gifts do you like to receive?

【Sample Answer】 I think I'm fine with any kind of ordinary birthday presents like stuffed animals, flowers, accessories, and cosmetics. I'm happy as long as my friends and parents can remember my birthday and give me wishes.

词汇和句型

Children in China are no exception 中国的儿童也不例外
in the middle of my final exam week 处在期末考试周之中
ordinary birthday presents 普通的生日礼物
stuffed animals 毛绒玩具
cosmetics 化妆品

31. Weekends 周末

考试原题和范文

What do you do on weekends?

【Sample Answer】 On Saturdays I tend to sleep in and when I wake up, I do things on impulse, like seeing friends, watching movies, etc. On Sundays I do my laundry, finish up my assignments, and get ready for the school week.

What did you do last weekend?

【Sample Answer】 It was actually pretty uneventful, to be honest with you, because I basically just chilled out at home. On Saturday I had a lie-in until about midday, and then spent the rest of the day on the computer.

Do you think weekends are important to you?

【Sample Answer】 Yes, weekends are very important because I have a rigorous schedule during the week and weekends help me forget about all my work and I can do whatever I want instead of rushing from class to class.

How do people in your country spend the weekend?

【Sample Answer】 University students tend to enjoy the weekends by doing whatever they want. Most adults would go grocery shopping or play with their children. For older people, they don't work, so they do the same thing as they do all week. To them, the weekend is just another day.

What do you plan to do next weekend?

【Sample Answer】 I haven't really given much thought to it actually, but I guess I'll probably just end up staying at home, watching TV, and surfing the Internet, which is what I do on most weekends. Having said that though, I suppose it's also quite possible that I'll go out and do something with my friends, as I don't think I'll have much work to do.

词汇和句型

sleep in 睡懒觉

on impulse 一时心血来潮

do my laundry 洗衣服

finish up my assignments 完成作业

uneventful 平静的,平凡的

chilled out at home 在家放松休息

I had a lie-in until about midday 睡懒觉到中午

rigorous schedule 很紧凑的时间表

go grocery shopping 采购各种东西

I haven't really given much thought to it actually 我其实真的没有想过这个问题

32. Sleeping 睡眠

考试原题和范文

How many hours do you sleep every day?

【Sample Answer】

Sample 1:

On weekdays, I sleep about 7 – 8 hours a day, from around 11:00p. m. to 6:00a. m.

Sometimes I doze off after lunch if I am really tired and exhausted, but my nap won't last more than half an hour. But during weekends or holidays, I spend a little bit more time on sleeping — usually 8 - 10 hours every night.

Sample 2:

It's hard to say for sure, but I guess on average, I probably get about 7 or 8 hours of sleep a day, something like that. I'm normally in bed at about 11, and I usually get up sometime around 7. So yeah, 7 to 8 hours is about the norm for me.

Is it necessary to take a nap at noon?

【Sample Answer】

Sample 1:

It depends. Taking a nap at noon proves to be essential for children; however, it is not as important for grown-ups, so the idea that people must have a nap at noon is mistaken. Basically, I believe that it is not necessary for people, except young children, to nap in the middle of the day.

Sample 2:

No, I wouldn't say it is. And also I think it depends on the person, because some people do feel the need to have a nap to give them energy for the rest of the day. But for others, like me, we can quite easily get through the day without taking a nap.

Do old people sleep a lot, why or why not?

【Sample Answer】 No, they definitely don't sleep for a long time. As people get older, they sleep less simply because they don't need a lot of sleep any more, which is a universal law. I think they sleep around 5 - 6 hours every day, and that is about 2 hours less than others.

Do you think younger people sleep more than old people?

【Sample Answer】 Yeah, absolutely. Generally speaking, infants and young children sleep the most because they need to. Teenagers, who sleep less than children, spend a little bit more time on sleep than adults. And the sleep time of elders is the shortest of all.

What are the effects of sleeping too little on people?

【Sample Answer】 There will be a number of bad results from the lack of sleep. If one fails to sleep enough at night, he or she can be exhausted the next day and have no energy to do anything. Sleeping too little in the long term can cause more serious consequences, such as bad health, and even a shorter life span.

How can one sleep well?

【Sample Answer】 I'd say it differs between people, because what works well for one person might not work well for another. But by and large I'd say most people sleep well when it's quiet around them. And I think it helps too if you've had a fulfilling day. Because I mean，for me，I always tend to sleep better if I've done a lot that day，like doing exercise and stuff.

Do you like to get up early in the morning?
【Sample Answer】
If no:
No，not particularly. I'm not really a morning person，and if I do get up early，I always fccl extremely groggy，and it takes me awhile to feel fully awake.
If yes:
Yeah，I do actually. It feels quite good getting up early while everyone else is still sleeping. Sometimes I find it difficult to drag myself out of bed，but once I'm up，I feel pretty good，and it means I can get more things done that day.

Can you sleep well if you're in a noisy environment?
【Sample Answer】 No，definitely not. I find it very difficult to fall asleep if there's lots of noise around me，which I guess is the same for most people.

词汇和句型
doze off 打盹儿
7 to 8 hours is about the norm for me 对我来说，大概每天要睡 7 - 8 小时
grown-ups 成年人
in the middle of the day 在中午
a universal law 一个普遍规律
elders 老年人
lack of sleep 缺乏睡眠
one fails to sleep enough at night 一个人在晚上没有充分的睡眠
cause more serious consequences 引起严重结果
what works well for one person might not work well for another 对某个人有用的方法对另外一个人不一定有用
a fulfilling day 充实忙碌的一天
I'm not really a morning person 我真的不是一个喜欢早起的人
groggy 虚弱无力
it takes me a while to feel fully awake 要过一会儿才能完全清醒

33. Robots 机器人

考试原题和范文
Are you interested in robots?
【Sample Answer】 Yes，I'm interested in robots. I really like the fact that we are able to

use robots to improve our lives by having them perform tasks that are dangerous, dreary, or difficult. When I ask my robot to do something, it does it. My robot's name is Robert. He's the coolest robot ever, and he even goes skiing or running with me.

Do you like robots to work at your home?

【Sample Answer】 Yes, sure. Robots could relieve the burden of dreary domestic tasks, such as mopping the floor, scrubbing the grill, cutting the lawn, watering plants, changing cat litter, and vacuuming the carpet.

Do you want to take a car in which a robot is the driver?

【Sample Answer】 No, probably not, even if Google has developed this kind of technology. Robot-driven cars will be completely autonomous. There will be no need for the vehicles to be equipped with steering wheels or brake pedals. Everything will be controlled through a combination of sensors, lasers, software and intricate maps. So it requires a sense of adventure. I don't like this feeling when I'm in a car.

Will robots replace human beings in the workplace completely?

【Sample Answer】 No, they won't fully replace human workers. Robots are able to work on repetitive tasks tirelessly and continuously and in many businesses they are welcomed as valuable team members because they do the work that humans don't want to do. Robots will replace most of human workers, but not all of them. Perhaps 75% of the jobs will be gone in 50 years because robots are generally smarter, less error-prone, and more creative than humans.

词汇和句型

perform tasks that are dangerous, dreary or difficult 完成一些危险的、枯燥的或困难的任务

relieve the burden of dreary domestic tasks 减少无聊的家务负担

scrubbing the grill 擦洗烧烤架

cutting the lawn 修剪草坪

watering plants 给植物浇水

changing cat litter 换猫砂

vacuuming the carpet 给地毯吸尘

Robots-driven cars 机器人驾驶的汽车

steering wheels 方向盘

brake pedals 刹车板

intricate maps 复杂的地图

fully replace 完全代替

error-prone 容易出错的

34. Sounds & Noise 声音和噪声

考试原题和范文

Do you prefer to study in a quiet environment or an environment with some sounds?

【Sample Answer】 I guess on the whole I prefer to study in a quiet environment. The main reason is that I find it easier to concentrate, because noises or sounds tend to distract me. So in other words, I tend to get more work done when I can't hear anything around me. But saying that, I do occasionally like to listen to some music while I'm studying, because it can make studying a little bit more enjoyable.

Does your school have any quiet places for studying?

【Sample Answer】 Yeah, I guess I'm quite lucky in this respect, because there's a pretty big library on our campus with loads of desks for studying, and I'm always able to get quite a lot of work done there, as it's really nice and quiet.

What natural sound do you like the most?

【Sample Answer】 I guess I would probably say the natural sound I like most is that of waves hitting the seashore, because it's just really soothing. And it's a sound I only really get to hear when I'm on holiday, so I also probably associate it with being on holiday, which would be another reason why I like it so much.

Are there any sounds that you dislike?

【Sample Answer】 Yeah, for sure. I mean, firstly, I really can't stand the sound of drilling, simply because it's just such a loud and unpleasant noise, so that would definitely be at the top of my list. And I guess the next one would be the sound of cars hooting, mainly because I hear it all the time where I live, and it gets quite irritating after a while, especially when I'm trying to concentrate on something.

Are you ever bothered by noise?

【Sample Answer】 Yeah, for sure, especially when I'm trying to get to sleep. If there's a dog barking or something, it can be really maddening, but during the day I'd say I can put up with pretty much most noise, unless, of course, the noise is really loud and relentless, like if there's construction or renovation work going on around me.

Do you think that cities will become noisier in the future?

【Sample Answer】 I guess my feeling would be that they probably will get noisier, yeah, basically because if you compare the situation in cities now to what it was like 10 or 15 years ago, then it's obvious that cities have become a lot noisier, mainly, of course, due to the increase in traffic on the roads. So unless something changes, I would say that, unfortunately, this trend is likely to continue into the future.

What sounds remind you of your childhood?

【Sample Answer】　I would say that one sound that especially reminds me of my childhood is，interestingly enough，the sound of firecrackers because when I was young，I used to love setting off firecrackers with my friends，especially during the Spring Festival. So now when I hear firecrackers now，it always brings back good memories of my childhood. And another sound I've just thought of would be the sound of morning exercises going on，because schools always play music through a microphone along with a voice counting the beat of the exercise，which students have to move along with. So whenever I walk past a school and hear the morning exercises going on，it always reminds me of the time when I had to do them，and I'm glad I don't have to anymore.

词汇和句型

distract me　分散我的注意力

in other words　换句话说

get more work done　做完更多的事情

in this respect　在这方面

there's a pretty big library on our campus　在我们校园里有一个很大的图书馆

loads of desks　很多课桌

really soothing　真的很让人放松

the sound of drilling　钻孔的声音

simply because　主要是因为

hooting　汽车喇叭鸣笛

mainly because　主要是因为

quite irritating　非常令人不快的

there's a dog barking　有只狗在叫

maddening　令人气恼的

put up with　忍受

relentless　不间断的

construction or renovation work　建筑或装修工程

basically because　主要是因为

compare the situation in cities now to what it was like 10 or 15 years ago　比较一下现在和10年或15年前城市中的这种情况

due to the increase in traffic on the roads　因为道路交通量的增长

I would say that this trend is likely to continue into the future　我觉得这个趋势将来很有可能会持续下去

sound of firecrackers　鞭炮的声音

setting off firecrackers　放鞭炮

it always brings back good memories of my childhood　这总是会把我带回童年的记忆中

35. Sky 天空

考试原题和范文

Do you like watching the sky?

【Sample Answer】 If it's a nice day, I do, yeah, because the sky can be quite pretty on a sunny day. But unfortunately, most of the time there's not much to look at. Normally it's just a blanket of grey.

What's the sky like at night in your hometown?

【Sample Answer】 It's nothing spectacular — I can tell you that. I mean, you're lucky to even see one star. So um, yeah, there's pretty much nothing to look at, apart from the moon.

Have you ever taken a course about stars?

【Sample Answer】 No I haven't, it's never crossed my mind. And I think it would be a bit pointless, seeing as I can't even see the stars most nights.

Is it important to study stars?

【Sample Answer】 I wouldn't say it's important for everyone to study stars, but I think it's pretty important that at least some scientists study them, like the Sun, to get a better understanding of how they work, because after all, we rely on the Sun to survive. So it makes sense to understand it as much as possible.

What's your favorite star?

【Sample Answer】 I honestly don't have a favorite star. I mean, they all look pretty much the same to me. Some might shine a bit brighter than others, but that's about it.

词汇和句型

a blanket of grey 　厚厚的一层灰色
it's nothing spectacular 　没有什么特别之处
apart from the moon 　除了月亮之外
it's never crossed my mind 　我从来没有想过

36. Sunny Days 晴天

考试原题和范文

Do you like sunny days?

【Sample Answer】 No. I feel dizzy when the sunlight is too strong. Another reason why I don't like sunny days is that I would get tanned after being exposed to the sunlight for some time. Let me explain this. I know most westerners appreciate tan skin, but here in

China we don't think dark skin is beautiful. So I make sure that I won't be exposed to direct sunlight for a long time to keep my skin white. That's why I don't like sunny days so much.

What do you do in sunny days?

【Sample Answer】　I usually stay indoors on sunny days to avoid direct sunlight because as I mentioned，I don't want to get a tan. If I have to go outside，I would apply sunscreen，wear a pair of sunglasses，and use a hat or an umbrella to block the sunlight.

What do people do in sunny days in your country?

【Sample Answer】　In China，there are two interesting traditional activities which have to be done in sunny days. Chinese people believe that strong sunlight could sterilize things. One activity is to take out the bedding such as sheets，blankets，and covers that are used on beds，and put them under the sunshine for a few hours. This is because Chinese people believe that sunshine can kill the bacteria in the bedding. Another activity is to put books in the sunlight to kill the mold on the books.

词汇和句型

I feel dizzy　我会感到头晕

get tanned　晒黑

tan skin　黝黑的皮肤

apply sunscreen　涂一些防晒霜

wear a pair of sunglasses　戴一副太阳眼镜

block the sunlight　防止阳光的直射

sterilize　杀菌

bedding　寝具,床上用品

37. Rainy Days 雨天

考试原题和范文

Do you like rainy days?

【Sample Answer】　No，not that much to be honest with you，because I mean，when it rains，you can't really do anything outside，unless you don't mind getting wet of course. And also for me，I find it a bit of a hassle having to carry an umbrella around with me everywhere I go.

What do you do on rainy days?

【Sample Answer】　It depends really，because there are some things I have to do regardless of whether it's raining or not，like going to lectures and stuff. But when I'm free，I tend to just chill out at home if it's raining. So for example，I might read a book or watch TV, and I'll only leave the flat if I absolutely have to.

Do you think rain is good?

【Sample Answer】　Yeah, for sure. I mean, for one thing, it helps get rid of all the dust in the air. For another, it's good for the natural environment. It helps all the plants and vegetation stay alive. So although I don't particularly like the rain, I understand the need for it.

Does rain ever affect transportation in your hometown?

【Sample Answer】　Yeah, most definitely, because whenever it rains, the traffic always seems to get a lot more congested. I'm not exactly sure why, but I guess it's probably because people have to drive slower in the rain.

Is there any part of China where it doesn't rain much?

【Sample Answer】　Yeah, I'd say there are a quite a few areas of the country where it doesn't rain a lot, the most obvious place being the Gobi Desert, which I guess never gets any rain, what with being a desert and all. And also I'd say the north of China, in general, doesn't all get that much rain, at least compared with the south, so a lot of that part of the country is quite dry and arid.

What effects can a shortage of rain have on people's lives?

【Sample Answer】　I suppose one of the biggest effects it can have is on our food supply, because things like fruits and vegetables need water to grow, and rain provides the water. So I think it's pretty safe to say that a shortage of rain is likely to result in a decrease in our overall food supply. It could result in the government controlling how much water we can use. For example, I think I'm right in saying that in some parts of Australia, people can only spend a certain amount of time each day having a shower.

Can you remember a time when it rained particularly heavily in your hometown?

【Sample Answer】　Yeah, I can. About a year or so ago, we had, like, several days of torrential rain, almost non-stop, and so the whole of my neighborhood got flooded. The water was like, up to my knees, and so traffic came to a complete standstill. So yeah, that was probably the worst time I can remember.

Do you think the seasons have changed in recent years, compared to the past?

【Sample Answer】　Yeah, I'd say they have. I think it's fair to say the summer has got quite a lot hotter, because I mean, it seems to be hitting 40 degrees centigrade every year now, and that definitely wasn't the case in the past. And also the winter isn't as cold as it used to be, because if I think back to when I was a child, it used to snow quite a lot during the winter，but now it hardly snows at all.

词汇和句型

not that much to be honest with you　说实话不是那的(喜欢)

hassle　烦恼，困扰

there are some things I have to do regardless of whether it's raining or not　有一些不管下不下雨我都要做的事情

like going to lectures and stuff　比如去听课之类的

get a lot more congested　变得更加拥堵

arid　干旱的

food supply　食物供应

having a shower　洗澡

38. Advertisements 广告

考试原题和范文

Do you like advertisements?

【Sample Answer】 Yes. I like advertisements because I can learn more about a range of products and compare the advantages and disadvantages of different products in order to find the best deal. What's more，some ads，such as iPhone and iPad ads，are fun and attractive.

What kind of advertisements do you like?

【Sample Answer】 I like TV commercials，which combine music and images. Some well-produced TV commercial could be regarded as short movies.

What kind of advertisements is common in China?

【Sample Answer】 In China，Internet advertisements are common because there are more than 1 billion Internet users and most young people use their smart phones all day long. So Internet ads are prevalent.

How do advertisements influence your life?

【Sample Answer】 Advertisements influence my life quite a lot. When I'm walking on the street，I see billboards on the outside wall of the buildings. On the screen of my smart phone，ads pop up from time to time. My life is flooded with all kinds of advertisements.

Have you ever bought advertised products?

【Sample Answer】 Yes. I have bought some advertised products. I get the email ads of Amazon.com every day and there are bargains，which give me good opportunities to save money. So I often buy advertised products.

Do you like street advertisements?

【Sample Answer】　Yes. I like street advertisements, which make the city view vivid. Without street ads, the whole city would be boring. For example, H&M street ads are well-made. When I see them, they take me out of the daily worries and cares, and remind me of the beauty in my life.

词汇和句型

a range of products　各种各样产品
find the best deal　找到价钱最划算的商品
some ads　一些广告
TV commercials　电视广告
combine music and images　把音乐和图像结合在一起
Internet advertisements　网络广告
use their smart phones all day long　成天都在用智能手机
Internet ads are prevalent　网络广告是很普遍的
influence my life quite a lot　对我的生活影响很大
billboards on the outside wall of the buildings　建筑外面的广告牌
On the screen of my smart phone　在我智能手机的屏幕上
ads would pop up from time to time　广告会时不时弹出来
My life is flooded with all kinds of advertisements　我的生活充斥着各种各样的广告
advertised products　广告产品
email ads　邮件广告
bargains　特价商品
street advertisements　街头广告
make the city view vivid　使得城市景观生动
take me out of the daily worries and cares　让我摆脱日常的烦恼
remind me of the beauty in my life　提醒我生活中的美

39. Social Networking 社交网络

考试原题和范文

What kinds of social networking websites do you like to use?

【Sample Answer】　I suppose the main one I use is Weibo, which is basically the equivalent of Twitter in the West. And as well as that, I occasionally use a website called Facebook, although I don't really use it as much as I used to, because I think Weibo's a bit better.

What kinds of people do you like to be friends with on those websites?

【Sample Answer】　I'm not really that picky actually. I mean, if anyone's interested enough to get in touch with me on a social networking site，then I will definitely respond. Someone's gone out of their way to contact me. So I appreciate it，and I'm generally willing to make friends with them.

Are you a social person?

【Sample Answer】

If yes:

Yeah，I'd say I am，because I mean，I like hanging out with my friends a lot and doing stuff with them. And ... yeah，I just enjoy being around others，and I've always found it quite easy to strike up conversations with people，even complete strangers. So yeah，I'd say I am quite a social person.

If no:

Not really，if I'm going to be totally honest with you，I'm just not the kind of person who actively strikes up conversations with others. To me，that's just too much effort，and I always worry that I'll run out of things to talk about. So I tend to just keep to myself.

Is it easy to find real friends on a social networking site?

【Sample Answer】 I'm honestly not that sure because I've never really made a big effort to find friends on the Internet，but thinking about it，I'd say it's probably not that easy，although it's definitely possible，because I think you never quite know someone properly until you've met them face to face. At least that's been my experience anyway.

What kinds of chatting APPs or software do Chinese people like to use?

【Sample Answer】 The most popular APP right now is definitely WeChat，because I mean，literally everyone in China uses it. And as well as this，QQ is the other popular way of communicating with people. If you've been in China for any length of time，I'm sure you've been asked for your WeChat or even QQ number.

词汇和句型

the equivalent of Twitter in the West　等同于西方国家的推特

as well as that　除此之外

I'm not really that picky　我这个人不是那么挑剔

make friends with them　和他们交朋友

strike up conversations　开始交谈

a social person　一个喜欢社交的人

I'm honestly not that sure　我真的不是那么确定

literally　确实,实际上

第六节 雅思口语 Part 1 动植物类 话题真题及范文

1. Animals 动物

考试原题和范文

Do you like birds?

【Sample Answer】 Yeah. I'd say birds are lovely creatures. I mean，they look really graceful when they fly，especially doves and eagles，and I love waking up to the sound of them chirping and singing away in the morning. It's just a shame that there aren't more of them around.

What kinds of pets do people have?

【Sample Answer】 I suppose it's true to say that people have all sorts of pets，like dogs，cats，goldfish，and even turtles，but from what I see around my apartment complex，it seems that the most popular pets right now are little dogs，especially fluffy brown poodles. And I guess the main reason for this is that poodles require relatively low maintenance. They don't shed that much fur，unlike big dogs.

Do you like animals?

【Sample Answer】 Yeah，I really love animals，mostly because they're just so cute and cuddly，and they tend to be good company，especially dogs. But I should also admit that there are some animals I'm terrified of，such as cockroaches，which really give me the creeps.

Do birds have special meanings in China?

【Sample Answer】 Yeah，I guess it's probably true to say that some birds do have special meanings here，such as swallows，which represent the coming of spring，and Mandarin ducks，which，if I'm not mistaken，symbolize love and commitment，due to the fact that they are apparently meant to be the most faithful lovers in the animal kingdom. Whether it's actually true or not，I have no idea.

How can we protect birds?

【Sample Answer】 One way，I guess，might be to refrain from throwing the chewing gum on the ground，because apparently birds can choke on it. And as well as this，maybe a law could be introduced to forbid people to eat birds，although I can't really see that happening any time in the near future.

Why do people have pets?

【Sample Answer】 I suppose there are a handful of reasons，one of which would be that pets keep people company，and as a pet owner myself，I know that they are really good at cheering you up if you're feeling a little down. So they are great companions.

词汇和句型

I'd say . . . 我认为……

I mean . . . 我的意思是……

look really graceful 看上去很优雅

doves and eagles 鸽子和老鹰

I love waking up to the sound of them chirping and singing away in the morning 我喜欢清晨在叽叽喳喳的鸟鸣声中醒来。

It's just a shame that . . . 很遗憾……

I suppose 我认为

it's true to say that 可以这样说

from what I see around my apartment complex 从我所住的公寓大楼的情况来看

it seems that . . . 情况好像是……

fluffy brown poodles 棕色毛茸茸的狮子狗

And I guess the main reason for this is that . . . 而且我觉得这个现象的主要原因是……

poodles require relatively low maintenance 养狮子狗相对比较好打理

they don't shed that much fur 它们(狮子狗)不会脱很多毛

basically because 主要是因为

cute and cuddly 可爱的而且令人想抱抱的

and also 而且

good company 好伙伴

But I should also admit that 但我也承认

there are some animals I'm terrified of 也有一些我害怕的动物

cockroaches 蟑螂(复数)

give me the creeps 让我毛骨悚然

I guess 我认为

swallows 燕子(复数)

represent the coming of spring 代表着春天的到来

Mandarin ducks 鸳鸯(复数)

if I'm not mistaken 如果我没记错的话

symbolize love and commitment 象征着爱和承诺

due to the fact that . . . 因为……

the most faithful lovers 最忠诚的爱人

in the animal kingdom 在动物王国中

Whether it's actually true or not，I have no idea 我不知道我刚说的是不是真的

refrain from 制止

throwing the chewing gum on the ground　把口香糖扔在地上

choke on it　由于(口香糖)而窒息

And as well as this　除此之外

forbid people to eat birds　禁止人们吃鸟类

I can't really see that happening any time in the near future　我觉得近期人们是做不到这点的

there are a handful of reasons　有各种理由

as a pet owner myself　我自己作为一个养宠物的人

they are really good at cheering you up　宠物可以让你振作起来

if you're feeling a little down　如果你心情低落

they are great companions　宠物是很好的伙伴

2. Flowers 花

考试原题和范文

What flowers do you like?

【Sample Answer】 I like rose because it is common in Shanghai and I can find it in almost all flower shops. I can give roses as gifts in most cases. For example，if I go to a wedding ceremony，I can bring roses with me to give to the new couple. When I go to hospital to see a patient，I will give him or her rose to wish him or her to recover soon.

Why do people give flowers to others as gifts?

【Sample Answer】 There are several reasons. The most important one I think is that flowers have special aroma，which could cheer people up and make them feel peaceful.

Which flower have a special meaning in China?

【Sample Answer】 In China，we consider peony a symbol of good fortune and plum blossom as a representation of iron will and elegance. Another popular flower，the daffodil，symbolizes nobility and a little arrogance for Chinese people.

词汇和句型

in most cases　在大多数场合

wedding ceremony　婚礼

the new couple　新婚夫妇

wish him or her to recover soon　祝愿他/她早日康复

special aroma　特别的香味

cheer people up　使人精神振奋

make them feel peaceful　让他们感到平和

peony　牡丹

plum blossom　梅花

iron will　钢铁般的意志

daffodil　水仙花

symbolizes nobility and a little arrogance　象征高贵和一点点傲慢

3. Fruits & Vegetables 水果和蔬菜

考试原题和范文

Do you like eating fruits?

【Sample Answer】　Yes，I like eating different fruits. I eat apples and bananas most of the year，not only because they are delicious and nutritious but also because they are easy to carry. I also eat seasonal fruits. For example，I eat a lot of watermelons in summer，as they can help quench my thirst.

Do you like eating vegetables?

【Sample Answer】　Of course，I like eating vegetables. There are so many different types of vegetables for me to choose from. I know vegetables of different colors represent different vitamins and minerals. Eating them can satisfy our basic need for nutrition. That's the main reason. And the second reason is that most of the vegetables are delicious. I like broccoli and carrot the most. Also，compared to meat，they are easier to digest.

Did you like eating vegetables when you were a child?

【Sample Answer】　Actually I didn't like eating vegetables very much when I was a child. This was due to an unpleasant experience with eating green vegetables. That day，the vegetable I ate tasted a little bitter，but I did not dare to spit it out because my father always said vegetables were good for children. I forced myself to swallow it，but the bad taste had a lasting impression.

Is it convenient for you to buy vegetables and fruits near where you live?

【Sample Answer】　Yes，it is quite convenient for me to buy vegetables and fruits because the food market is only 200 meters away from my neighborhood. It is open until 7 p.m. so most people can still buy what they need for dinner after they get off work. The only inconvenient occasion is before the Spring Festival，when most vendors go back to their hometowns. Then we have to take a bus and go to a supermarket to buy vegetables and fruits.

What are the benefits of eating fruits and vegetables?

【Sample Answer】　There are many advantages of eating fruits and vegetables every day. First of all，they provide almost all the necessary vitamins and trace minerals our body needs. Second，eating them a lot will not make us fat. And health experts say they are good for skin. That's why many girls like to have different fruits every day. Also，some vegetables such as celery contain a lot of fiber，which helps our digestion.

Are there any special fruits in your hometown?

【Sample Answer】 No，I'm afraid not. There are no special fruits in Shanghai，which is why most people here buy imported fruits. For example，people in my hometown buy kiwi fruits grown in New Zealand. And they also buy coconuts produced in Thailand. The climate condition and soil quality make it difficult to plant special fruits. But the commonly seen fruits such as apples and oranges are still popular with the local dwellers.

词汇和句型

seasonal fruits 季节性水果

quench my thirst 解渴

vegetables of different colors represent different vitamins and minerals 不同颜色的水果代表了其中含有的维生素和矿物质

broccoli and carrot 花椰菜和胡萝卜

an unpleasant experience 不愉快的体验

swallow it 把它吞下

had a lasting impression 留下了持久的印象

the food market is only 200 meters away from my neighborhood 食品市场离我住的小区只有 200 米距离

after they get off work 他们下班以后

The only inconvenient occasion 唯一不方便的情况

most vendors 大多数小贩

trace minerals 微量元素

celery 芹菜

a lot of fiber 大量纤维

helps us digest 有助于消化

imported fruits 进口水果

kiwi fruits 猕猴桃

coconuts 椰子

local dwellers 当地居民

4. Trees 树木

考试原题和范文

Do you like trees?

【Sample Answer】

Yeah，I do. And I don't think there's anything not to like about them. They look nice， they add more color to a place, so yeah I think trees are great.

What kind of trees do you like?

【Sample Answer】 I prefer those big trees with plenty of green leaves, such as oak and pine. Evergreen trees are my favorite because I can enjoy their beauty all year around. I also like trees which have special sweet smells, for they are not only beautiful but also bring me good aromas.

What kind of trees is popular in your country?

【Sample Answer】 Generally speaking, the plane tree is the most common kind and people can see them anywhere across the country, because they are suitable for the weather in most areas in China. In the northern part of China, there are large white birch forests. And in the southern area, it is popular to plant banyan along the streets in the cities and countryside.

Are there any important trees in your country?

【Sample Answer】 Yes, that's bamboo, which I'd say is pretty important here in China, first of all, because a lot of stuff's made out of bamboo here, like chopsticks, and also because it's closely tied to Chinese culture. For instance, bamboo appears quite a lot in Chinese art. So um, yeah, I'd say bamboo is probably the most important kind of tree here.

Is there a forest near your hometown?

【Sample Answer】

If yes:

Yeah, I suppose there is, because there's quite a lot of natural scenery surrounding our city, much of which is covered with trees.

If no:

No, there isn't, at least not that I'm aware of. It's mainly just farmland and small towns and villages around my hometown.

Where can one find trees in your country?

【Sample Answer】 All over the place. For example, in the cities, you can find them in parks, and also a lot of the streets are lined with trees. But I guess to find the most trees, you have to leave the urban areas and venture into the countryside, especially the hills and mountains, because these are the places which are still in their natural state, and you'll find that many of the mountainous areas are covered with trees.

Do you think places with trees attract more visitors than places with few trees?

【Sample Answer】 I guess it depends on why the visitor is going to a certain place. So for instance, if they're going to enjoy the natural environment and scenery, then yeah, I think having trees will obviously attract more visitors. But if the visitors are going for a different reason, for example to visit a famous tourist attraction or something, then I think trees aren't really going to have any impact on the number of visitors. So it's hard to generalize.

Did you ever climb trees when you were a child?

【Sample Answer】 Yeah, I did. I had great fun climbing trees when I was little. I really enjoyed it, and I even remember when my mum took me to buy new shoes, I always chose the ones with the best grip, because they would be the best for climbing trees in. So yeah, it was something I really enjoyed doing.

Have you ever planted a tree?

【Sample Answer】 No, I can't say that I have. First of all, I don't think it's that easy to do, because you've got to find somewhere that sells the seeds, and then you've got to find a suitable place to plant one. So yeah, it's not something I've ever done before.

Do you think more people should plant trees?

【Sample Answer】

Sample 1:

Yeah, I think more people should. At least in theory it sounds like a good idea, although I don't know how well it would actually work in practice, because I mean, you can't just go around planting trees anywhere. There needs to be a certain amount of planning. So it might be better to give this responsibility to a limited number of people who know what they are doing.

Sample 2:

Yes, of course people should plant more trees because trees can clean the air and reduce the pollutants in it, and without enough trees, people breathe in bad air which will damage their health. Trees can also help create a better environment, so people should definitely plant more trees in our cities.

词汇和句型

oak and pine 橡树和松树

Evergreen trees 常青树,常绿植物

plane tree 悬铃木,法国梧桐

across the country 遍及全国

white birch forests 白桦林

banyan 榕树

chopped them down 把(树)砍断

chopsticks 筷子

natural scenery　自然风景
leave the urban areas and venture into the countryside　敢于走出城市地区去到农村
the mountainous areas　山区
a famous tourist attraction　一个知名景点
shoes with the best grip　有最好抓地力的鞋子
in theory　理论上来说
damage their health　损害他们的健康
help create a better environment　使环境更好

第七节　雅思口语 Part 1 学科类 话题真题及范文

1. Science 科学

考试原题和范文

Do you like science?

【Sample Answer】 It's ok I suppose，but I have to admit I'm not particularly interested in it. It's not something I've ever got really excited about. Having said that though，science is such a broad subject，so although I'm not really that interested in most of it，there are some areas of it that I think are pretty cool，such as astronomy，which studies how the universe came into being.

Are there many science museums in your hometown?

【Sample Answer】 No，not really. I mean，there's only one I can think of，which is the Science & Technology Museum. That's the one.

Did you like science classes when you were young?

【Sample Answer】 No. I didn't really enjoy most of the science classes I had at all，because I was never any good at science，and if I'm going to be totally honest with you，most of the classes were pretty boring，which is a bit of a pity. I think I could have actually really enjoyed science if it was taught in a more fun way. So yeah，I guess I was just unlucky with my teachers.

Do you think children should have both art classes and science classes?

【Sample Answer】 Yeah，I'd say it is a good thing to have both，because I think it helps children discover where their interests lie. If，for example，they didn't have art classes，then they would probably never know whether they had a gift for it or not. So I think being exposed to as many things as possible at an early age really helps children develop their talents and interests.

Do you think science is important to our society?

【Sample Answer】 Yeah，I'd say it's extremely important，because I mean，science helps us to continue improving our standard of living. Without science，technology wouldn't be able to progress，and in terms of combating diseases，we wouldn't be able to come up with new vaccines. So yeah，it's incredibly important to us.

词汇和句型

I'm not particularly interested in it　我对这个不是特别感兴趣

how the universe came into being　宇宙是如何形成的

in a more fun way　以一种更加好玩的方式

discover where their interests lie　发现他们的兴趣所在

being exposed to as many things as possible at an early age really helps children develop their talents and interests　在小时候尽可能多地接触各种事物确实能帮助小孩子开发天赋和兴趣。

extremely important　特别重要

in terms of combating diseases　就治疗疾病而言

vaccines　疫苗

incredibly important　非常重要

2. Dictionary 词典

考试原题和范文

Do you often use a dictionary?

【Sample Answer】 Yeah，I use it a lot，especially in the last few months，while I've been preparing for my IELTS test.

How often do you use a dictionary?

【Sample Answer】

Sample 1:

Basically whenever I'm studying English，so that would be about two or three times a day，something like that.

Sample 2:

Quite a lot I suppose. I mean，whenever I'm studying English，I'll refer to a dictionary at some point. So I'd say I use one at least once a day.

Do you prefer paper or electronic dictionaries?

【Sample Answer】 Electronic dictionaries，without a doubt. I mean，for me it's a no-brainer，because electronic dictionaries can pronounce the word for you，and it's also a lot quicker looking up words on them. So yeah，I can't really see why people would still want to use a paper dictionary.

What kinds of dictionaries have you used before?

【Sample Answer】 When I was younger, I used a Chinese dictionary at lot. And in particular, I used what I suppose I could call a character dictionary, because it gives the definition of individual Chinese characters as opposed to words. But now I use a Chinese-English dictionary more, and I have also started using just English dictionaries to try and help me learn the language faster.

How will dictionaries change in the future?

【Sample Answer】 I'm honestly not that sure, because I mean, dictionaries have pretty much everything we need to know in them, like pronunciation, parts of speech, and word origins. But I suppose it's possible that in the future they might use voice recognition, which will allow us to just say the word into the App, and the definition will come up.

How would you feel if you received a dictionary as a gift?

【Sample Answer】 I suppose I wouldn't mind it, because after all, they're pretty useful to have, but I mean, they're not exactly the most exciting gift in the world. But I would still feel grateful, because I'm grateful for every gift I receive, regardless of what it is.

词汇和句型

refer to a dictionary 查词典
it's a no-brainer 答案很明显,不需要思考的问题
electronic dictionaries 电子词典
character dictionary 字典
as opposed to 而不是
parts of speech 词性
word origins 词源
voice recognition 语音识别
come up 出现
grateful 感激的

3. Math 数学

考试原题和范文

When did you learn math?

【Sample Answer】 I started to learn math formally when I was in primary school, but before I went to school, my father had taught me a little bit about calculation within 20.

Was it easy for you to learn math?

【Sample Answer】 Yes, I think it was quite easy for me to learn math throughout the period from primary school to high school. The teachers I met were good at teaching and patient，and I seemed to be very sensitive to numbers and was always quick in solving math problems.

Do you like math?

【Sample Answer】　Yes，I like math. Maybe some will say math is not as useful as Economics or English in our daily life or finding a good job，but I think learning math is the training of logical thinking. To figure out a math problem，we need to think hard from different angles. This way of thinking can positively affect our way of tackling other problems in life.

Did you use the calculator?

【Sample Answer】　I know now most students use calculators in school. However，when I was still in high school，we were not allowed to use a calculator in math class，and nobody thought it strange. I think that was because the teachers wanted to exercise our calculating ability. They wanted to train us to think without relying on any tool.

词汇和句型

primary school　小学
before I went to school　在我上学前
calculation within 20　二十以内的加减法
be very sensitive to numbers　对数字非常敏感
the training of logical thinking　逻辑思维的训练
figure out a math problem　解决一个数学问题
from different angles　从不同的角度

4. Teachers 教师

考试原题和范文

Do you have a favorite teacher?

【Sample Answer】　Yeah，I suppose I do，but it's actually hard to pick out a favorite because I've been really lucky with all my teachers. They've been really great，at least most of them anyway，but I guess my favorite teacher would have to be my Chinese language teacher，because she was incredible. I mean，the amount of effort she put into her teaching，and her attention to detail，were just amazing. And not only that，but she also genuinely cared for all of us，which left a really deep impression on me. So yeah，out of all my teachers，I'd say she was probably my favorite.

What kinds of teachers do you like?

【Sample Answer】　I guess first of all，teachers who are passionate about their subject， because if they show enthusiasm for what they're teaching, I'm much more likely to be interested in that subject and do well in it. And as well as this, I also like teachers that are supportive and approachable. So in other words, teachers who show patience and understanding, and are there for you if you need help.

What are the qualities of a good teacher?

【Sample Answer】 The good teachers I've had have shown a genuine care for their students. They genuinely want their students to learn and develop. It's not just simply a job to them. So yeah I think that's the most important thing — taking their job seriously and really caring about their students' development.

Do you think teachers should be angry at students or not?

【Sample Answer】 No, I think as a general rule, teachers shouldn't get angry at students. It never ends well when teachers get angry, at least in my experience. So in my view, I think teachers should always control their temper, whatever the situation, and instead use other means to get their point across. I mean, I'm sure you've experienced it before, that when a teacher gets angry, the whole atmosphere in the class changes and everyone is scared, which is definitely not conducive to learning.

Do you like strict teachers?

【Sample Answer】 Yeah, I do. I have no problem with them at all, as long as they're fair. Because I think, on the whole, they tend to set high standards, and so consequently, that makes us work harder and learn more. And the other good thing about strict teachers is that they keep students in line, which means that the class won't be interrupted by slackers who just want to joke around and be a nuisance.

What's the difference between young and old teachers?

【Sample Answer】 There's probably not all that much of a difference, but I guess the main one would be the level of experience. I think it's fair to say that old teachers tend to have more experience, and so they'll be more skilled at adapting to any kind of situation that might arise in class, whereas young teachers might struggle. So that's one difference, and I suppose another might be the use of technology, because a lot of old teachers might stick to the traditional teaching methods they're familiar with, whereas young teachers, I think, are more likely to bring technology into their teaching, such as using iPads and laptops in class. So yeah, I'd say these are probably the main differences.

词汇和句型

pick out　选出来

And not only that　而且不止如此

genuinely cared for all of us　对我们的真正关心

left a really deep impression on me 给我留下了非常深刻的印象

teachers who are passionate about their subject 对他们所教科目有热情的老师

show enthusiasm 表现出热情

And as well as this 除此之外

So in other words 所以换句话说

taking their job seriously 认真对待工作

control their temper 控制他们的脾气

use other means to get their point across 用其他方法来让别人理解他们的意图

is definitely not conducive to learning 绝对无助于学习

as long as 只要

on the whole 总的来说

the other good thing about ... is that ... 关于……的另外一个优点是……

keep students in line 让学生守规矩

slackers who just want to joke around and be a nuisance 那些偷懒成天想着讲笑话的讨厌鬼

be more skilled at adapting to any kind of situation that might arise in class 更有能力适应课堂中有可能出现的不同种类的情况

young teachers might struggle 年轻的老师可能会疲于奔命

stick to the traditional teaching methods they're familiar with 坚持他们所熟悉的传统教学方法

So yeah，I'd say these are probably the main differences 所以说，我觉得这些可能就是主要的区别

第三章　IELTS Speaking Part 2 Questions and Sample Answers 雅思口语 Part 2 真题和范文

第一节　雅思口语 Part 2 核心技巧

核心技巧 1

话题归类,拓展思维。雅思口语 Part 2 考题有几百题,但是我们归类之后就几大主题类别,每个类别准备的内容不需要很多,这样可以充分熟悉话题,考生所要做的就是考试中快速反应,灵活应变。

核心技巧 2

充分利用 1 分钟准备时间构思答案,这点非常重要,要做好笔记。

核心技巧 3

注意 Part 2 长段子的连接词使用,如果没有连接词将会失分。

核心技巧 4

注意过去时态的使用,雅思口语 Part 2 百分之五十的题目牵涉过去时态。

核心技巧 5

最好说足两分钟时间,确保语言能力充分展现。

核心技巧 6

提示卡上的四个问题最好能全部涉及,否则可能说不满 2 分钟。

核心技巧 7

注意语速,不要太快。太快的话你在一分钟就把两分钟内容说完了,造成冷场。太慢的话,两分钟内说不完会被考官打断。

核心技巧 8

尽量表现自然,不要出现刻意准备过答案的感觉,否则会让考官觉得你在背书,出现低分现象。

第二节 People 人物类话题真题及范文

1. **Describe a family member you would like to spend most time with** 描述一个你想要与其共度时光的家人

You should say:
Who he or she is
What you do with him or her
What the person is like
And explain why you would like to spend most time with him or her

Sample Answer

The person I would like to spend most time with is my mum. We often go shopping together.

I like shopping with my mum because she has great taste in clothes. At least，she has better taste than me. Sometimes I cannot find a suitable dress for myself but she always can. She also encourages me to try new styles and the result is always good. I help her choose clothes too and she also takes my advice. We have great fun when we pick clothes for each other.

We also do other things together，such as having dinner and going to the gym，and we have many common interests.

Another reason why I would like to spend time with my mum is that she can always give me good advice. My mum is a very wise person and she is good at making the right choices in life. When we hang out together，we talk about what's new in our lives. If my mum gives me some advice on my work or my relationship with others，I will take them very seriously. In most cases，I take her advice because I know that there is a great chance that she is right.

I can learn a lot from my mum and I am happier when I spend time with her. So I would like to spend most time with my mum.

词汇和句型
has great taste in clothes 对衣服有很好的品位
new styles 新的款式
pick clothes 挑选衣服
going to the gym 去健身

2. Describe a child who makes you laugh 描述一个使你笑的小孩

You should say:
Who the child is
What the child is like
What the child often does
And explain why the child makes you laugh

Sample Answer

The most adorable child who makes me laugh a lot is my niece，who is only two months old. Before I saw her in person，I learned a lot about her through the pictures and videos sent by her mother，my sister.

She is a fat baby with little hair. Her face is so fat that her nose and mouth appear very small. She spends a great part of a day sleeping，but she has a lot of facial expressions while she is asleep. Sometimes，she pouts，seeming to show some dissatisfaction；other times，she frowns，like a young philosopher. And sometimes she smiles，making us wonder what she has dreamed of. Seeing her change of expressions always amuses me a lot. The most interesting video I saw about her is the moment she wakes up. She waves her four limbs wildly，twisting her features before she sighs and shows a kind of relief one minute later.

A week ago，I visited my sister and got the chance to hold the baby. It was an amazing feeling，having such a soft and tender body in my arms. She stared at me，moved her lips and made some unidentified sound，seeming to communicate with me，though I didn't know what she tried to convey. However，she didn't always behave well. Whenever I held her and sat，she cried desperately，protesting against my stillness. She wanted me to hold her and keep walking. In this way，she can watch the world around her.

When I laid her down in her own bed and put a blanket over her，I found her legs kept kicking and arms kept waving. The more the blanket was kicked away，the happier she was. Her mother told me that she was trying to feel her legs.

All the things my little niece has done seem so interesting to me，because I never knew a new-born baby could have such rich means of expression.

词汇和句型
adorable child　可爱的小孩
niece　侄女，外甥女
facial expressions　脸部表情
pout　噘嘴

frown　皱眉

amuses me a lot　让我感到很好玩

four limbs　四肢

unidentified sound　听不清的声音

cried desperately　号啕大哭

put a blanket over her　帮她盖上一条毯子

a new-born baby　新生儿

such rich means of expression　这么丰富的表情方式

3. Describe a polite person you know 描述一个你认识的礼貌的人

You should say:

Who the person is

How you knew the person

What the person looks like

And explain why you think the person is polite

Sample Answer

The person I'd like to talk to you about is a very good friend of mine called Matthew. He must be one of the nicest and most polite people I know, which I'll explain in a moment.

As for how I knew him, we've basically known each other since middle school, because we were in the same class together, and we still hang out quite a lot. If I feel like going out and doing something, I normally give him a call and see if he's free to meet up.

And moving on to why I think he's so polite, it's basically because he's just got really good manners. And just to give you an example. He always says thank you to people, even for the slightest thing. For instance, I've noticed that whenever we're eating at a restaurant, he will thank the waiters and waitresses every time they bring a dish to the table. And another example would be that whenever he gets off a bus, he will always say thank you to the driver, which a lot of people probably think isn't necessary, but I'm sure the bus drivers really appreciate it, as do the waiters and waitresses, because it's not all that often they hear people thanking them.

So yeah, that's basically why I'd say he's such a polite person, and I'm just trying to think if there's anything to add, and one other thing to mention would be that he's always very complimentary to people. So what I mean is that he tends to always say nice things to people. For example, he might make a comment about how nice someone's looking, or how good their cooking is, which I know might be seen as being a bit insincere, but I think he genuinely means what he says, at least most of the time anyway.

And I mean, I can't remember a single time when he's ever been rude or unpleasant to anyone, and I also can't really imagine him being nasty to anyone either. So yeah, that's pretty much it.

词汇和句型

as for how I knew him　关于我是怎么认识他的

we've basically known each other since middle school　从中学开始我们就认识了

give him a call　给他打个电话

meet up　见面

And moving on to why I think he's so polite　至于说到为什么我认为他很礼貌

good manners　好习惯,有礼貌

gets off a bus　下公交车

one other thing to mention would be that　我要提一下另外一件事情

complimentary　称赞的,赞美的

make a comment about　做出关于……的评论

he genuinely means what he says　他是真心诚意这么说的

I can't remember a single time when he's ever been rude or unpleasant to anyone.　他从来都没有对别人发过脾气。

being nasty to anyone　对任何人使坏

4. Describe a person you know who dresses well 描述一个你认识的穿着得体的人

You should say:

Who the person is

How you knew them

What clothes they like to wear

And explain why you think they dress well

Sample Answer

The person that I'd like to talk to you about is a good friend of mine called Franc, because he always dresses really well, at least whenever I see him anyway.

As for how I knew him, I basically got to know him at a company I used to work at. We've actually both left that company now but we still stay in touch.

Going on to what clothes he likes to wear, I guess it's mainly formal clothes, like a suit, tie, long-sleeve shirt, dark trousers, leather shoes, that kind of thing. And even when he's not working, he still dresses smartly. For example, I've noticed that he always wears collared shirts, and I don't think I've ever seen him in a T-Shirt.

In terms of why I think he dresses well, firstly, his shirts are always impeccably ironed.

There's never a crease in them. And another thing is that he usually wears cufflinks instead of plain buttoned sleeves, which looks super smart. And his shoes are always nicely polished and shiny, not dirty and scruffy like a lot of the shoes you see guys wearing.

And he also wears a waistcoat underneath his suit, which I think really gives a positive impression in terms of his professionalism. The fact that he goes to such lengths to look smart and presentable gives the impression that he puts the same amount of care and attention into his work as well.

词汇和句型

as for how I knew him　关于我是如何认识他的
we still stay in touch　我们仍然保持联系
suit　西装
tie　领带
long-sleeve shirt　长袖衬衫
dark trousers　长裤
leather shoes　皮鞋
dresses smartly　穿着非常得体
his shirts are always impeccably ironed　他的衬衫总是熨烫得完美无瑕
crease　折皱，折痕
cufflinks　（衬衫的）袖钉
plain buttoned sleeves　普通纽扣的袖子
his shoes are always nicely polished and shiny　他的鞋子总是擦得很亮
scruffy　肮脏的，破旧的
waistcoat　背心，马甲
professionalism　专业性，职业性
smart and presentable　得体和体面的

5. Describe a singer or band you like 描述一个你喜欢的歌手或乐队
You should say:
Who the singer or band is
How you knew the singer or the band
What you know about the singer or the band
And explain why you like the singer or the band

Sample 1

Sample Answer

The singer I would like to describe is Gloria Tang Tsz-kci, who is a Chinese singer and songwriter. She is better known by her stage name G. E. M., an acronym for Get

Everybody Moving. She is one of best-selling musical artists，winning IFPI Hong Kong's Top Selling Female Artist award.

Gloria Tang Tsz-kei was born in Shanghai and moved to Hong Kong at the age of four. She grew up with a musical background，with her mother being a graduate of the Shanghai Conservatory of Music，her uncle playing violin，her grandfather playing saxophone in an orchestra，and her grandmother teaching her how to sing. She appeared on Educational Television in Hong Kong at the age of seven. By that age she was already writing songs and entering school singing competitions. At the age of thirteen，she achieved grade eight in piano.

Her debut EP，GEM，was released in 2008. She won several awards for the album，earning the nicknames "girl with giant lungs" and "young diva with giant lungs"，for her vocal range and covers of Whitney Houston and Beyoncé songs.

She gained popularity in China after her appearance on the program "*I Am a Singer*" in 2014. Her fan base also extends to the United States，Canada，Australia，and Southeast Asia.

I like this singer because her singing skills are exceptionally high. Her live performance could prove this. When she sings the song called "Bubbles"，all the fans on the spot are fascinated by the flexible switch of the low pitch and the high pitch. Another aspect I like about her is that she is good at composing music and she always make innovations in her music style.

Gloria Tang Tsz-kei is my favorite singer.

词汇和句型
stage name　艺名
Shanghai Conservatory of Music　上海音乐学院
singing competitions　歌唱比赛
fan base　粉丝群
exceptionally high　特别高
live performance　现场表演
on the spot　在现场
the flexible switch of the low pitch and the high pitch　高低音的灵活转换
make innovations　创新

Sample 2

Sample Answer
The singer I would like to describe is Hua Chenyu，who is a Chinese singer and

songwriter. He was the winner of the Super Boy Singing Contest. Hua is well known for his powerful vocal，dramatic stage performance，and composing talents.

Hua Chenyu was born on February 7，1990. He began playing the flute at the age of 6 and playing the piano in the fifth grade when he realized flute was not enough to express his ideas. He soon mastered piano and wrote his first song at the age of twelve.

After finishing middle school，he moved to Wuhan，which is the provincial city of Hubei Province in China，to receive professional music training. In 2010，he entered Wuhan Conservatory of Music，where he studied vocal performance and gained more stage experience as the vocalist of a college rock band.

In 2013，shortly before graduating from the conservatory，Hua entered the casting for the Super Boy contest. The young singer stood out among the contestants. Since then，Hua Chenyu officially started his career as a singer.

I like this singer because Hua Chenyu is a gifted and diligent singer. Although he is one of the most popular singers in China，he still puts in effort to make breakthroughs in his music style. Innovation is always his concern and that's why his fans are so crazy about him as well as his music. Additionally，as a songwriter，Hua Chenyu has solid theoretical foundation and abundant practical experience. Therefore，Hua Chenyu is regarded as an all-round music superstar.

One more thing I would like to mention is that Hua Chenyu is a very optimistic person. Even if he came across a lot of obstacles in his life，he stuck to his goal and dream，which is a good virtue for a successful singer. That is another reason why his fans like him so much.

词汇和句型

singer and songwriter　歌手和流行歌曲创作人
powerful vocal，dramatic stage performance　强大的声音表现以及令人印象深刻的舞台表现
composing talents　作曲方面的天赋
playing the flute　吹长笛
professional music training　专业的音乐培训
Wuhan Conservatory of Music　武汉音乐学院
the vocalist of a college rock band　一个大学摇滚乐队的主唱
casting　挑选角色，海选
a gifted and diligent singer　一个有天赋并且勤奋的歌手
make breakthroughs in his music style　在他的音乐风格上有所突破

solid theoretical foundation and abundant practical experience 坚实的理论基础和丰富的实践经验

an all-round music superstar 一个全能的音乐超级明星

come across a lot of obstacles 经历许多坎坷

stuck to his goal 坚持他的梦想

6. Describe a friend who you think is a good leader 描述一个你认为是好的领导者的你的朋友

You should say:

Who he or she is

How you knew him or her

What he or she did

And explain why you think the friend is a good leader

Sample Answer

The friend who is a good leader I would like to describe is Jack Williams，who is also an engineering major in my university. Although he is two years older than me，we are good brothers and the best friends.

I knew Jack two years ago when I entered Shanghai Jiao Tong University. At that time，I planned to participate in the Students' Union and Jack was the Vice President of the Students' Union. On the occasion of filling out the application form，Jack introduced the features of different clubs. Since then，we have become friends.

Jack is so interested in the Information Technology that he led a team to develop iOS Apps and other websites. The most important thing he did at university was that his group developed an App for learning English vocabulary，which was particularly popular with students in China. Another significant thing he accomplished was that his team launched a website last year. That website was similar to Facebook，but it provided the Internet users with more opportunities to work part-time so that students from poor families could afford the tuition fee.

As to the reasons why I think he is a good leader，I would say that there are three main reasons. The first one is that he has a glamorous personality，so people around him are willing to do things for him. People regard him as a trustworthy person. Another reason why I consider him to be a good leader is that he has leadership skills. He knows how to manage people in a team and allocate the tasks to different people who are good at specific aspects. More importantly，he excels in information technology so that everyone in our university respects him and would like to work for him.

Jack is a friend who is a good leader.

词汇和句型

participate in the Student Union　参加学生会

filling out the application form　填写申请表

was particularly popular with the students　在学生中特别受欢迎

launched a website　发布了一个网站

afford the tuition fee　付得起学费

a trustworthy person　一个值得信任的人

allocate the tasks to different people who are good at specific aspects　把任务分配给擅长不同方面的人

he excels in information technology　他对信息技术很擅长

7. Describe a person who apologized to you 描述一个跟你道过歉的人

You should say:

Who the person is

What the person is like

What the person did

And explain why this person apologized to you

Sample Answer

The person who apologized to me is Jeff，who is my dorm mate in my university.

Jeff and I are big fans of music. My favorite singer is Taylor Swift and his favorite singer is Adele. Jeff has collected all the CDs and DVDs of Adele and he even flew to London to attend her concert. He told me that he wished to work with Adele one day in the future.

On a sunny weekend afternoon in the dorm，after finishing our paperwork，we talked about our idols. When I said that Adele never came to Shanghai to hold her concert while Taylor Swift did last year in Mercedes-Benz Arena，Jeff suddenly got angry and shouted at me. I was completely shocked by his rude behavior. He said nothing but slammed the door and left the dorm room.

In the evening that day，Jeff came back to the dorm room with some snacks. He told me that he was out of control in the afternoon because he misunderstood what I meant. He thought that I looked down upon Adele，but he realized that I said that without offence. He apologized to me sincerely because what he did was so ridiculous and he hoped I didn't feel hurt. He also said that he will invite me to listen to Adele's concert in Shanghai in the future as an apology. Then，we ate some snacks Jeff bought and talked more about our idols.

I accepted his apology and we are still best friends.

词汇和句型

dorm mate （寝室)室友

big fans 超级粉丝

flew to London to attend her concert 坐飞机去伦敦看她的演唱会

hold her concert 举办演唱会

slammed the door 把门猛然关上

without offence 没有冒犯的意思

8. Describe a person you know who is good at cooking 描述一个你认识的擅长烹饪的人

You should say:

Who it is

How they learned to cook

What they like to cook

And explain why you think their cooking is good.

Sample Answer

The person that I'd like to talk to you about is my mum，which I guess comes as no surprise to you，seeing as most people enjoy their mother's cooking. But I honestly think my mum is an amazing cook，and as for how she got to being so good at cooking，I guess she basically picked it up from her mother，in other words my granny，who was also incredibly good at cooking. So yeah，I suppose it kind of runs in the family. Although unfortunately，I haven't inherited this skill myself. My cooking's pretty awful.

But anyway，whatever my mom cooks，it's amazing，without exception. I mean，everything she's ever cooked for me has been absolutely delicious. I don't really know how else to describe it. And out of all of the dishes she's made for me，I'd say my favorite one would probably be roast chicken，because it's always so succulent and tender. And my mouth's actually starting to water just thinking of it.

Anyway finally，before I finish，I'd just like to mention one time which really left an impression on me，and it was when my mum was feeling a bit down，for some reason or other，and basically what happened was that the potatoes she'd cooked were a bit underdone; they were a bit hard. And when I mentioned this to her，she said to me，"I'm sorry, my heart just wasn't in it". And that was when I realized that every single dish she had cooked for me in my life had been done out of love. And that's really，I think，the main reason as to why she cooks so well.

So yeah，I'm super lucky to have such a wonderful mum who cooks nice food for me.

词汇和句型

an amazing cook　一个很棒的厨师
incredibly good at cooking　非常擅长烹饪
I haven't inherited this skill myself　我没有继承这个技能
my cooking's pretty awful　我做饭水平很差
absolutely delicious　非常可口
roast chicken　烤鸡
succulent and tender　（鸡肉）多汁鲜嫩
my mouth's actually starting to water just thinking of it　想到这个我就要开始流口水了
I'd just like to mention one time which really left an impression on me　我要提一下我记忆中印象很深刻的一次经历
my mum was feeling a bit down　我妈妈心情不太好
for some reason or other　某种原因
the potatoes she'd cooked were a bit underdone　她煮的土豆有点不熟
every single dish she had cooked for me in my life had been done out of love　她为我做的每道菜都是用爱精心烹饪的

9. Describe a character or personality of yours 描述一个你的个性特征

You should say:
What the character or personality
When you had this character or personality
What influence of this character or personality exerts on you
And explain why you have this character or personality

Sample Answer

My personality I would like to describe is patience，which is a good virtue to deal with the hustle and bustle of life.

I had the character when I was in primary school. During that period，I was required to learn a variety of subjects including arithmetic，Chinese，English，science，and so on. What's more，teachers demanded us to finish homework within two hours for every subject. Initially，I thought it was impossible to fulfill the task because math and science were so complicated and I needed time to review the formulas learned in classroom before I could start doing the homework. However，at that point，I noted that everything would be chaotic if I was in a hurry. Then，I took my time and thought over the priority in doing the things. Eventually，I did a good job in doing the homework.

Since then，I have been a patient person.

Patience exerts positive influences on me. The first benefit is that I can avoid mistakes. Patience gives me a second chance in reviewing my work. I can figure out the correct ways to do a job. Plus，in most cases，I am able to find better ways to solve problems. When I am under time pressure，more often than not，I would be hasty in doing things. If I get the solution，I would be inclined to regard it as the best one. But if I am patient，sometimes I would think twice about the way things are done. So innovative ideas always come to my mind.

As to why I have this personality，I guess it is related to the childhood education given by my parents. They are nice people. And they are always able to address problems，even when facing urgent situations. Because of this，I learned the importance of being patient. Additionally，from primary school to college，I saw many peers who possess the same personality as I do. We often do class assignments and hang out together，which reinforces this personality.

词汇和句型
a good virtue　一个优良品德
the hustle and bustle of life　生活的喧闹繁忙
learn a variety of subjects　学习各种课程
Initially　一开始
fulfill the task　完成任务
everything would be chaotic if I was in a hurry　如果我很急，事情就会很混乱
took my time　慢慢来
thought over the priority　思考事情的优先顺序
exerts positive influences on me　……对我造成积极影响
I can figure out the correct ways to do a job　我可以找到做事情的正确方法
under time pressure　处于时间压力中
more often than not　往往，多半
be hasty in doing things　做事情很匆忙
think twice　三思，谨慎考虑
innovative ideas　创新的想法
address problems　解决问题
reinforces this personality　强化了这种个性

10. Describe a creative person you admire 描述一个你钦佩的有创造力的人
You should say:
Who he / she is
What he / she is like

What he / she has done
And explain why you admire him / her

Sample Answer

A creative person I admire is, definitely, Mark Zuckerberg, who initiated an era of social networking system. He is the most innovative person on a global scale.

Mark Elliot Zuckerberg is an American computer programmer, Internet entrepreneur, and philanthropist. He is the chairman, chief executive, and co-founder of the social networking website Facebook. His net worth is estimated to be $48. 2 billion. Zuckerberg and his wife Priscilla Chan announced they would donate the majority of their wealth to charity.

Zuckerberg began using computers and writing software in middle school. By the time he began classes at Harvard, Zuckerberg had already achieved a "reputation as a programming prodigy". Zuckerberg launched Facebook from his Harvard dormitory room on February 4, 2004. It published its own student directory, "The Photo Address Book", which students referred to as "The Facebook". Such photo directories were an important part of the student social experience at many private schools. With them, students were able to list attributes such as their class years, their friends, and their telephone numbers.

I admire him for the following reasons. Although he's wealthy, he never shows off what he owns in public. Every time he gives speeches, he just wears the same T-shirt, by which I mean the same color and style exactly. Unlike other tycoons who drive luxury cars, Zuckerberg drives Volkswagen Golf. I respect this kind of thrifty lifestyle. Another reason I admire him is that he donated a huge sum of money to charitable organizations. In this way, many youngsters are encouraged to do the same thing, which could help a lot of people in need all over the world. The most important reason I admire him is that he is by far the most creative person. Not satisfied with the achievement in the Internet industry, he has launched programs in other fields such as Virtual Reality and Artificial Intelligence. Hopefully, I will have the chance to work for him after graduation.

词汇和句型

initiated an era of social networking system　开启了社交网络的时代
computer programmer　电脑程序员
Internet entrepreneur　因特网企业家
philanthropist　慈善家
donate the majority of their wealth to charity　把他们大多数的财产捐献给慈善事业

a programming prodigy　一个电脑编程神童
attribute　标志,特征
Unlike other tycoons who drive luxury cars　跟其他企业界大亨开豪车不同
charitable organizations　慈善组织
Virtual Reality VR　虚拟现实

11. Describe a person you do not like but have to be friendly to 描述一个你不喜欢但不得不友好对待的人

You should say:
Who the person is
What this person is like
Why you do not like him or her
And explain why you have to be friendly to him or her

Sample Answer

It was several years ago when I was in a summer camp held by my school. I lived with three other girls in the dorm room in the suburban area. I was quite good friends with all the other girls except one of them，a senior student whose name was Amy，because she was too noisy and arrogant.

She spoke on her phone for more than an hour every night，which was so disturbing. And her voice was so loud that I could hear her clearly even when I was listening to music with my earphones. I couldn't focus when she was making so much noise in the room. Neither could I have a rest. That was so annoying.

Also，she thought that she was smarter and more experienced than us because she was two years older than all of us. But in fact，she was neither smart nor experienced.

I didn't want to speak to her but I was forced to because we happened to be in the same team in the summer camp. The teacher had put us in the same team and I had no choice. I basically had to do everything with her. We had to share plenty of resources and we had to finish a lot of projects together. Therefore，I decided to be smart and to befriend her even though I didn't like her at all.

In order to make up for the relationship，I tried to be nice to her. Her birthday was during the summer，so I helped her hold a birthday party. I bought a lot of pretty decorations and she loved them. Then our relationship became better and we could work with each other and communicate with each other properly.

词汇和句型

a summer camp　夏令营

in the suburban area　在郊区

too noisy and arrogant　太吵闹和傲慢了

She spoke on her phone for more than an hour every night　她每晚打电话超过 1 小时

I couldn't focus　我不能集中注意力

befriend her　对她如朋友一般

12. Describe a person who is fashionable in clothes 描述一个穿着时尚的人

You should say:

Who the person is

What clothes this person often wears

What is special about this person

And explain why you think this person is fashionable in clothes

Sample Answer

The person who is fashionable in clothes I would like to describe is my older sister. Her name is Crystal and she is a fashion model. I regard her as the most attractive girl among my family members because of her awesome appearance，in particular her great figure.

Crystal often wears tight dresses，especially mini-skirts，and she looks fabulous. Besides，she is obsessed with collecting various skirts，so her room is full of different styles of clothing. She can find whatever she likes wearing in her bedroom.

As for what is special about my older sister，I would say she is the craziest person that I have met in my daily life. Can you guys imagine that a person refuses to eat any food for a week just to wear an extremely tight dress? Honestly speaking，I cannot do that because I will starve to death.

When it comes to the reason why I regard her as the someone who is fashionable in clothes，the main reason is that she has a unique taste about clothes. She always provides me with precise and creative advice when we go shopping for clothes together. Apart from this，she is good at choosing and combining colors. So I would say that she has a special sense of fashion.

My older sister Crystal is the person who is fashionable in clothes.

词汇和句型

a fashion model　时装模特

awesome appearance   极好的外貌

in particular   特别是

great figure   好身材

she looks fabulous   她看起来太棒了

she is obsessed with collecting various skirts   她热衷于收藏各种裙子

She can find whatever she likes wearing in her bedroom   她可以在她卧室找到任何她想穿的衣服

tight dress   紧身女装

Honestly speaking   说实话

a unique taste about clothes   对服饰有独特的品位

Apart from this   除此之外

she is good at choosing and combining colors   她善于选择和搭配色彩

13. Describe a person who is good at a foreign language 描述一个擅长外语的人

You should say:

Who the person is

What language she is good at

How often that person uses that language

And explain why this person is good at this foreign language

Sample Answer

The person who is good at a foreign language I would like to describe is one of my good friends. His name is Tony，and he is a junior student in my university. His major is English and he excels in writing awesome essays as well as speaking English.

Since Tony is an English major，I would say he uses English almost every day. I guess he has to speak that foreign language with classmates in the classroom and discuss with foreign professors in English during the break，which can be an excellent way for him to speak very good English.

As for why Tony is good at this foreign language，I think there are two main reasons. First of all，he has been studying English for more than 10 years，which has laid a solid foundation for him. Meanwhile，he devotes plenty of time and energy to learning English. In his spare time，he goes to the library to study English grammar and analyze grammatical structure of English sentences，which enables him to have a deeper understanding of this language than other students do. Another reason is his pronunciation is pretty good，which is similar to the accent of native speakers. He is a Hollywood-movie fan and is crazy about imitating intonations of oral English，so he can pronounce English sentences accurately. To be honest，it is comfortable to hear his voice.

Tony is the person who is good at a foreign language.

词汇和句型

a junior student 一个大三学生

he excels in ... 他擅长······

As for why Tony is good at this foreign language 至于说为什么托尼擅长这门外语

Meanwhile 同时

analyze grammatical structure of English sentences 分析英语句子的语法结构

enables him to have a deeper understanding of this language than other students do 使他比其他学生对这门语言有更深的理解

14. Describe a good parent you know 描述你认识的一个好父亲或者好母亲

You should say:

Who the parent is

How you knew the parent

What the parent looks like

And explain why you think the parent is good.

Sample Answer

The parent I'd like to talk about is the mother of a good friend of mine, and the reason for choosing to talk about her is that my friend is always going on about how lucky he is to have such a nice mum. And from what I know about her, I'd say he's absolutely right.

Anyway, as for how I knew her, it's basically due to the fact that I went to the same middle school as her son. And because we became pretty good friends, we ended up seeing quite a lot of each other's parents, especially during the holidays when we often went over to each other's homes.

And regarding what his mother looks like, well interestingly enough, she actually looks pretty similar to my own mother, because they both have round faces and long wavy hair. Having said that though, I've noticed that my friend's mother often ties her hair up in a bun, whereas my mother usually always keeps it down. And another thing to mention would be that whenever I see her, she seems to be wearing red, which I guess is probably because red suits her quite well.

But anyway, as to why I think she's a good parent, I'd say there are quite a few reasons, one of which would be that she's always been very supportive to her son. And just to give you an example. When he was deciding what major to study at university, he ended up choosing music. And his mother gave him her full support, which is probably not what many other parents would have done, as music doesn't really leave open a lot of career choices.

And I think it's fair to say that currently，a lot of parents persuade their children to do things which they think are best for them，but my friend has said that his parents have never been like this with him，especially his mother. So I get the impression that she's never forced him to do anything against his will，and has always let him make his own decisions，which I think's really great.

词汇和句型

it's basically due to the fact that ...　主要是因为……

we often went over to each other's homes　我们经常去对方家里玩

she actually looks pretty similar to my own mother　她看起来和我的妈妈很像

long wavy hair　长波浪卷发

Having said that though　尽管这样说

ties her hair up in a bun　把她的头发绑成一个髻

And another thing to mention would be that ...　另外一个我要提及的事情是……

red suits her quite well　红色非常适合她

as to why I think she's a good parent　关于为什么我认为她是一个好母亲

she's always been very supportive to her son　她一直以来都很支持她的儿子

just to give you an example　给你举个例子

he ended up choosing music　他最终选择了音乐(专业)

his mother gave him her full support　他的妈妈给了他全力支持

leave open a lot of career choices　留待很多职业供选择

a lot of parents persuade their children to do things which they think are best for them　许多父母劝说他们的孩子去做一些他们所认为对他们孩子好的事情

she's never forced him to do anything against his will　她从未强迫过他做违背他意愿的事情

make his own decisions　他自己做决定

15. Describe a couple you know who have a happy marriage 描述一对有幸福婚姻的夫妻
You should say:
Who they are
How you knew them
How long they have been married
And explain why you think they are happily married

Sample Answer

The first married couple that came to mind when I saw this topic were some neighbors of mine，because as far as I know，they are very happy together，so I'd like to tell you a little bit about them.

So firstly, as for how I knew them, I basically got to know them when I moved into my flat here, because they live just next door to me, so we often bump into each other, and we've now become pretty good friends.

And as for how long they've been married, I think it's only been for about two or three years, because they're both quite young and only in their mid-twenties. Although if I remember correctly, I think one of them told me that they were together for quite a few years before they got married, because they met each other in high school, so taking that into account, they've actually been together for about ten years or so.

But anyway, regarding why I think they're happily married, I would say one reason is that, whenever I see them, they always seem to be happy and cheerful. I mean, I've never seen them argue or shout at each other before, and they've also never said anything bad about each other, apart from when they're joking of course.

And I get the impression that they treat each other really well. For example, I've noticed that the husband always drives his wife to and from work every day, and she often buys clothes for him, which I know because I once saw him wearing a nice-looking shirt and asked him where he got it, and he told me that his wife got it for him.

So yeah, there's no doubt that they're really happy together, and I think they're great role models for how to keep a marriage strong and healthy.

词汇和句型

as far as I know   据我所知
they live just next door to me   他们住在我隔壁
we often bump into each other   我们经常不期而遇
they're both quite young and only in their mid-twenties   他们很年轻,只有二十五六岁
I've never seen them argue or shout at each other before   我从来没有看到过他们吵架
And I get the impression that ...   我觉得……
role models   榜样
keep a marriage strong and healthy   使得婚姻牢固持久

16. Describe two people from the same family 描述来自相同家庭的两个人
You should say:
Who they are
How you knew them
What are their features
And explain what are the similarities and difference between them

Sample Answer

I would like to describe my best friend Jenny and her mother Mrs. Patrol.

I knew Jenny when I was in primary school. At that time，I often visited her home and that's why I got acquainted with her mother Mrs. Patrol as well. I would say that Jenny and her mother are fairly nice people not only because they are well-educated but also because they have good personalities.

Jenny is an extroverted person，similar to her mom，which is why they are very friendly to others，even to strangers on the street. It is a great pleasure to talk to them. Whenever I felt depressed and frustrated，I would talk to them and feel a lot better. That's one thing. And another feature I would like to mention is that Jenny and her mom are optimistic about their life. Even if they encounter obstacles，they would solve the problems with a positive attitude.

But there are some differences between Jenny and Mrs. Patrol. For one thing, Jenny's hobby is doing outdoor activities. For example，she likes extreme sports. She went to some cliffs to do bungee-jumping, which is so terrifying to me and I would never dare to do that. However，her mother likes shopping. So on weekends and holidays，what she does is to rush to the shopping malls to purchase luxury bags and shoes. Another thing is that their preference of music is different. Jenny prefers to listen to R&B music such as Beyoncé's songs，while her mother likes listening to pop music such as Adele's songs.

Anyway，they are both really nice people.

词汇和句型
that's why I got acquainted with her mother　这就是为什么我认识她的妈妈
not only because they are well-educated but also because they have good personalities　不仅是因为他们受过良好教育,而且是因为他们有很好的性格
an extroverted person　一个开朗的人
which is why they are very friendly to others　这就是为什么她们对待其他人非常友好
are optimistic about their life　对她们的生活很乐观
encounter obstacles　遇到挫折
solve the problems with a positive attitude　以积极态度来解决问题

17. Describe a comic actor who is popular in your country 描述一个在你的国家受欢迎的喜
　　剧演员
You should say:
Who the actor is
How you know him / her

What kind of person he/she is
And explain why he/she is popular in your country.

The actor that I've decided to talk about is Stephen Chow，who，I think it's fair to say，is one of the most famous and popular comedians in China.

I've watched his films ever since I was a child，which I'm sure could also be said for the majority of people of my age in China. And the reason is simply that he's incredibly funny. I mean，whenever I watch his films，I can't stop myself from laughing. And I'm not sure if you've watched any of his films before，but I guess you could compare him to Jim Carrey，in the sense that they can both pull really funny faces. And that's probably what sets him apart from most other comedians in China. He's got such an array of different facial expressions.

Anyway，as for what kind of person he is，I don't know him personally of course，but the impression I get of him is that he's a very down-to-earth guy. So I mean，although he's super famous and rich，he seems to carry himself in a very unassuming manner. For example，in the interviews I've seen of him，he comes across as being a very modest and likeable guy.

So yeah，that's pretty much all there is to say really，and if you haven't seen any of his films before，you should definitely watch one.

词汇和句型

one of the most famous and popular comedians　最著名和最受欢迎的喜剧演员之一
the majority of people of my age　和我相同年龄中的大部分人
the reason is simply that ...　原因主要是……
I can't stop myself from laughing　我会情不自禁地笑起来
in the sense that ...　从……角度来说，从……意义上而言
pull really funny faces　装出滑稽的面孔
that's probably what sets him apart from most other comedians　这可能就是区分他和大多数其他喜剧演员的重要方面
he's got such an array of different facial expressions　他有各种不同的脸部表情
the impression I get of him is that　我对他的印象是……
he's a very down-to-earth guy　他是一个非常脚踏实地的人
super famous and rich　非常有名和有钱
he seems to carry himself in a very unassuming manner　他看起来总是非常谦和
he comes across as being a very modest and likeable guy　他给人的印象是一个非常谦虚和讨人喜欢的人

第三节　Places 地点类话题真题及范文

1. **Describe a place you visited that has been affected by pollution** 描述一个你去过的被污染的地方

You should say:
Where it is
When you visited that place
Why you visited that place
And explain how serious that place has been polluted

Sample Answer

The place I visited that has been seriously polluted，without doubt，is Beijing，the capital of China. It is by far the most severely contaminated city in China because of its large population and fastest industrial development.

I went to Beijing last October to attend a conference. Autumn should be a season full of colors and fresh air. However，what I experienced at that time was dust storms as well as fog and haze，which made Beijing an uninhabitable place.

Beijing is a historic city with more than 5,000 years of history，which is why I was eager to go there although I would be on a business trip. There are a variety of cultural relics and well-preserved historical buildings，which make Beijing an appealing city. Nevertheless，the unbearable pollution ruined all the cultural treasures.

Beijing has been extremely polluted to a large extent. For one thing，natural disasters，such as dust storms，invariably occur annually. When it happens，people cannot leave their houses and apartments because the air is unbreathable. For another，the booming economic development is at the cost of environment pollution. Indeed，factories of heavy industries，such as iron industry，are emitting toxic gases every single day. Waste water is another by-product of industrial progress. As for the public，most people drive private cars instead of taking public transportation. Therefore，the amount of waste gas discharged by vehicles is alarmingly huge. All these factors contribute to the large-scale contamination of Beijing.

Hopefully，this polluted city will become better in the near future.

词汇和句型
without doubt　毫无疑问

by far the most severely contaminated city in China　目前中国污染最严重的城市

attend a conference　参加一次会议

an uninhabitable place　不适于居住的地方

be on a business trip　去出差

a variety of cultural relics　各种文物

well-preserved historical buildings　保护良好的历史建筑

an appealing city　一座有吸引力的城市

the unbearable pollution　无法忍受的污染

dust storms　沙尘暴

invariably occur annually　每年总是发生

the booming economic development　繁荣的经济发展

toxic gases　有毒气体

every single day　每一天

the amount of waste gas discharged by vehicles is alarmingly huge　汽车排放出的尾气量很大

All these factors contribute to the large-scale contamination　这些因素导致了大规模的污染

2. **Describe a place you know where people go to listen to music（such as a theatre or a music hall）** 描述一个你了解的人们去听音乐的地方(比如戏院或者音乐厅)

You should say:
Where it is
What kind of music is performed
What type of people go there
And explain your impressions of this place

Sample Answer

Talking about a place where people like to go and listen to the music，I guess Shanghai Grand Theater in my hometown is a perfect place for me to describe.

It is located at the east of the People's Square，which is the center of Shanghai，and shaped like a triangular box. The architectural style is absolutely distinctive. When night falls，it resembles a crystal palace. This unique design has made it a famous landmark in our city that attracts millions of visitors every year.

The audiences there are mainly students majoring in music and middle-aged music lovers as well as senior citizens. Visitors can enjoy a range of elegant music types such as symphonies，dramas，and traditional Chinese operas. Every year many preeminent musicians would choose this place as their major performing stage and thousands of world-class musical artworks would also show up on the stages for us to appreciate.

I think it's an extraordinary place for people to listen to music because of its top-quality acoustic settings. The floor is constructed with massive rubber pads, so they are able to absorb any vibrations. The walls are made of several layers of brown timber, which are all curved instead of being straight in order to improve the acoustic properties and to amplify the sound.

That's why I believe Shanghai Grand Theater is a great place for people to enjoy music.

词汇和句型

Shanghai Grand Theater 上海大剧院

architectural style 建筑风格

unique design 独特的设计

a famous landmark 一个著名的地标

students majoring in music 音乐专业的学生

middle-aged music lovers 中年音乐爱好者

senior citizens 老年人

symphony 交响乐

traditional Chinese operas 中国戏曲

preeminent musicians 卓越的音乐家

major performing stage 主要的表演舞台

world-class musical artworks 世界级的音乐作品

top-quality acoustic settings 顶级的音响设置

rubber pads 橡胶垫

absorb any vibrations 吸收震动

improve the acoustic properties 提高声音特性

amplify the sound 放大声音

3. Describe an interesting public place that you like 描述一个你喜欢的令人感兴趣的公共场所

You should say:

Where it is

What can be seen there

How often you go there

And explain why you like it.

Sample Answer

The interesting public place I would like to describe is Shanghai Library, which is one of the most popular places in Shanghai. The library is located in the downtown area in the city. To be specific, it is in a central business area, so most commuters could access it on weekdays.

A variety of things are available in Shanghai Library. What I love the most is the foreign-magazine area. In this area, I could find the most popular magazines from the US and the UK. I like reading *Time*, *National Geographic*, and *the Economist*. With a transparent glass ceiling, I can enjoy sunshine when I read these magazines. It is the utmost enjoyment for me if I also have a cup of coffee.

Another special aspect is that there is a video room in Shanghai Library. In this room, I can watch any video in history by clicking the mouse on the screen as the storage of video files is huge. When I feel tired, I watch Disney animation movies. And if I feel depressed, I would choose Mr. Bean to cheer me up.

I visit Shanghai Library every weekend, spending two hours in reading books and magazines there. After that, I would borrow six to eight books to read from Monday to Friday. Sometimes I would buy a cup of coffee and some cheese cakes in the coffee bar.

Everyone likes Shanghai Library including me. The main reason is that it provides me with a quiet environment to relieve stress and acquire knowledge. If I read books and write papers in Starbucks, people around me would distract me. However, Shanghai Library is a spacious and absolutely tranquil place, so I could focus on the things I'm working on.

That's why I like Shanghai Library, which is the best public place everybody should visit.

词汇和句型
the downtown area 市中心地区
To be specific 具体而言
a central business area 中心商业区
most commuters could access it on weekdays 大多数通勤者可以在工作日方便地去那里
Time，National Geographic，and The Economist 《时代周刊》、《国家地理》和《经济学人》
a transparent glass ceiling 透明的玻璃天花板
Disney animation movies 迪士尼动画电影
relieve stress 缓解压力
acquire knowledge 学习知识
tranquil place 安静的地方
I could focus on the things I'm working on 我可以集中注意力做我的事情

4. Describe a place that was full of colors you remember going to 描述一个你记得去过的充满色彩的地方
   You should say:
   What the place was

When you went to that place
What the place was like
And explain why that place was full of colors

Sample Answer

Last Monday evening, I went to the kindergarten to pick up my niece. When I entered the classroom, I noticed that the room was very colorful. I also observed that there were no dark colors like black and brown but only light ones such as pink and yellow, for children usually prefer light colors and dark colors are considered unsuitable for young children.

Everything in the room had been carefully painted, and the whole room looked so sweet as if it was made of candies. The walls were mint green and the floor was lemon yellow with a large piece of orange carpet on it. All the tiny chairs were sky blue and the little desks were pink and decorated with red glitter. Various kinds of toys, dolls, and models were placed in pinky-white baskets behind the door. There was a giant puppet, which was almost as tall as the children, beside the whiteboard. Two shelves stood in the corner, and there were cups for each student — blue ones for boys and pink ones for girls. The most interesting part in the classroom was the ceiling, because there was a fresco of sky on it. The blue sky and the white clouds in the fresco were so real that I felt as if I was standing under the sky.

I think there are two main reasons why the interior of the room and the furniture are multi-colored. Young children love colorful stuff and they feel delighted in a colorful room. Those bright colors can cheer children up. A colorful room also makes it easier for teachers to teach the children all kinds of colors. For example, the teacher can let the children look at the chairs and tell them that the chairs are blue.

词汇和句型
pick up my niece 接我的侄女
light colors 浅色
dark colors 深色
mint green 薄荷绿
lemon yellow 柠檬黄
sky blue 天空蓝
red glitter 红色亮片
Various kinds of toys, dolls and models 各种玩具、洋娃娃和模型
pinky-white baskets 粉白色篮子
a giant puppet 巨型木偶
a fresco of sky 一幅天空的壁画
the interior of the room 房间内部

multi-colored　多彩的
feel delighted　感到开心
cheer children up　使儿童开心

5. Describe a stadium in your town or city 描述一个你所在城市的体育场
You should say:
What the stadium is
Where it is located
What events were held there
And explain why you like this stadium

Sample Answer

The stadium that I'd particularly like to introduce is Shanghai Stadium，which was constructed for the 8th National Games held in Shanghai in 1997. The 2008 Olympic football games were held in that stadium as well. This stadium lies in the southwest of Shanghai，which is the downtown area. It is both a field for football games and a venue for outdoor concerts. In particular，the superstar Celine Dion has held a concert in Shanghai Stadium.

Basically，it now serves as a home field for the local football team — Shanghai SIPG Football Club. Besides，it's now open to the public，which is also the chief reason why I go there frequently. On average，I play badminton there once a week and some male friends of mine enjoy playing basketball there almost every week. I suppose that local residents tend to go there because the sports facilities are of high quality. Also，the ancillary facilities，such as the bathroom，the lounge，and of course the service center，outstandingly cater to residents' needs. And one thing I'd also like to mention is that Shanghai Stadium is now holding almost all concerts in the city. I have already been to many pop music concerts there.

Finally，I'd like to discuss more benefits of this stadium. It provides the public with a terrific opportunity to enjoy sports，improving public health and local dwellers' life quality. Likewise，the society has benefited from that stadium as well，such as tax revenues they get from visitors and from the charge for facility use.

词汇和句型
National Games　全国运动会
a venue for outdoor concerts　室外音乐会场地
Celine Dion　席琳·迪翁
a home field　主场
Shanghai SIPG Football Club　上海上港足球俱乐部

the chief reason 主要原因

play badminton 打羽毛球

the sports facilities are of high quality 体育设施质量很高

ancillary facilities 附属设施

cater to residents' need 迎合了居民的需求

terrific opportunity 极好的机会

local dwellers' life quality 当地居民的生活质量

tax revenue 税收收入

the charge for facility use 设施使用收费

6. **Describe a café (or restaurant) that you know in your hometown** 描述一个你家乡的咖啡馆或者餐厅

Sample Answer

You should say:

Where it is

How often you go there

What kind of food they serve there（or，what service they provide）

And explain why you like to eat at this place.

The cafe that I'd like to talk to you about is one called SD Cafe，which is somewhere in the outskirts of the city，just a few minutes' walk from where I live.

And as for how often I go there，I actually go there quite a lot，probably something like once or twice a week. Having said that though，it really depends on how busy I am. I mean，there are times when I don't go for weeks on end because I'm simply too busy with stuff，but normally that's not the case，and I'm there pretty regularly，as I just mentioned.

Anyway，regarding what kind of things they serve there，it's great，because they've got a really good selection of both Chinese and Western food，so there's a lot to choose from. And in terms of drinks，there's also quite a lot on the menu，especially coffee. I tend to go for the Americano coffee，because I think they do it really well，and so I've never really felt the need to try any of the other drinks on the menu.

But anyway，moving on to why I like this place so much，I'd say it's a combination of reasons，one of which would be that it's really big and spacious，at least compared to most of the other cafes I've been to，so you never have to worry about not being able to find a place to sit. Although having said that，it can sometimes get pretty busy at night，so I usually go in the morning or afternoon. Anyway，another thing to mention would be that the food and drinks there are pretty good-value because I mean most of the western food there only costs between 30 to 50 RMB，which is a lot cheaper than most of the other western restaurants in the city. And the price of the coffee there is about the same price as Starbucks'，which some people might see as expensive，but considering the fact that you're paying for the environment as well as the drink，I'd say it's definitely worth it.

The other thing I really like about it is that you can spend as much time as you want there，without being bothered by the waiters. And the chairs there are nice and comfy，so it's actually very easy to spend half the day there using the free WIFI or doing whatever.

So yeah，I guess that's about it.

词汇和句型

the outskirts of the city　市郊

a few minutes' walk from where I live　我住的地方走过去几分钟时间

Having said that though　话虽如此

something like once or twice a week　大约一周一两次

there are times when I don't go for weeks on end　有时候我连续几周不去

that's not the case　不是这样的

a really good selection of both Chinese and Western food　中西方美食汇聚

And in terms of drinks　谈到饮料

I tend to go for the Americano coffee　我通常会选择喝美式咖啡

the other drinks on the menu　菜单上的其他饮料

moving on to why I like this place so much　继续说我为什么这么喜欢这个地方

I'd say it's a combination of reasons　我觉得有各种原因

it's really big and spacious　占地很大很宽敞

you never have to worry about not being able to find a place to sit　你永远不必担心找不到地方坐

Although having said that　话虽这样说

the food and drinks there are pretty good-value　食物和饮料物有所值

the price of the coffee there is about the same price as Starbucks'　这个咖啡馆的咖啡和星巴克的咖啡价格差不多

you can spend as much time as you want there，without being bothered by the waiters　你在那里想待多久待多久,不必担心服务员赶你走

nice and comfy　既漂亮又舒服

I guess that's about it　我觉得说得差不多了

7. Describe a country you would like to visit for the first time 描述你想要去一次的国家
You should say:
What country it is

How long you would stay there
What you would like to do there
And explain why you would like to visit this particular country

Sample Answer

One country that I'd really love to go and visit sometime is the United States. And there are a few reasons. First of all, I have some really good friends living there, and they told me if I ever get round to going there, then I'm welcome to stay at their place, which would be great.

And another thing is that I've always wanted to go there, but have never had the opportunity, so I really hope that sometime in the future I'll be able to go there.

I think there would be so much to do there. I mean, first of all, I'd definitely go and see Hollywood. And if I'm not mistaken, that's also where Universal Studios is, where you can, like, go around and check out all the sets from famous movies that have been filmed there. So that would be pretty cool. And the weather's meant to be really great there, sunny the whole time, at least in California anyway, which is where I'd spend my time.

And as for how long I would stay there, I'm not actually that sure, but I suppose two or three weeks would be about right. I think I'd be able to do and see most things in that time. And if I stayed any longer, I'd probably end up spending far more money than I can afford to.

I think it would be an amazing place to visit, and hopefully I'll have the chance to do so in the near future.

词汇和句型

I have some really good friends living there　我有些好朋友住在那里
get round to ...　开始考虑……;抽出时间去……
stay at their place　住在他们那里
I think there would be so much to do there　我觉得在那里有很多事情可以做
if I'm not mistaken　如果我没记错的话
Universal Studios　环球影城
the sets from famous movies that have been filmed there　在那里拍的著名电影中的场景
I'm not actually that sure　我其实不是那么确定

8. **Describe a foreign country you would like to work in for a short period of time** 描述一个你想要去短暂工作一段时间的国家
   You should say:

Where it is
When would you like to go there
What you would like to do there
And explain why you would like to work in that country

Sample Answer

The foreign country I would like to work for a relatively short period of time is the United States，which is the biggest superpower in the world with the most advanced working methods.

I plan to go to work in the US after my graduation from a local university here in Shanghai. My major is engineering so I would like to work in the Silicon Valley in the Bay Area of California. Many high-tech companies set their headquarters there so perhaps I could find a decent job out there.

I would like to do various types of jobs in the field of engineering in California. To be specific，my favorite job is the software designer. which is completely connected with my major. I would love to do that because there are so many distinguished software experts from all over the world in the Silicon Valley，so I could benefit a lot from working with them.

Being a software designer means I need to be creative. But what I lack the most is innovative ideas. If I were offered a chance to work in the United States，I would have a chance to improve my creativity because the US is a free country that promotes innovation everywhere.

There are other reasons why I would like to work in that country. The weather in California is pretty cozy so I could enjoy the sunshine while I work every day. I could work in a happy mood. And the interpersonal relationship is quite good. Even if people have arguments in their work，they would not quarrel with each other；instead，they would persuade others by rational reasoning. That's why I would like to work there.

But I would not work there for a long time because I plan to have my career in Shanghai. And I have many friends here and there are no cultural barriers between us. One more thing is that my parents would not go to the US with me. So I would have to stay here to accompany them.

Ok，that is all I would like to say. Thanks.

词汇和句型

the most advanced working methods 最先进的工作方法

the Silicon Valley　硅谷
the Bay Area of California　加州湾区
high-tech companies　高科技公司
find a decent job　找到一个体面的工作
many distinguished software experts　许多优秀的软件专家
innovative ideas　创新的想法
cultural barriers　文化障碍
stay here to accompany them　留在这里陪伴他们

9. Describe your favorite park or garden 描述你最喜欢的公园或者花园
You should say:
Where it is
What can be seen there
How often you go there
And explain why you like it

Sample Answer

As you can imagine，I've been to quite a few parks and gardens，but if I had to pick a favorite，I guess I would probably say Prince's Bay Park，which is somewhere in the center of Hangzhou，not far from the West Lake.

And regarding what you can see there，I guess the first thing to mention would be the tulips，which is what the park's famous for，because it's full of them，and they're really gorgeous. In fact，I'm sure if you looked on the internet，you'd probably be able to see some photos of the park and the flowers yourself. Another thing that a lot of people go there to see is the cherry blossom，which is quite literally stunning，especially in the spring time. Unfortunately though，I've seen quite a number of people shaking the blossom off the branches，which means it disappears quicker than it would naturally，so it's a bit of a pity. But anyway，it's honestly no exaggeration to say that the park is incredibly beautiful，and that's why you'll also see a lot of young couples taking their wedding photos there.

Anyway，as for how often I go there，I don't really go there that often，probably only something like once or twice a month. The main reason is that it gets pretty crowded on weekends，so I normally go on weekdays.

And finally，with regard to why I like this park，there's not really that much more to say about it，apart from the fact that it's just a really nice and scenic place to go and relax，and simply enjoy the beauty of nature. The other great thing about it is that it's free entrance，which wasn't the case a while ago，so I'll probably be going there more often in the future.

词汇和句型

pick a favorite　选择一个最喜欢的

I guess the first thing to mention would be ...　我觉得首先要提一下的是……

the tulips　郁金香

really gorgeous　真的很美

the cherry blossom　樱花

literally stunning　真的非常漂亮

especially in the spring time　特别是在春天期间

Unfortunately though　但是

I've seen quite a number of people shaking the blossom off the branches　我看到过很多人把花从树枝上摇下来

it's honestly no exaggeration to say that　真的毫不夸张地说

incredibly beautiful　非常漂亮

you'll also see a lot of young couples taking their wedding photos there　你会看到很多年轻夫妇在那里拍结婚照

on weekdays　在工作日

10. Describe a shop that was just opened in your hometown 描述一个你家乡刚刚开的商店

You should say:

What shop it is

What it sells

When you first started going to this shop

And explain why you like this shop.

Sample Answer

A shop that was just opened in my hometown is H&M，so that's the one I'm going to describe.

With regard to what it sells，I'm not sure if you're familiar with H&M or not，but it's basically a mid-end clothes shop which sells a variety of women's and men's clothing，mostly geared towards young adults like myself. And as well as clothing，the shop also has a small accessories section for women，with things like hair bands，bracelets and earrings，but the main focus is definitely on clothes.

Anyway，as for when I first started going to this shop，to be totally honest with you，I'm really not that sure，but I guess I must have first started shopping there about two or three years ago，round about the time I was in high school，because I seem to vaguely remember one of my high-school classmates telling me about how good it was.

So that's kind of how I got to know about H&M, and finally, regarding why I like shopping there, I suppose it's really a combination of reasons, one of which would be that the clothes there, on the whole, tend to be quite fashionable and trendy, unlike the stuff I see in many other shops. And the clothes are pretty simplistic, which is exactly what I like. So that's one thing, and I guess another reason would be that everything there is really good-value, and just to give you an example, a decent pair of jeans there costs around three hundred RMB, whereas a similar pair at another shop would probably set you back a thousand RMB or so. And in terms of quality, there's really not that much difference between H&M's clothes and the higher-end brands, but you're paying considerably less.

So yeah, I would say these are, more or less, the main reasons why I like shopping there.

词汇和句型

that's the one I'm going to describe　这就是我将要描述的

with regard to what it sells　关于它卖什么

it's basically a mid-end clothes shop　这基本上是一个中档服装店

a variety of women's and men's clothing　卖各种各样的男女装

mostly geared towards young adults like myself　主要是适用于像我这样的年轻人

a small accessories section for women　一小块女性配件区

hair bands，bracelets and earrings　发带、手镯和耳环

vaguely remember　模糊地记得

a combination of reasons　各种理由

quite fashionable and trendy　非常时尚和流行

the clothes are pretty simplistic　衣服款式非常简约

which is exactly what I like　这就是我所喜欢的

a decent pair of jeans　一条像样的牛仔裤

set you back a thousand RMB or so　大约花费你1000元人民币

in terms of quality　就质量而言

the higher-end brands　更高档的品牌

you're paying considerably less　你花费少得多

I would say these are，more or less，the main reasons why I like shopping there.　我觉得这些基本上就是我喜欢在那里购物的主要原因。

11. Describe a tall building you like or dislike 描述一个你喜欢或不喜欢的高层建筑

You should say:

What the building is

Where the building is located

How you got to know the building

And explain why you like or dislike this building

Sample Answer

The tall building I would like to describe is the Shanghai Center，which is by far the highest architecture in the world. It is so tall that you can see the building anywhere in the downtown area. I would say that it is a magnificent piece of art work because no building in history has been so aesthetically appealing.

As to the location of the building，I will give you a brief introduction. Shanghai Center is at the center of the financial area，in which there are many multinational companies，some of which set their headquarters there. Shanghai Center is close to the Huangpu River，which is the most popular sightseeing spot in Shanghai.

I got to know the building by several means. Initially，I read the news on local newspaper that there was an incredibly high-rise building that would be completed in 2016. After that，local and national TV programs reported the construction process of the amazing building. When I watched some BBC and CNN news programs，overseas media focused on this building as well.

Regarding the reasons why I like this tall building，I would say that，first，this building represents the highest architectural skills. And the design of this building has no parallels in the world. In addition，Shanghai Center is regarded as the financial hub of Asia. At least 100 international companies have signed the contract to move their global head offices into the Shanghai Center. Because of the architectural and business aspects，I would definitely say that Shanghai Center is my favorite tall building.

词汇和句型

by far the highest architecture in the world 目前世界上最高的建筑
in the downtown area 在市中心区域
a magnificent piece of art work 一件杰出的艺术作品
aesthetically appealing 具备审美上的吸引力
multinational companies 跨国公司
the most popular sightseeing spot 最受欢迎的观光景点
overseas media 国外媒体
this building represents the highest architectural skills 这个建筑代表了最高的建筑技能
the design of this building has no parallels in the world 这个建筑的设计在全世界也无可匹敌
the financial hub 金融中心

12. Describe a small business that you think is successful 描述一个你认为成功的小公司
You should say:
What the company is

What this company produces
How you know about this company
And explain why you think this company is successful

Sample Answer

I'm going to describe a small company which I think is successful. I should admit that I'm not really familiar with that many small companies in my hometown, but the one that I do know a little bit about and which I believe to be quite successful is my neighbor's company.

And as for what it produces, if I'm not mistaken, his company mainly focuses on women's clothing, such as dresses, cardigans, and blouses. I actually asked my neighbor if he had ever considered making men's clothes too, as I would be interested in buying some, but unfortunately he said that for the time being, they are just going to stick with women's clothes, because that's what they are most experienced in.

Anyway, with regard to how I got to know about this company, as I mentioned earlier, it's run by my neighbor, and I seem to remember him telling me about it not long after we first met, which must have been about two or three years ago. Since then, I've had the pleasure of visiting the office a few times and meeting some of the employees. One of the reasons is that they've got a pool table there, and my neighbor often invites me over to have a few games of pool during his lunch break.

And that brings me onto my last point, which is regarding why I think the company is successful. In a nutshell, I would say it's basically because the company has managed to grow from two staff to over 50 over the course of just 3 years, which I think is staggering. And another thing to mention would be that, if I remember correctly, most of his business comes from return customers, which I think shows that the company has been able to maintain good product quality and keep their customers happy.

So I guess that's pretty much everything.

词汇和句型

if I'm not mistaken　如果我没搞错的话
his company mainly focuses on women's clothing　他的公司主打女性服装
dresses, cardigans and blouses　连衣裙、开襟羊毛衫和女式衬衫
for the time being　暂且
stick with women's clothes　坚持继续做女装
that's what they are most experienced in　那是他们最擅长的
it's run by my neighbor　这个公司是我邻居开的
a pool table　台球桌

pool　美式撞球
in a nutshell　简单来说
staggering　惊人的
return customers　回头客
maintain good product quality　保持良好产品质量
that's pretty much everything　这就是我所要说的

第四节　Objects 物品类话题真题及范文

1. Describe an exciting book you read 描述一本你看过的令人兴奋的书
You should say:
What kind of book it was
What it was about
Why you read this book
And explain why you found it exciting

Sample Answer

The exciting book I read was called *Gone Girl*, which was written by Gillian Flynn. Undoubtedly, it was by far the most thrilling book I have ever read.

I read this book a couple of months ago, when I accidentally saw the reviews of the book posted on the Internet and the rating was amazingly high so I was interested in reading the novel. Then I bought it from amazon.com. I read the novel with my best friend John in a local Starbucks.

This book is about marriage. On the occasion of his fifth wedding anniversary, Nick Dunne reports that his wife, Amy, has gone missing. Under pressure from the police and growing media attention, Nick's portrait of a happy marriage begins to crumble. Soon his lies, deceits, and strange behavior have everyone asking the same dark question: Did Nick Dunne kill his wife? After I read this novel, I had the feeling that loyalty and honesty are the keys to a successful marriage or any good relationship between men and women. If someone lies, he or she will experience the devastating consequences sooner or later.

The main reason why this is an exciting book is that the plot of this novel is excellent and it has twists and turns, partly because the writer has full imagination and she was probably inspired by some true life stories.

Gone Girl is an exciting novel I like the most. Two thumbs up.

词汇和句型

it was by far the most thrilling book I have ever read 这是一本我所看过的最令人兴奋的书

a couple of months ago 两个月前

I accidentally saw the reviews of the book posted on the Internet 我偶然看到网上贴出的书评

the rating was amazingly high 评分非常高

Under pressure from the police and growing media attention 在警察和媒体不断关注的压力下

crumble 开始崩塌

lies，deceits，and strange behavior 谎言、欺骗和奇怪的行为

loyalty and honesty 忠实和诚实

the devastating consequences 毁灭性的结果

sooner or later 迟早

twists and turns 迂回曲折

Two thumbs up 赞

2. Describe a gift you made by hand for your friend 描述一个你手工制作的给朋友的礼物

You should say:

What the gift was

When and where you made it by hand

How you made that gift

And explain why you made it by hand

Sample Answer

A gift I made by hand was a scarf that I wove last year for my friend Alice. Actually she was my classmate in primary school，so we've known each other over a decade.

But last year she told me that she would go to the UK to study in a prestigious university. Although I was proud of what she had achieved，I felt a bit upset，because we couldn't see each other every day. Then I decided to make something that was useful and meaningful for her，and weaving a scarf seemed like a good choice，because the weather in the UK is not so pleasant. I mean it is normally very cold in winter. In order to weave it well，I asked my mom to tell me some tips. And I also bought high-quality materials. I remembered that it was really challenging at the beginning，because I had never woven a scarf before. It took me one month to make the scarf，but it was worthwhile. Alice was totally moved by this meaningful present.

As for why I decided to make this gift by hand，the main reason is that I think the handcraft has some sentimental value，as the scarf can reflect our friendship and show how much I care about her. Another reason is that it is more affordable for me to buy good materials rather than a high-quality scarf.

词汇和句型

a scarf that I wove　我所织的一条围巾
a prestigious university　一所知名大学
totally moved　非常受感动
this meaningful present　有意义的礼物
sentimental value　情感价值

3. **Describe a photograph you took that you like** 描述一张你喜欢的你拍摄的照片
You should say:
When and where you took the photograph
What the photograph is about
Where the photograph is
And why you like this photograph

Sample Answer

I took a good picture of my cute little niece when we were on holiday last summer. It was a sunny afternoon and we were playing on the beach of a small island near Shanghai. My four-year-old niece looked very cute，and I decided to take a picture of her so that I could remember this moment many years later. The daylight was perfect，so I didn't use the flash light. My niece didn't know I was taking pictures and she just kept running and jumping on the beach.

I took four pictures and one of them is amazing. The background is a row of black houses and the white sand. My niece who was wearing a bright yellow dress is so eye-catching in the picture. The colors are just black，white，and yellow，which makes the picture look clean and beautiful. The timing is perfect too. In the picture，the little girl is jumping high up. Her smile is sweet and warm.

I like this picture because it reminds me of the happy time we spent that summer whenever I see it. I'm also very satisfied with the lighting，the color，and the composition. I call it "the girl in the yellow dress" and it is my favorite. I put it in a photo frame. Now it is on the table in my living room.

词汇和句型

my cute little niece　我可爱的小侄女
the flash light　闪光灯
a row of black houses　一排黑色的房子
I'm also very satisfied with the lighting，the color and the composition　我也很满意光线、

色彩以及构图

a photo frame　相框

4. Describe a piece of equipment which you found hard to use for the first time 描述一件你第
一次很难使用的设备

You should say:

What it was

What difficulties there were

What you felt when you used it

What was done to solve the problem

Sample Answer

The piece of equipment I found difficult to use for the first time is the iPad Air. My friend Lee bought it for me as a birthday gift, and it cost him US＄499. The iPad Air is quite common in university these days because it can be used to take notes or record lectures.

However, at first, I thought it was very difficult to use. As I always bring the Google Nexus 10 with me, which is an Android phone, I had no idea how to use the iOS system. The first aspect was that I didn't know how to activate the system when I switched on the iPad Air. There were so many steps to the setup. I thought there was something wrong with the iPad Air at that moment. Another thing was that there was only one pressing button on the front of the machine so I had no idea how to shut down the Apps.

I felt confused when I first used the iPad Air. I didn't think it was as good as most people thought it was. I got a little bit annoyed because my friends told me that it was very convenient to use but actually it wasn't.

However, I eventually figured out how to use that eventually by means of the following ways. The first means was that I watched some instruction videos on Youtube. I thought it was a straightforward way to get things clear. Another thing I did to solve the problem was that I called my friend Lee to ask him to teach me how to use it. After these two problem-solving methods, I fell in love with the fancy iPad Air and took it with me everywhere.

词汇和句型

take notes　记笔记

record lectures　录讲座

an Android phone　一个安卓手机

I had no idea how to use the iOS system　我不知道如何使用它

activate the system　激活系统

switched on the iPad Air　打开 iPad Air

There were so many steps to the setup　设置过程有许多步骤

one pressing button　一个按钮

shut down the Apps　关闭应用

I eventually figured out how to use that eventually　最终我搞清楚了如何来使用它

The first means was that ...　第一个方法是······

a straightforward way　一个直接的方法

get things clear　把事情弄明白

5. Describe a product you bought that made you happy 描述一件你购买的令你开心的产品

You should say:

What it is

Where you bought it

Why you bought it

And explain why it made you happy

Sample Answer

The product I bought that made me happy is my Macbook Air，which I think is the most useful tool for my study and entertainment. It cost me 10,000 RMB，which is equivalent to US $1,500. As is known to all，the Macbook Air is by far the most popular product with youngsters who are enthusiastic about high-tech products.

I bought this laptop in a local authorized Apple Store，which is totally trustworthy. I remember that three months ago，I went to that place，which was full of customers choosing their favorite iPhones，Apple Watches，and Macbooks. The sales people in that store were very friendly and willing to introduce the basic skills about how to use these devices. One sale person suggested me to buy the Macbook Air because it is not only thin and streamlined but also highly-efficient.

There are several reasons why I bought the Macbook Air. The most important reason is that this machine is lightweight，so I can bring it with me to different places，such as Starbucks，without any effort. Another reason is that I love the Mackintosh operating system，which will not be infected with computer viruses. This is not the case with many Windows-system laptops. Therefore，I do not need to worry about my computer system crashing. And the data in the hard drive can be safe.

The Macbook Air really made me happy not only because the design of the laptop is so exquisite but also because the functions of the laptop are so powerful that it improves my efficiency in my study and life. On one hand，I could use the note-taking App downloaded from Mac App Store to take notes in class. And I can write essays and other paperwork immediately after classes or lectures，which saves a huge amount of time for me. On the other hand，when I feel tired，I can watch some movies on the Macbook Air or listen to some pieces of music with iTunes. The battery can sustain 10-hour consecutive operation so I don't need to plug in power for a whole day.

The Macbook Air is the best product I bought and it made me so happy.

词汇和句型

which is equivalent to US $1,500　相当于 1500 美元

by far the most popular product with youngsters who are enthusiastic about high-tech products　目前最受对高科技产品着迷的年轻人的欢迎

a local authorized Apple Store　一个当地的授权苹果经销商

totally trustworthy　完全值得信任的

highly-efficient　很高效

this machine is lightweight　这个机器很轻

will not be infected with computer viruses　不会中电脑病毒

the computer system crashing　电脑系统会崩溃

the data in the hard drive　硬盘的数据

the design of the laptop is so exquisite　这台笔记本的设计很精致

The battery can sustain 10-hour consecutive operation　电池可以支持连续 10 小时的操作

plug in power　插上电源

6. Describe an important plant in your country 描述你的国家中的一个重要植物

You should say:

What the plant is

How you knew it

Why it is important

And explain how much you like the plant

Sample Answer

Ok then，after a bit of thought，I've decided to talk to you about bamboo.

So first of all，as for how I knew about bamboo，I can't really remember exactly how I first got to know about it. It could have been in a biology class at school，or when I was out somewhere with my parents，but my guess would be that I probably first knew about it in primary school，because that was about the time when we first started learning about things like that.

Anyway，moving on to why bamboo is important，I'd say it's pretty important for a number of reasons，the main one of which would be that it can be used to make so many different things，such as chopsticks，chopping boards，flooring，and musical instruments，like the bamboo flute.

And another thing to mention is that bamboo is also used a lot for carrying stuff. For example，what I've seen people do is to rest it on their shoulders，and then hang things on each end，because as well as being strong，it's also very flexible，so it won't break，even with very heavy loads.

So it's extremely useful，and what's good about it is that it grows incredibly fast，unlike most other trees，and so although a lot of it is cut down to make stuff，there will still be an abundant supply of it here.

But anyway，finally then，as for how much I like bamboo，I'd say it's actually probably one of my favorite plants. Because I mean，it gives me a nice，pleasant feeling whenever I see it. And it's also a plant which is often associated with China，because we grow so much of it here，so it's something that reminds me of my own culture.

So yeah I guess that's pretty much it then. Thanks for listening.

词汇和句型

in primary school　在小学
moving on to why bamboo is important　继续谈为什么竹子重要
a number of reasons　许多原因
chopsticks，chopping boards，flooring　筷子、切菜板、地板
musical instruments　乐器
bamboo flute　竹笛
rest it on their shoulders　把它放在肩膀上
hang things on each end　两头挂东西
as well as being strong，it's also very flexible　除了强度高之外，它也非常柔韧
it won't break　它不会断
very heavy loads　很重的货物
extremely useful　非常有用
it grows incredibly fast　它生长非常快
an abundant supply　充分供应
reminds me of my own culture　提醒我记起自己的文化

7. Describe something you bought but did not use for a long time 描述一件你买的但很长时间没有用的东西
You should say:
What the thing is
When and where you bought the thing

What features the thing had
And explain why you did not use that for a long time

Sample Answer

The thing I bought but did not use for a long time is the Nikon Digital camera，the model of which is D800.

It was launched by the Nikon corporation five years ago as one of the high-end products. I bought the camera at a specialized store that sold cameras and related accessories.

This camera featured many advantages. The most obvious aspect was that it had extremely quick focus speed，requiring only 0.3 seconds to focus on the object or people，much faster than that of cell phones. The second feature was that this camera was designed for taking pictures of people，by which I mean，the portrait of people. So I took a lot of photos of my family members and my friends.

However，I haven't used that camera for at least three years. There are several reasons for that. The first one is that this camera was too big to carry to different places when I went traveling. I remember that I brought it with me to climb a mountain，and it was a painful journey because of the size and weight of the Nikon camera. The second reason is that the iPhone is very popular now and it also has great photo quality. I can simply put my iPhone into my pocket and carry it around. I don't need to bear the heavy weight of large Nikon camera any more.

That's something I bought but did not use for a long time.

词汇和句型

It was launched by the Nikon corporation five years ago 它是尼康公司五年前发布的产品
the high-end products 顶级产品
cameras and related accessories 照相机和相关配件
This camera featured many advantages 这个照相机有许多优点
extremely quick focus speed 非常快的对焦速度
focus on the object or people 聚焦物体或人物
by which I mean 我的意思是
the portrait of people 人物肖像
climb a mountain 登山

8. **Describe a car or vehicle you would like to have in the future** 描述你将来想拥有的一辆车或者交通工具

You should say:

Which you would choose
What it would look like
How much it will cost
And explain why you'd like to buy it.

Sample Answer
We're spoilt for choices with the huge range of vehicles on the market，but one car that appeals to me a lot is an SUV.

And as for what it will look like，I wouldn't want it to be too flashy，as it might draw unwanted attention，so I'd rather go for something relatively low-key. I would choose a plain and simple color like white，because although it's one of the most common car colors，I reckon it looks the best，as long as the car is kept clean.

Going on to my next point then，which is regarding how much it will cost，to be honest with you，I'm not really that sure as I haven't done any research，but I guess the price range of a mid-end SUV would be somewhere between three hundred and four hundred thousand RMB. So it won't be cheap，but hopefully by the time I need one I'll have sufficient funds.

Finally，with regard to why I'd choose an SUV over other cars，to put it simply，I reckon SUVs are among the safest cars on the road，and the reason is that you are sitting higher up. So on the off chance you collide with another car，you're less likely to get injured than if you were sitting in a normal car. And just one final thing to add would be that I would definitely make sure the car is equipped with something called ESC，which means that if you make a sudden turn to avoid something，your car will automatically remain in control. So this，for me，would be an essential feature，as the traffic in China is pretty chaotic.

Ok，I think that's about everything，so thanks for listening.

词汇和句型
We're spoilt for choices　选择太多我们反而不适应
the huge range of vehicles　各种汽车
on the market　在市场上（等待出售）
appeals to me a lot　非常吸引我
an SUV = a sport-utility vehicle　一辆多用途跑车
too flashy　太闪耀，太花哨
draw unwanted attention　引起不必要的关注
relatively low-key　相对低调

a plain and simple color 一个平凡简单的颜色
as long as the car is kept clean 只要车辆保持干净
Going on to my next point then 然后说到下一个点
price range of a mid-end SUV 一款中档的多用途跑车的价格区间
have sufficient funds 有充分的资金
to put it simply 简单来说
on the off chance 万一
collide with another car 和其他汽车碰撞
get injured 会受伤
which means that 这意味着……
make a sudden turn 突然转弯
automatically remain in control 自动保持控制
pretty chaotic 非常混乱

9. Describe a toy you played with in your childhood 描述你在儿童时期玩过的一个玩具
You should say:
What it was
When you played with it
With whom you played with it
And explain why you used to like playing with this toy

Sample Answer

The toy I played with in my childhood was the Transformers，which were quite popular among the boys in my childhood. My favorite toy in the series of Transformers was the Bumblebee，which was a yellow car with a lot of fancy functions and appearances. My father bought it for me as a birthday gift.

I played with the toy when I was five or six years old. Many kids in my primary school played with the same toy，so I always played with some of my friends after school. Although that toy was not expensive，I had a lot fun playing with it.

I used to play with the toy for a lot of reasons. The most important one was that the functions of the transformer were amazing. The Bumblebee was a sports car when it was in its normal appearance. However，it could be transformed into a robot if the car parts were reinstalled. The second reason I used to like playing with it was that this toy had its TV animation series，which was shown on TV every other evening. After watching the Transformers TV program，I got more interested in the toy. The third reason I liked this toy was that I could make more friends by playing with it. Most boys liked playing with the Transformers，which means that if I brought the toy to school，I could find many common grounds with the boys in the primary school. And I could meet many new friends. That was why the Transformer Bumblebee was the toy I liked in my childhood.

词汇和句型

Transformers　变形金刚

Bumblebee　大黄蜂

fancy functions and appearance　酷炫的功能和造型

I had a lot fun playing with it　我玩这个玩具玩得很开心

a sports car　一辆跑车

TV animation series　电视动画片系列

every other evening　每两晚一次

find many common grounds　找到许多共同点

第五节　Events 事件类话题真题及范文

1. Describe a change that will improve your local area 描述一个将会提升你所在区域的变化

You should say:

What the change is

When it will happen

Where it will happen

And explain how your local area will benefit from this change

Sample Answer

There will be a new gym in my neighborhood this year, which I think will be a great change for us. The local government made the decision earlier this year to build the gym in the central area of our community. The gym is expected to be open to the public at the end of this year after a six-month construction.

The new gym will include all sorts of facilities, such as exercise bikes, rowing machines, and weights. There will also be places for people to do other kinds of sports. I've heard that they will build a badminton court, a tennis court, several table tennis courts, and even a swimming pool. People who live in our community can have a discount for booking the facility or renting the sports equipment. For the locals, the annual membership fee will be much lower than that of any other gyms.

Swimming lessons will be available during the summer and people can attend yoga classes and tennis classes all year round. I suppose this is great news for people who want to learn to practice these sports.

The gym will run from 10.00 a.m. to 22.00 p.m. every day，which means that people can go there after work or on weekends. To make a reservation，all we need to do is to contact the gym by phone，by email，or by WeChat.

We are all looking forward to this new gym because it will be much cheaper and more convenient for us to get some exercise and keep fit.

词汇和句型

a new gym　一座新的健身房

made the decision earlier this year　今年早些时候做出决定

exercise bikes　室内健身自行车

rowing machines　划船健身器

weights　哑铃

a badminton court　一个羽毛球场

a tennis court　一个网球场

the annual membership fee　年费

all year round　全年

make a reservation　预订场地

keep fit　保持健康好身材

2. **Describe a positive change that you have made to your life** 描述一个你对你的生活做出的
   积极变化
   You should say:
   What the change was
   When it happened
   Where it happened
   And explain how you have benefited from this change

Sample Answer

The positive change which I would like to tell you about was actually a pretty simple one，but it has improved my life a great deal，and basically it was getting up an hour earlier every day.

The reason I started doing it was that my whole day was taken up with various stuff，like classes and homework，and I found that I hardly had any free time left，so I realized that the only way to make more time for myself was to get up earlier，and that's what I decided to do. It wasn't easy at first，especially when it was cold，but thankfully it got a lot easier，and now I find it so habitual getting out of bed at five in the morning.

Anyway，as for when I first started doing this，I guess it must have probably been about two or three years ago, around the time when I was busy preparing for my university entrance exams, and I got up at something like five or six every morning to review. And after my exams finished, I remember thinking to myself, wouldn't it be good to continue getting up early and have all this extra time to do things at the beginning of the day.

So that's pretty much how it all started, and finally, with regard to how I've benefited from this change. I'd say I've benefited immensely in numerous ways. For example, it has given me time to do a bit of exercise every day, which I didn't have time for, so now I've become fitter. And as well as this, I also have the time to eat a proper breakfast every day, instead of skipping it, like I used to do, and as a result, I've become much healthier.

That's more or less everything, I guess, so thanks for listening.

词汇和句型

improved my life a great deal　大幅提高了我的生活
getting up an hour earlier every day　每天早起一小时
my whole day was taken up with various stuff　我一整天都被各种事情占据
university entrance exams　大学入学考试
I've benefited immensely　我受益良多
in numerous ways　从很多方面
I've become fitter　我现在身材好多了

3. Describe a goal you want to achieve in the future 描述一个将来你想要达成的目标
You should say:
What the goal is
What should be done to achieve the goal
What difficulties you would come across
And explain why you want to achieve the goal

Sample Answer

The goal I want to achieve is to run the 21 km marathon next year. It is not an easy task for ordinary people who have never been trained before. But I have made up my mind and I have made plans of how I should practice during this whole year. I am going to start training myself next week on the campus of Shanghai University, which is close to where I live.

This week, before the training starts, I must make some preparations. I am going to buy some accessories in a sports shop, such as a pair of running shoes and a pair of kneecaps. In my free time, I will search online for tips on how to successfully run a marathon. I will also talk to my friends who ran the marathon last year to get some advice and to learn from their experience. However，although I would do a lot of preparation beforehand，I am sure I would face new problems during the training process.

To make sure that I won't give up halfway，I will stick a poster of a famous marathon runner on the wall of my room. The poster will remind me of my goal whenever I see it. In case that I would feel lonely，I will ask a friend to join me. My friend and I will train together and encourage each other.

Another problem I face is that I am not fit enough，which means that it is possible that I will be exhausted before I arrive at the destination and I will have to give up halfway. To solve this problem，I have decided to go to the gym twice a week to do workouts. Therefore，my training consists of two parts — running and body building.

There are two reasons why I want to run the marathon race. Training for marathons can help people become stronger and more persevering. And I want to be tougher so that I won't give up when I face the difficulties in life in the future. In the meantime，I can keep fit and become healthier.

词汇和句型

run the 21 km marathon　跑半程马拉松

ordinary people who have never been trained before　从前没有训练过的普通人

I have made up my mind　我已经决定了

on the campus of Shanghai University　在上海大学的校园里

make some preparations　做一些准备

a pair of running shoes　一双跑步鞋

a pair of kneecaps　一双护膝

To make sure that ...　为了确保……

I won't give up halfway　我不会中途放弃

I will stick a poster of a famous marathon runner on the wall of my room　我会在卧室墙上贴一张著名马拉松选手的海报

In case that ...　以防万一……

I will be exhausted before I arrive at the destination　到达终点前我就会筋疲力尽

go to the gym　去健身房锻炼

do workouts　锻炼身体

help people become stronger and more persevering　使人变得更强壮和更有意志力

4. Describe a journey you would like to go on by car 描述一个你想要去的开车旅行

You should say:

What the journey would be

When you would like go on the journey
What you would you do during the journey
And explain why you would like to go on the journey by car

Sample Answer

As for the car journey I would like to go on, I will talk about the journey to the Mount Yellow, which is renowned as one of the five most famous mountains in China. It is roughly 4-hour driving distance. I plan to go with two of my intimate friends to spend the weekend. One of them, who has got the driver's license for approximately ten years, will be the driver of the trip.

In terms of the itinerary, actually, we spent nearly two months creating it. A month ago, we made reservations for the rooms of a local hot spring hotel, which is at the foot of the mountain. We will take the ropeway to where we are halfway up the mountain and then climb the mountain while taking photos at different tourist attractions. Also, we plan to get up early and enjoy the sunrise together.

As for the reasons why I would like to go on the journey by car, the main one is that the car trip will be the most convenient and economical way. If we take the train, we have to spend 10 more hours on the way and then switch to other means of transportation in order to get to the destination. Additionally, we could chat around and have some snacks without worrying about disturbing other people.

So I'm looking forward to the car journey.

词汇和句型

roughly 4-hour driving distance 大约 4 小时的车程
my intimate friends 我的好朋友
the driver's license 驾照
In terms of the itinerary 关于旅行计划
A local hot spring hotel 一个温泉酒店
at the foot of the mountain 在山脚下
take the ropeway 坐索道
tourist attractions 旅游景点
get to the destination 到达目的地
without worrying about disturbing other people 不用担心打扰其他人

5. Describe a mistake you once made 描述一个你犯过的错误
You should say:
What the mistake was

When you made the mistake
What you did
And explain what the result of the mistake was

Sample Answer

The horrible mistake I would like to describe happened a week ago.

I was preparing for a surprise party because it was my boyfriend's birthday. I made some fruit puddings for the party. To make puddings，I first mixed all the ingredients with flour and water. Then I was supposed to put some sugar into the mixture to make it sweet. Unfortunately，I mistook the salt jar for the sugar jar，because the two jars were exactly the same in shape and color. Usually，I would make sure which one is sugar and which one is salt before I use them by observing the grains in the jar. The salt grains are bigger and irregular，while the sugar grains should be small globular ones. However，this time I forgot to distinguish the two jars. I was in a hurry and was afraid that I couldn't finish baking before the guests came because it was only half an hour before the party and I was running out of time.

At that time，I didn't realize the mistake. After putting some salt，which I though was sugar，into the mixture，I put the mixture into the paper cups. Then I baked them. I was quite delighted as I managed to complete all these steps before the guests showed up.

The party went on well until I served the puddings. One of guests took a bite of the salt puddings，and he coughed furiously. I didn't know what happened. A few minutes later，I noticed that everyone's facial expression was so weird. But no one said anything. It turned out that they were so kind that they didn't want me to know about the pudding because they didn't want me to be embarrassed. But finally I found about the mistake anyway.

So yeah，I guess that's pretty much of it.

词汇和句型
a surprise party　一个惊喜派对
fruit puddings　水果布丁
mixed all the ingredients with flour and water　把原料和面粉与水混合
I mistook the salt jar for the sugar jar　我错把盐罐当作了糖罐
the two jars were exactly the same in shape and color　这两个罐子形状和颜色完全相同
observing the grains in the jar　观察罐子里的颗粒
small globular ones　小球状(颗粒)
distinguish the two jars　区分这两个罐子

I was running out of time 我快没时间了

I didn't realize the mistake 我没有意识到这个错误

I was quite delighted 我非常开心

I managed to complete all these steps before the guests showed up 我在客人到来之前成功完成了所有的步骤

took a bite of ... 咬一口……

coughed furiously 猛烈咳嗽

facial expression 脸部表情

so weird 很奇怪

6. **Describe a time when you needed to use the imagination** 描述一次你需要使用想象力的经历

You should say:

What was the situation

When it happened

Why you needed to use imagination

And explain what the result was after you used the imagination

Sample Answer

The time when I was required to use imagination was when I was in the Colosseum，which is in Rome，Italy. I pictured the scene that occurred thousands of years ago.

In June 2018，I went on holiday in Italy. During the holiday，I spent a couple of days in Rome，home to the most ancient culture in the world. The Colosseum is one of the most popular cultural relics. Around two thousand years ago，it was the place where slaves fought against fierce beasts in order to please their masters. However，history has totally changed the place. It is no longer a venue for killing；rather，it is a place for tourists.

There are a variety of reasons why I needed to use my imagination. The most obvious one is that the remains of the Colosseum are nothing but piles of walls and columns. So I had to imagine there were thousands of cheering audiences in terms of the details described in the books and films like the *Gladiator*. And the effect was overwhelming. I also envisioned that the slaves were fighting for survival. I felt sympathetic with those slaves whose lives were controlled by others. At this time，imagination was so important；otherwise，all I could do was to appreciate the architectural art of the Colosseum. Another reason why I needed to use imagination was that I read the book *The History of the Decline and Fall of the Roman Empire*，so I could relate the book content to the Colosseum.

After I used the imagination，the Colosseum changed from a magnificent building to a lively scene. And I was deeply impacted by the ancient Roman culture.

Many places in Rome needed me to use imagination to feel the city. I love this feeling.

词汇和句型

the Colosseum　罗马斗兽场/角斗场
pictured the scene　描绘场景
I went on holiday in Italy　我去意大利度假
Colosseum is one of the most popular cultural relics　斗兽场是最受欢迎的文化遗迹之一
walls and columns　墙和柱子
the details described in books　书中所描绘的细节
I also envisioned that …　我也想象……
appreciate the architectural art　欣赏建筑艺术
relate the book content to the Colosseum　把书的内容和斗兽场联系在一起

7. Describe a time when you got up early in the morning 描述一次你早起的经历
You should say:
When it was
How you felt
What you did
And explain why you got up early in the morning

Sample Answer

I remember clearly that I got up at 4:30 a. m. one day while I travelled in America last October. Actually I didn't mean to but I was told to get up early to catch the tourist bus heading for a faraway scenic spot.

At first，I felt sleepy and，like others，made some complaints about the guide. However，when I sat near the window of the bus，I caught sight of the sun rising from the horizon，rushing out of thick clouds and casting light. I thought，wow，what a fantastic view. All of us shouted and we were stunned. We took out our cameras or held up our cell phones to take pictures of the amazing sunrise view. I still remember the many "likes" I received after I uploaded those pictures on WeChat，a famous Chinese social networking system. Then I felt I should thank the guide for arranging such a special tour.

After that，we stopped at a forest called Yosemite. It was still early，around 6:30 a.m. There were few visitors. We enjoyed the extremely fresh air. I could even smell oxygen. Besides，we heard birds singing and squirrels squeaking. Those little cute squirrels were not afraid of humans at all. I even got a chance to feed them. But they seemed to be shy and were really naughty when I tried to take a photo of them. They kept jumping or hiding in a hole of a rock. Of course，during the one-hour stay，we went on a hike up the mountain，and we felt completely refreshed.

Anyway，I felt that morning was really rewarding，for I got the chance to appreciate the real beauty of nature.

词汇和句型

catch the tourist bus 赶上旅游巴士

a faraway scenic spot 一个遥远的旅游景点

I caught sight of the sun rising from the horizon 我看到太阳从地平线升起

took out our cameras or held up our cell phones 拿出我们的相机或拿起我们的手机

the many "likes" 许多"赞"

social networking system 社交网络工具

the extremely fresh air 非常新鲜的空气

we heard birds singing and squirrels squeaking 我们听到了鸟鸣和松鼠的吱吱声

during the one-hour stay 在一个小时的逗留途中

we went on a hike up the mountain 我们去爬山

that morning was really rewarding 那个早晨确实有很大收获

appreciate the real beauty of nature 欣赏自然的真实美景

8. Describe a time when you missed an appointment 描述一次你错过约定会面的经历

You should say:

What the appointment was

When and where it happened

Why you missed the appointment

And explain how you felt about missing the appointment

Sample Answer

Two years ago I missed an important appointment with the investors for the website www.m-e-e-t.com.

I co-founded the education website www.m-e-e-t.com with several of my friends three years ago. After we launched the website，we lacked the funds to promote it to more users. So we made an appointment with the local investors, who were from a well-known investment company，Delta Investment.

I made the appointment with the investors in Costa Coffee because it was not as crowded as Starbucks was and we would be able to talk about things without disturbance. We planned to see them on a Saturday afternoon because most people were not busy at that period of time and I was also available as I would not work in those hours.

However，I missed that appointment because something serious occurred that afternoon. The server of the website crashed just before we were supposed to meet each other. So one of our team members had to stay in the office to fix the problem. So I chose to stay to solve the problem and my team members went to see the investors. The server of the website was in HongKong，so I spent a couple of hours fixing it and I had no chance to attend the appointment.

This was the first time I would see the investors. I felt disappointed to miss that chance because I had prepared for this meeting by doing a lot of things. For example，I wrote the business plan in detail and did the benchmark investigations. It was a pity to miss the appointment. But my team members went to the appointment and negotiated with the investors in a smooth way. So I still felt happy although I didn't show up to that appointment.

词汇和句型

I co-founded the education website　我联合创始了这个教育网站
launched the website　发布了这个网站
we lacked the funds to promote it to more users　我们缺乏资金把这个网站介绍给更多的用户
made the appointment with the investors　和投资人约定见面
talk about things without disturbance　没有干扰地讨论事情
something serious occurred that afternoon　那天下午发生了一件严重的事情
The server of the website crashed　网站的服务器崩溃了
fix the problem　修复问题
I spent a couple of hours fixing it　我花了几个小时来解决问题
I wrote the business plan in detail　我把商业计划写得很详细
negotiated with the investors in a smooth way　和投资人谈判得很顺利

9. Describe something important you do to keep you healthy and fit 描述你经常做的保持健康和体格强健的重要事情

You should say:
What it is
When and where you do it
How you do it
And explain why it could keep you healthy and fit

Sample Answer
The important thing that keeps me healthy and fit is playing basketball，which is one of the most popular sports in the world.

In most cases，I play basketball in the basketball courts in my neighborhood，and I can walk there in about 5 to 10 minutes. I usually play basketball in the evenings or on the weekends because I need to go to school or do some part-time jobs in the daytime.

I play basketball in several ways. Sometimes I would train throwing balls by myself because this skill is very essential in winning a game. On other occasions，I would arrange a basketball game. I would call my friends in advance so that they will show up on time．

As to why it could keep me healthy and fit，I think there are several reasons. The first one is that playing basketball could train my arm and leg muscles，which is paramount to my overall health and could prevent me from developing cardiovascular diseases. The second reason is that by playing basketball，I could relieve stress so that I would be psychologically healthy. Therefore，playing basketball is an efficient activity to keep me healthy and fit.

词汇和句型

In most cases 在大多数情况下

the basketball courts 篮球场

in my neighborhood 在我居住的小区中

I usually play basketball in the evenings or on the weekends 我打篮球的时间大多数是在晚上和周末

I need to go to school or do some part time jobs in the daytime 白天我要去上学或做一些兼职工作

this skill is very essential in winning a game 这个技能对于赢得比赛来说是非常重要的

On other occasions 在其他情况下

call my friends in advance 事先打电话给我的朋友们

they will show up on time 他们可以准时出现

train my arm and leg muscles 训练我的手臂和腿部肌肉

is paramount to 对……重要的

cardiovascular diseases 心血管疾病

relieve stress 缓解压力

psychologically healthy 心理健康

10. Describe a wedding you attended 描述你参加过的一个婚礼

You should say:

Whose wedding it was

Who was there

Where it was

And explain how you felt at this wedding.

Sample Answer

I've actually been to quite a few weddings, because I'm now at the age when a lot of my friends are starting to get married, so it is kind of difficult choosing which one to describe, but I guess probably the easiest for me to talk about would be the most recent one I went to, which was that of a neighbor of mine.

Also, what I should probably make clear to you first is that weddings here in China tend to just involve the wedding reception, and not the signing of marriage documents, which is usually done in private several months before the wedding, so it's just that I'm going to talk about.

And, as for who was there, I can't tell you about everyone, because there were loads of people. The hall was packed, so my guess would be that there were probably 250 to 300 guests, and if I'm not mistaken, the majority were friends and relatives of the bride and groom, although I also noticed that they had invited quite a few of their colleagues from work as well, because one of them, who I think was her boss, went up on stage to make a speech at some point.

With regard to where the wedding was held, it was actually in a small city, which is about an hour's drive just to the south east of Shanghai, because that's where the bride comes from, and the reception itself was held in a nice-looking hotel, which was easy to spot because it was about 10 times higher than all the buildings around it.

Regarding how I felt at the wedding, to put it simply, it was a really wonderful wedding, and there were some parts of it that moved me quite a lot, such as when the bride broke down into tears when she was on stage thanking her parents for all the support they had given her. It was also really clear how much the bride and groom loved each other, as they couldn't take their eyes off each other the whole evening, so I was really happy for them and was glad that I made it to their wedding.

That's pretty much it, I think, so thanks a lot for listening.

词汇和句型

weddings here in China tend to just involve the wedding reception　在中国这边的婚礼往往只包括婚宴

in private　私下地

loads of people　很多人

the hall was packed　大厅里挤满了人

there were probably 250 to 300 guests　大概有 250—300 个客人

if I'm not mistaken　如果我没搞错的话

the majority were friends and relatives of the bride and groom　大多数是新娘和新郎的朋友和亲戚

I also noticed that …　我也注意到……

they had invited quite a few of their colleagues from work as well　他们也邀请了一些工作中的同事

went up on stage to make a speech　上台发言

in quite a nice-looking hotel　在一个看起来很不错的饭店

was easy to spot　很容易找到

to put it simply　简而言之

moved me quite a lot　让我很感动

broke down into tears　泪流满面

they couldn't take their eyes off each other the whole evening　整晚他们都无法将视线离开对方

11. Describe a situation that made you a little angry 描述一个让你有点生气的经历
You should say:
What it was that made you angry
Where you were when this happened
What you were doing at the time
And explain why you felt angry

Sample Answer

I'm not the kind of person who gets angry easily, but if I had to recall a time when I did get slightly angry, then one experience that comes to mind was when I recently went out for a meal together with my family at a local Indian restaurant.

I guess it must have been about three or four months ago, and we hadn't seen each other for quite a while, so we thought it would be nice to all go out somewhere for dinner, which would save us the hassle of cooking and washing at home.

And as for what happened at the restaurant, when we got there, we were all in really good spirits, because we'd had a nice day together, and we were looking forward to eating a good curry. Unfortunately though, we ended up waiting absolutely ages for our food to come, and, to make matters worse, I had a train to catch later that night, so I was in a bit of a hurry.

What was particularly infuriating was the fact that we noticed that some of the other customers, who had arrived quite a while after us, received their meals first, so as you can imagine, we weren't too happy about that.

So just before we left, I made it very clear to the manager that the service wasn't up to scratch, and we were totally unsatisfied with the way we were treated. He did apologize, but he still made some feeble excuse that they were really busy that night and were finding it hard to cope with all the orders.

Anyway, I'm glad to say that this kind of thing hasn't happened to me too often.

词汇和句型

I'm not the kind of person who gets angry easily 我不是那种容易生气的人
get slightly angry 有一点点生气
went out for a meal 出去吃饭
save us the hassle of cooking and washing at home 省的在家做饭洗碗的麻烦
we were all in really good spirits 我们都情绪不错
Unfortunately though 但不幸的是
we ended up waiting absolutely ages for our food to come 我们最终等了很久食物才来
to make matters worse 更糟糕的是
I had a train to catch later that night 那晚我要赶火车
I was in a little bit of a hurry 我有点着急
What was particularly infuriating was the fact that ... 特别令我们生气的是……
the service wasn't up to scratch 服务达不到标准
made some feeble excuse 找某种站不住脚的借口

12. Describe a time when you and your friend had a disagreement 描述一次你和你的朋友发生意见分歧的经历
You should say:
When it was
Who you disagreed with
What you did together
And explain why you and your friend had a disagreement

Sample Answer

I am a person who is seldom in conflict with others, but there is indeed one time that I was really in disagreement with one of my friends. It happened on the first day of our trip to the USA last October. My friend Kathy and I arrived at the airport of San Francisco and then the minibus from the local tourist agency took us to a suburban hotel. Our tour around the west America would officially start the next day. We had a whole afternoon free, and we decided to go somewhere by ourselves.

We asked the receptionist about what place around the hotel was worth visiting. The answer was a shopping mall about a 15-minute drive away. Later we enquired about the taxi fee，but both of us felt it was too expensive. Then came the disagreement between us. I suggested staying in the hotel to rest since we had a long journey ahead of us，or just strolling around since the scenery nearby was quite beautiful，while Kathy insisted on walking to the mall or getting a ride in a stranger's car. I thought it was impossible to walk that far，and the receptionist agreed with me. And getting a ride in a stranger's car would be dangerous since we knew nothing about the local people. Kathy said the meaning of traveling is to take risks and make full use of the time. We argued a bit with controlled emotions. Luckily，a family living in the hotel also wanted to go to that shopping mall and came to ask the receptionist about the route. Finally，the five of us called a taxi and shared the fee.

Reflecting on that disagreement，I think the reason lies in our personalities. It is a gap between personalities，which won't be revealed until a choice has to be made. Kathy is adventurous，willing to explore anything new，while I am relatively conservative and give priority to safety. Anyway，that one disagreement didn't affect our friendship. It just helped us know each other better.

词汇和句型

I am a person who is seldom in conflict with others 我是一个很少和别人产生矛盾的人
the local tourist agency 当地旅行社
Then came the disagreement between us 然后我们产生意见分歧了
strolling around 闲逛
getting a ride in a stranger's car 搭陌生人的车
take risks 冒险
make full use of the time 充分利用时间
shared the fee 分摊费用
I am relatively conservative 我比较保守
give priority to safety 以安全为优先

13. Describe a time you taught a new skill to someone you know，such as a relative or a friend
描述一次你教你认识的人新技能的经历 (比如教你的亲戚或朋友)
You should say:
Who this person was
What you taught this person
Whether it was easy or difficult
And explain how useful this skill was

Sample Answer
A couple of months ago，I taught my cousin John how to drive a car.

John is planning to go to study in the United States next year，which means that he has to grasp the skill of driving a car because in the US it is impossible to get a taxi in small towns and Uber service is not available in some cases. So I decided to teach him how to drive a car.

Teaching John how to drive a car was not that easy because he had no experience behind the wheel. In particular，he was extremely nervous when he turned on the engine. So I gave him the driving manual which includes the functions of different components and buttons. After getting to know the basic knowledge of functioning principles of cars，John started to gain confidence and became less nervous.

Teaching John how to drive was a complicated process because the training of driving forward，turning，and reversing would take a lot of time. And warning him to obey the traffic rules was my prime concern. But John is a smart boy and after struggling for two weeks，he was proficient in driving a car. Now he is a pro in driving despite the fact that he doesn't have a driving license. I advised him to get a driving license when he settles in the US.

This skill is particularly useful to him because it could save him precious time. Imagine waiting for the bus for 30 minutes with all the stuff you have just bought from Walmart. It's an awkward occasion if you don't drive a car. Additionally，John could put the learning stuff including the Macbook Pro，textbooks，and notebooks in the car. Whenever he needs those things，he could grab those things from the car. It's very convenient for him on campus.

Driving a car is the most useful skill I taught to my cousin John.

词汇和句型

A couple of months ago　几个月前

which means that ...　这意味着……

grasp the skill of driving a car　掌握开车技能

was not that easy　不是那么容易

he was extremely nervous when he turned on the engine　他开启发动机的时候就特别紧张

driving manual　驾驶手册

the functions of different components and buttons　不同零配件和按钮的功能

driving forward，turning and reversing　向前开，转弯和倒车

obey the traffic rules　遵守交通规则

prime concern　首要关注点

he was proficient in driving a car　他可以熟练开车了

Now he is a pro in driving　现在他是一个开车高手了

despite the fact that ...　尽管……
a driving license　一张驾驶执照
an awkward occasion　一个尴尬的情况
grab those things from the car　从车中拿出来
on campus　在校园中

14. **Describe an occasion that you ate a kind of food for the first time** 描述你第一次吃某种食物的经历

You should say:
What the food was
When you ate it
How you knew this kind of food
And explain why you ate this kind of food

Sample Answer

The occasion I ate a kind of food for the first time is that I ate sushi when I was in primary school. Sushi is a kind of Japanese food which has hundreds of years of history. This food is favored not only by the Asian people but also by Westerners such as Australians, Americans, and Europeans because this kind of food is very healthy and delicious.

If I remember correctly, in the 3rd grade of primary school, I participated in a weekend party, in which I tasted sushi. It seemed that this food was very simple when I tried it, by which I mean it was just the mixture of rice, vegetable, and seafood. But it was very tasty with sauces such as the mustard and soy sauce.

I knew sushi from a variety of sources. The first way was that I saw a TV documentary when I was five or six years old. In this program, I learned about the history of the food and how this food was made. In particular, I was aware of the cultural elements in sushi. It was not simply a kind of food; instead, it was a kind of lifestyle. Later on, I read many articles about sushi in the local newspaper during the first year in primary school. So I was interested in eating this kind of food.

When I saw sushi at that party, I was eager to eat it. Apart from the reasons I mentioned above, I had other reasons to try that. The most important one was that sushi was by far the healthiest food in the world as it contained seafood such as shrimps, salmon, and tuna. Long-term consumption of sushi is beneficial to the cardiovascular system.

After eating sushi for the first time, I eat that kind of food in a regular way, almost once or twice every week.

词汇和句型

Sushi is a kind of Japanese food which has hundreds of years of history. 寿司是一种有着几百年历史的日本食物

it was just the mixture of rice，vegetable，and seafood 它是米饭、蔬菜和海鲜的混合体

But it was very tasty with sauces such as the mustard and soy sauce. 但是它和诸如芥末和酱油等调料一起吃的时候很好吃。

a TV documentary 一部电视纪录片

I was aware of the cultural elements in sushi 我了解到了寿司中所包含的文化元素

Apart from the reasons I mentioned above 除了上述我提到的理由之外

by far the healthiest food in the world 到目前为止世界上最健康的食物

shrimps，salmon，and tuna 虾、三文鱼和金枪鱼

Long-term consumption of sushi 长期食用寿司

cardiovascular system 心血管系统

15. Describe a time you watched the sky 描述你看天空的一次经历

You should say:
When and where it was
Who was with you
What you saw
And explain how you felt about watching the sky

Sample Answer

Two years ago，I went to the Santa Monica Beach，which is located in Los Angeles. That place was very popular with tourists and it was the ideal place to lie down on the beach and watch the sky. My wife went there with me to enjoy the vacation.

The sky in the west of United States was crystal blue，which cannot be seen in China because of air pollution. I could see something different from the sky in China. The cloud was amazing because it had the blue-sky background and the shapes of clouds were various. I could see the shapes of elephants，ships，flowers，and so on. People who had rich imagination could see more shapes in the blue sky. Besides，I saw many people flying kites with different materials and forms. Dragon-shaped and phoenix-shaped kites were favored by kids. When I saw these things，they reminded me of my childhood.

Another special thing I would like to mention was that there were a variety of sea birds flying in the beach area. These birds were not afraid of human beings. In most cases，they flew very low just above my head and I could see their elegant flying postures，which was the most enjoyable thing because it is not possible to see such intimate behavior between wild animals and human beings.

Santa Monica Beach is close to the Santa Monica Airport. Therefore，I saw some planes from time to time. But it didn't matter to me because the noise was hardly audible.

The incredible thing was that I saw the moon and sun simultaneously in the sky. I didn't know why it occurred but it was true. I saw it with my own eyes. It must not have been an illusion.

I felt totally refreshed when I watched the sky in Santa Monica because unlike Chinese tourist attractions，Santa Monica Beach kept its natural environment. That's why the sky was crystal blue，which reminded me of my childhood when there was no pollution in most cities in China. And I wished to immigrate to the United States one day.

词汇和句型

the Santa Monica Beach　圣莫尼卡海滩

it was the ideal place to lie down on the beach and watch the sky　它是一个理想的躺在沙滩上看天空的地方

enjoy the vacation　享受假期

the shapes of clouds were various　云的形状各不相同

flying kites　放风筝

they reminded me of my childhood　这些东西让我想起了我的童年

there were a variety of sea birds flying in the beach area　有不同种类的海鸟在海滩地区飞翔

elegant flying postures　优雅的飞行姿势

from time to time　时不时地

the noise was hardly audible　噪声几乎听不见

I saw the moon and sun simultaneously in the sky　我在天空中同时看到了月亮和太阳

It must not have been an illusion　那绝不是幻觉

immigrate to the United States　移民去美国

第六节　Others 其他类话题真题及范文

1. Describe a dinner you had with your friends 描述一个你和你朋友吃的一顿晚餐

You should say:
Who you had the dinner with
Where you had the dinner
What you ate
And explain why you chose to eat the dinner

Sample Answer

After thinking long and hard about it just now，I suppose the dinner I had with my friends was a bit like this ...

First of all，it was at my home，and I was the one cooking，as I thought this was a lot better than just going out to some restaurants where we would not be able to fully enjoy ourselves. Whenever I had dinners at restaurants in the past，things invariably went wrong，such as waiters messing up the orders，or having to wait ages for the food to arrive. I wanted to be in full control of everything，and the best way of assuring this would be to have dinners in my own home. Of course，it was a bit more effort，but it was a lot more enjoyable.

So anyway，as for who I had the dinner with，because my dining table at home only seated about six，I invited a handful of friends；they were all long-time friends. And having them over for dinner was a good way of showing my gratitude to them for all the support they gave me over the years.

So with that in mind，I made sure that I cooked something really nice for them，and actually I made pasta in a tomato and cheese sauce，which I considered to be my best dish，as it really did taste amazingly good，if I may say so myself. So that was the main course，and for dessert，I served them chocolate cake，as I was a bit of a chocoholic，along with some ice cream and strawberries，as some of them didn't like eating cake.

I had a great time having the dinner with my friends.

词汇和句型

I was the one cooking　我是烧菜的那个人

things invariably went wrong　事情总是会出错

messing up the orders　搞错所点的菜

having to wait ages for the food to arrive　花很久的时间等食物来

I wanted to be in full control of everything　我喜欢完全掌控所有的事情

my dining table at home only seated about six　我的餐桌只能容纳大约 6 个人同时进餐

having them over for dinner　邀请他们过来吃晚餐

showing my gratitude to them for all the support they gave me over the years　我对他们这些年来给我的支持表示感谢

pasta in a tomato and cheese sauce　用番茄和芝士酱拌的意大利面

my best dish　我最拿手的一道菜

the main course　主菜

I am a bit of a chocoholic　我有点吃巧克力上瘾

along with ...　和……

2. Describe a film you like 描述一部你喜欢的电影

You should say:

What the film is

When and where you saw this film
What you felt after you saw this film
And explain why you like this film

Sample Answer

The film I like is called *Gone Girl*, which was adapted from the novel of the same title written by Gillian Flynn. That film was released in the US and the UK in 2014. Undoubtedly, it is by far the best film I have seen.

I saw this film three years ago, when I accidentally saw the reviews of the film on the Internet and the rating was amazingly high so I was interested in watching the film. Then I downloaded it from a popular film-downloading website (it's illegal to do that for sure). And I watched the film with my family members on the flat-screen TV at home.

This film is about marriage. On the occasion of his fifth wedding anniversary, Nick Dunne reports that his wife, Amy, has gone missing. Soon his lies, deceits, and strange behavior have everyone asking the same dark question: Did Nick Dunne kill his wife? After I saw this film, I had the feeling that loyalty and honesty are the keys to a successful marriage or any good relationship between men and women. If someone lies, he or she will experience the devastating consequences sooner or later.

There are several reasons why I like this film. The main one is that the plot of this film is excellent and it develops with twists and turns, partly because the film is the adaptation of the book so the screenplay is amazing. So that's the first reason I like this film. Another reason is that there are two superstars starring in this film. The main character Nick is acted by Ben Affleck, who is a famous actor and a film director. The female main actress is Rosamund Pike, who has a huge number of fans in the UK.

Gone Girl is my favorite film. Two thumbs up.

词汇和句型

was adapted from the novel of the same title　改编自同名小说
Undoubtedly, it is by far the best film I have seen　毫无疑问,这是我看过的最好的一部电影。
the reviews of the film　这部电影的评论
the rating was amazingly high　打分非常高
it's illegal to do that for sure　当然,这样做是非法的
the flat-screen TV　平板电视
lies, deceits and strange behavior　谎言、欺骗和奇怪的行为
loyalty and honesty　忠实和诚实

experience the devastating consequences sooner or later　迟早会得到毁灭性的结果

it develops with twists and turns　情节发展很曲折

there are two superstars starring in this film　有两个超级巨星主演这部电影

3. Describe a movie that you dislike 描述一部你不喜欢的电影

You should say:

What the movie is

When and where you saw this movie

Who you saw this movie with

And explain why you dislike the movie

Sample Answer

One of the movies I really hated was *Titanic*.

I saw this movie when I was in high school and at that time I was into action movies. So I asked my friend if he wanted to go with me to the cinema and he said sure.

Now the story gets funny，because our English wasn't great so we looked up the meaning of *Titanic* on our electronic dictionaries. What is funny is the definition means having great stature or enormous strength，huge, or colossal. We were convinced this would be a movie about something powerful and full of action. Then we watched the movie and we were shocked，because this movie is actually a love story and it was very boring. Besides，the ending was horrible too. I think that Jack should have actually survived and met Rose later in the future and they could have sold the necklace and traveled together. Even worse，our friends made fun of us for seeing a romantic movie together because we are both boys.

To this day I will never forget the meaning of *Titanic*.

词汇和句型

I was into action movies　我对动作电影着迷

electronic dictionaries　电子词典

enormous strength　巨大的力量

We were convinced　我们确信

our friends made fun of us　我们的朋友取笑我们

4. Describe an educational TV program you like 描述一个你喜欢的教育类电视节目

You should say:

What it is

When and where you saw this educational TV program

What the features of this program are
And explain why you like this educational program

Sample Answer

A TV program that I've seen and found really interesting was a Wildlife Program named *Adventure and Discovery*. It was on CCTV 10 last month.

I saw it at home with my family and a couple of friends who came around for the evening. The program was about scuba diving, and it showed all sorts of fantastic animals. There were lots of different types of sharks, including hammerheads and white tipped sharks. And there were turtles, stingrays, and lots of other really beautiful fish as well.

But the thing that surprised me was the penguins and the seals, because I didn't know there are penguins or seals living on the equator; I thought they only live in the seas near the north and south poles.

I was amazed to learn that there are penguins and seals living on the equator because of very cold water there. I was also excited to learn that the animals are not frightened of divers and that you can swim really close to them. Obviously, they previously had almost no contact with human beings and that's why they were unafraid of people.

This program was really educational because it was very informative and I knew nothing about the sea world before. After watching this program, I could tell lots of names of unknown animals, which offers me a sense of achievement. So I love this program very much.

Adventure and Discovery is the educational program I like.

词汇和句型
scuba diving　戴水肺潜水
there are penguins or seals living on the equator　有企鹅和海豹生活在赤道
the animals are not frightened of divers　这些动物不害怕潜水者
a sense of achievement　成就感

5. Describe a good service that a company or shop offers 描述一个公司或商店提供的好服务
You should say:
What service a company or shop offers
Where you knew the service
Who provides the service

And explain why you think it is a good service

Sample Answer

The service I want to describe is the IKEA paper-and-pencil service.

The first time I knew this service was two years ago，when I was buying some pieces of furniture for my new apartment. One afternoon I went to IKEA Shanghai Flagship Store to buy the couch，chairs，and lamps. What I needed to do was to compare and contrast the color，size，and function of the furniture. But the problem was that I could not memorize the codes of the items I had seen. At that moment，I had no idea what to do because I did not bring paper and pencils with me. My smart phone was out of battery as well，so I could not use the memo App in the cell phone. Suddenly I saw a small desk in one corner. There was an employee-use-only computer，beside which were a pile of small pieces of paper and a bunch of pencils. I went closer and I saw the instruction of how to use the paper and pencil. Specifically，there were some key words on the paper，such as the name of the item，the array of picking up the item，the item code，and so on. Beside these key words were some spaces for the customer to take notes. Customers could use the pencils for free to record the information of the commodities they would like to buy.

I think the service provided by IKEA is really considerate. This service reflects their human-centered service philosophy. Although the cost of the service is relatively low，the result is amazing because customers think that they are taken good care of and they are highly valued. So they would like to visit IKEA more frequently.

词汇和句型

some pieces of furniture　一些家具

IKEA Shanghai Flagship Store　宜家上海旗舰店

the couch，chairs and lamps　沙发、椅子和灯

I did not bring paper and pencils with me　我没有带纸和笔

My smart phone was out of battery as well　我的智能手机也没电了

the memo App　备忘录应用

an employee-use-only computer　一台仅供员工使用的电脑

Beside these key words were some spaces for the customer to take notes.　在这些关键字旁边有些空白处可以让顾客做笔记。

the service provided by IKEA is really considerate　宜家所提供的服务是为顾客考虑得非常周到的

the human-centered service philosophy　以人为本的服务理念

6. Describe a job you would like to do in the future 描述一个你将来想要做的工作

You should say:

What the job is
How you knew this job
What are involved in doing this job
And explain why you would like to do this job

Sample Answer
The job I would like to do in the future is the IT specialist because currently the world is based on the Internet.

Two decades ago，the Internet commenced its era. Information technology employees are increasingly needed in the process of its development. I knew this job when my desktop computer crashed in primary school. An IT specialist came to my home and fixed the problem in 10 minutes. Thus，if I had the chance，I would try the job in the future.

There are demanding duties involved in this job. The most important requirement of the job is sound theoretical knowledge，which includes math，physics，and statistics. In other words，it is a comprehensive job. This job requires patience as well. An IT specialist should be extremely patient because major problems are not readily identified in some cases. It will cost people hours to find out the root cause of a problem. Additionally，IT specialists should have at least five years of experience to do this job well.

I would like to do this job for the following reasons. The first one is that most people communicate with each other or do business by means of the Internet. Facebook，eBay，and Amazon are good examples. If I work as an IT specialist，I will have more chances of being successful. The second one is that I am good at science subjects such as math and physics so I am confident that I will be proficient in doing the job. The most significant reason is that I would like to launch a social networking system like Facebook and Wechat. Therefore，I would like to start working with basic tasks to get more experience.

Hopefully，I can work in the IT field and become a professional in the future.

词汇和句型
Two decades ago 20 年前
the Internet commenced its era 因特网的时代开启了
Information technology employees are increasingly needed in the process of its development
在它的发展过程中，越来越需要信息技术人员。
fixed the problem 修复问题
demanding duties 要求很高的职责
sound theoretical knowledge 扎实的理论知识

math，*physics and statistics*　数学、物理和统计学
In other words　换句话说
it is a comprehensive job　它是一个综合性工作
major problems are not readily identified in some cases　在某些情况下主要问题并不会被轻易发现
the root cause　根本原因
I will be proficient in doing the job　我对这个工作会很熟练
launch a social networking system　发布一个社交网络工具

7. Describe a song you heard when you were a child 描述一首你儿童时期听过的歌
You should say:
What song it is
When you first heard it
What the song is about
And explain why this song had a special meaning to you

Sample Answer

The first song that comes to mind is *Mary had a little lamb* in English. This song is considered a nursery rhyme. I think this song is from America，but it is sung in many countries including China.

It is kind of funny but the first time I heard this song was in kindergarten about 15 years ago. It was the first day of class and a lot of children were crying and then the teacher played the song and everybody was quiet. I remember learning this song in Chinese from my grandma. This song has a good melody and is very easy to sing both in Chinese and English.

If I remember correctly，the song is about a girl named Mary and she had a little lamb with fur and the fur was as white as snow. The lamb followed Mary everywhere she went，even to school. Although Mary broke the school rules because lambs were not allowed in school，the teacher was nice and let the lamb wait outside for Mary.

This song still has a special meaning to me because it helped me remember school rules and the kindness of teachers，such as no eating in class and standing while answering the teachers' questions. I actually won an English singing contest in first grade by singing this song in front of a large audience.

词汇和句型
a nursery rhyme　一首童谣/儿歌
a good melody　好听的旋律

the fur was as white as snow　皮毛洁白如雪
The lamb followed Mary everywhere she went　玛丽去哪里，这只小羊就跟到哪里
broke the school rules　破坏校规
English singing contest　英语歌唱比赛
singing this song in front of a large audience　在大批观众面前唱这首歌

8. **Describe a law about the environment you would like to see in the future** 描述一个你将来想看到的关于环境的法律
   You should say:
   What the law is
   When and where you would like to see this law
   What will be the effect of the law
   And explain why you would like to see this law

Sample Answer

There will be an effective law in China which bans smoking in public places such as schools，hospitals，and movie theaters. I would like to see this law in the near future because smoking makes the indoor environments polluted and people would get hurt if they are surrounded by cigarette smoke.

The government will let people know that smoking is a serious issue by making a law about it. And I think the law will be quite influential. First of all，it will remind people that smoking is unhealthy and people should give up smoking as soon as possible. In addition，for those who cannot quit smoking，according to the law，they will be not allowed to smoke in public places. The law will make it clear that it is not acceptable to produce harmful gas in public places，because second-hand smoking can be a serious threat for others and it is immoral to force non-smokers to smoke passively.

Those who disobey the law and smoke in public places will be punished. For example，they will have to pay a certain amount of fine or they will be forbidden from entering the place again.

I wish the government will enforce this law as soon as possible in order to create a good environment for people to breathe fresh air in public places.

词汇和句型
bans smoking in public places　禁止公共场所吸烟
movie theaters　电影院
cigarette smoke　香烟的烟雾
a serious issue　一个严重问题

people should give up smoking as soon as possible　人们应该尽快戒烟

as for those who cannot quit smoking　对于那些无法戒烟的人

it is immoral to force non-smokers to smoke passively　强迫不吸烟的人被动吸烟是不道德的

Those who disobey the law　那些违反这个法律的人

pay a certain amount of fine　缴纳一定量的罚款

enforce this law　实施这个法律

9. Describe a method that helps you to save money 描述一个帮你省钱的方法

You should say:

What it is

How you knew this method

What you do to save money

And explain why you use this method

Sample Answer

An effective method for me to save money is to use the App downloaded from the App Store called Money Saver, which has been utilized by more than 7 million people in the world, most of whom are young people who are between 18–25 years old.

I knew this method from my best friend John, who used to be a person who spent out all the money his parents gave him and he earned from part-time jobs. However, recently, he always has spare money. A couple of weeks ago, I asked him what he did to save the money and he told me that he downloaded the Money Saver App and its functions are powerful enough for him to save money.

I used his way to save money. Specifically, what I need to do is to key in the amount of the total money I have to the Money Saver. The App would allocate the percentages into different sections including food, education, entertainment, and so on. Every time I spend money on something, I should record the amount in the App. If what I spend exceeds the budget limit of a section, the App would give me a warning. This can help me control my spending impulse. Another way the App helps me to save money is that it recommends me the best deals on the Internet so I can always get the best value for money.

I use the App every day because it is the most effective way to save money. I have tried other means such as saving the money in the bank or asking my parents to control my budget. But those methods do not work well. This App, however, could pop up some suggestions on my smart phone screen so I can know how much money I have spent and how much money I should save.

By using this method, I would say that my financial status is going on well.

词汇和句型

use the App downloaded from the App Store called Money Saver 使用一个从应用商店下载的被称为 Money Saver 的应用

a person who spent out all the money his parents gave him and he earned from part-time jobs 一个花光所有父母给的零花钱和兼职工作赚的钱的人

what I spend exceeds the budget limit 我的开支超过了预算限制

control my spending impulse 控制我的消费冲动

the best deals 最佳交易

get the best value for money 获得最佳性价比

those methods do not work well 那些方法不怎么起作用

pop up some suggestions on my smart phone screen 在我的手机屏幕上弹出一些建议

10. Describe an App (in your mobile phone) that you think is the most useful 描述一个(你手机中的)你认为最有用的应用

You should say:
What it is
How you knew the App
What the functions of the App are
And explain why the App is useful

Sample Answer

The most useful App I want to describe is Google Map. This App is the most popular one in the world. Almost everybody installs Google Map on his or her cell phone.

I knew this App about 5 years ago from one of my friends, Jack. He told me that Google Map was extremely useful if you could not find a place or you got lost in the wild.

As to the functions of Google Map, I would say that it is quite useful. For example, if I want to go to a specific place by driving a car, all I need to do is to locate where I am by the GPS function of the App. After that, I key in the address of the destination. Then I only need to press the navigation button. The App tells me how long it will take to get there and the nearest or the fastest route.

In terms of the reasons why it is useful, I think the first one is that I do not need to bring a map with me all the time and memorize the main routes or branch roads. The second reason is that it can be used to deal with emergencies. For example, when I am traveling in the wild but I cannot find my way back. At this time, Google Map could be helpful to locate the specific place and navigate the way back.

词汇和句型

extremely useful　非常有用

you got lost in the wild　在野外迷路

locate where I am by the GPS function　通过全球定位系统的功能定位我所在位置

key in the address of the destination　键入目的地的地址

press the navigation button　按下导航按钮

I do not need to bring a map with me all the time　我不需要一直带着地图

memorize the main routes or branch roads　记得主路和岔路

11. **Describe an area of science you studied that you are interested in（e. g.　the medicine, physics, or math）描述一个你学过的感兴趣的理科科目(比如医学、物理或数学)**

You should say:

What the area of science is

When and where you studied it

How you studied it

And explain why you are interested in it

Sample Answer

The area of science that I'm interested in is chemistry. I took chemistry classes during high school, which I guess must have been about six or seven years ago by now.

Anyway, as for why I'm interested in chemistry, to put it simply, it's because I remember we did a really cool experiment in the process of learning it, so it stands out in my memory over the other subjects, most of which I've pretty much forgotten.

So you're probably wondering what exactly the experiment was. If I remember correctly, we were basically testing the reaction of certain metals when you put them into water. And what made it so fun was the fact that the metals turned out to be really volatile. In other words, they literally exploded when they came into contact with water. And this was something that we had never seen before, so none of us expected such a big reaction. Anyway, after we finished the experiment, we had to write everything up, which was the boring part, but I guess doing that helped us analyze the results in a methodical way and draw conclusions.

And when you compare this to most of the other subjects of science we had, where we basically just went through the textbook and took notes, it was a thousand times more interesting, as I'm sure you can imagine, so none of us forgot that class, and we all wanted to do the experiment again, but unfortunately our teacher told us once was enough.

So yeah，I guess that's pretty much it.

词汇和句型

took the chemistry classes during middle school　在中学时上化学课
we were basically testing the reaction of certain metals when you put them into water　我们在测试某些金属放在水中的反应
really volatile　非常不稳定
so in other words　所以换句话说
they literally exploded　它们真的爆炸了
they came into contact with water　它们和水接触
this was something that we had never seen before　这是我们以前从来没有看到过的东西
write everything up　把所有东西完整清晰地记录下来
analyze the results in a methodical way　有条不紊地分析结果
draw conclusions　得出结论
went through the textbook　浏览课本
compare this to most of the other subjects of science　把这个和其他理科科目作比较
it was a thousand times more interesting　它要有趣得多

12. Describe an effective advertisement you saw 描述一个你看过的有效的广告
You should say:
What the advertisement is
When you saw this advertisement
What is special about the advertisement
And explain why you think this advertisement is effective

Sample Answer

The advertisement that has just come to my mind is a PSA，or a public service announcement that I saw on TV several days ago.

That PSA is against human consumption of wild animals. I remember that this advertisement starred Yao Ming，a former basketball star from China. He and some other people were having dinner in a well-decorated restaurant. Also in that restaurant，there was a huge fish tank，in which there was a shark swimming. The shark had no fin，and I could see the bleeding wound clearly. My heart was tightened because of that. Then the waiter served a dish，which was actually soup made with shark fin. Meanwhile，there was a striking voice，saying that about 70 million sharks were killed every year，just because human beings needed their fin on their dining table. Hearing that，all the people in the restaurant dropped their spoons and pushed the soup away from them. In the end，Yao Ming said a slogan：no trade，no killing.

I believe this advertisement is effective，because of Yao Ming，and，more importantly，because of the shocking facts and statistics that it had shown. After seeing this advertisement，I myself have not thought about enjoying shark fin any more.

词汇和句型

PSA（public service announcement） 公益广告
this advertisement starred Yao Ming 这个广告是姚明主演的
a former basketball star 一个前篮球明星
a huge fish tank 一个大鱼缸
The shark had no fin 这条鲨鱼没有鳍
the bleeding wound 流血的伤口
the waiter served a dish 服务员上了一道菜
soup made with shark fin 鱼翅汤
on their dining table 在他们的餐桌上
a slogan 一条广告语
no trade，no killing 没有买卖就没有杀害
the shocking facts 令人震惊的事实

13. Describe an important skill you learned when you were a child 描述你儿童时期学的一个重要技能
You should say:
What skill it was
When you learned the skill
How you learned the skill
And explain why you learned this skill

Sample Answer

The important skill I learned when I was a child was the communication skill，which is the key skill to the development of my life.

I learned this skill when I was in the first grade. It was a totally new environment for me and I was required to talk to my teachers and classmates. So I had to get rid of the shyness and communicate with them without any barriers. At that time，communication skill was an important ability to me. I thought I should try every means to grasp this skill.

The first way to master this skill was to ask my parents about how to communicate with my teachers and peers. My father told me that I should be honest and friendly when talking with others. Honesty is a crucial element in communication. If I was honest，he told me，others would be honest to me as well. Then we could continue communicating and making friends with each other.

Another thing was that I should be extroverted and optimistic. I learned from my parents and relatives that a good personality was critical to smooth communication. So I always kept smiling when talking to others. And it was effective in communication.

The reason I learned communication skill was that it is beneficial to my whole life. When I was in high school and university，this skill helped me a lot in overcoming difficulties. Now that I'm working in a big company，interpersonal relationship is particularly important to work efficiency. Thank to the skill I grasped in my childhood，I can solve tough problems and work well with others.

That is an important skill I learned when I was a child.

词汇和句型

the key skill 　关键技能

communicate with them without any barriers 　毫无障碍地跟他们交流

try every means to grasp this skill 　想尽办法掌握这个技能

Honesty is a crucial element in communication 　诚实是沟通中的一个重要元素

be extroverted and optimistic 　开朗和乐观

a good personality was critical to smooth communication 　一个好的个性对于流畅沟通来说是重要的

interpersonal relationship 　人际关系

solve tough problems 　解决棘手的问题

14. Describe an interesting website you have used 描述一个你用过的令你感兴趣的网站

You should say:
What the website is
What is on the website
How often you go on it
And explain why it is an interesting website

Sample Answer

The website I'd like to talk to you about is Ted. com，which you might have heard of before，and possibly even been on.

And as for what's on the website，it's basically a huge collection of video speeches by people from all kinds of fields. So it's a really great resource for learning stuff. It's completely free，which means that it doesn't cost anything to listen to the talks. And what's great about it is that you can choose Chinese or English subtitles for most of the talks，and also download them onto your computer. I also like to read the comments written by other people who have watched the talk.

I go on it two or three times a week，so pretty much every other day. I'm normally on it while I'm having lunch because most of the talks are between 10 to 20 minutes.

As for why I think it's an interesting website，first and foremost，it's because the vast majority of talks are incredibly appealing，at least in my opinion anyway，so there's a tremendous amount you can learn from them. I think it's wonderful to have a website like this，which brings all these great talks together in one place. And another interesting thing about it is that the talks on the website don't go on for too long. We've all listened to speeches which drag on and on，but these ones are generally quite short and to the point.

词汇和句型

a huge collection of video speeches　大量的视频演讲
it's a really great resource for learning stuff　它是学习材料极好的素材来源
which means that it doesn't cost anything to listen to the talks　这意味着听这些演讲不需要花任何钱
And what's great about it is that ...　这个(网站)的一大特点是……
Chinese or English subtitles　中文或英文字幕
download them onto your computer　把(这些视频)下载到你的电脑
I go on it two or three times a week　我一周两三次上(这个网站)
every other day　每两天
first and foremost　首先，最重要的是
the vast majority of talks　大量的演讲
incredibly appealing　非常吸引人的
at least in my opinion anyway　至少我是这么认为的
there's a tremendous amount you can learn from them　你可以从中学到大量东西
speeches which drag on and on　(时间)拖得很长的演讲
to the point　讲到点上，重点清晰

15. Describe another language (not English) that you would like to learn 描述另外一种你想学的语言(不包括英语)
You should say:
What language it would be
How you would learn it
What equipment or facilities you would need to study this language
And explain what difficulties you think you would have

Sample Answer

There are actually quite a few languages that I would like to learn，but probably the one I'd like to learn most is French，partly because I think it sounds really nice，and also because France is a country that I'd really love to visit sometime. And so if I was able to speak French，I would then be able to converse with the locals，which I think that would give me a much better understanding of the country and also make my time there a lot more interesting and enjoyable.

As for how I would learn it，I guess first of all I would try and find a decent self-study course on the Internet. And as well as that，I would look for a teacher，preferably a native speaker if possible，because I would then be able to get feedback on what I was doing right and wrong. And having a native speaker as my teacher would be extremely beneficial in terms of developing a good accent.

And regarding what equipment I would need to study French，I suppose it would be more or less the same as what I've been using for learning English，basically a laptop and a smartphone，with which I would be able to download various things like podcasts and other learning materials onto.

So that's probably how I would learn the language，and finally，with regard to what difficulties I think I might encounter，I imagine having quite a bit of difficulty with the pronunciation，as it's so different from Chinese. I mean，there are so many sounds in French which we don't have in our language，so I'm sure it would take an extremely long time to speak it well. And besides the pronunciation，I guess it might also be pretty difficult mastering the grammar，simply because every language has its own set of grammar rules，and I'm sure French is no exception.

So yeah，I suppose that's about it then. Thanks for listening.

词汇和句型
probably the one I'd like to learn most is French　我最想学的可能是法语
it sounds really nice　它听起来很好听
France is a country that I'd really love to visit　法国是一个我非常想去的国家
converse with the locals　和当地人谈话
make my time there a lot more interesting and enjoyable　使我在那里度过的时光更有趣更开心
I would try and find a decent self-study course on the Internet　我会在网上找一个不错的自学课程
And as well as that　除此之外
preferably a native speaker if possible　有可能的话，最好是一个讲母语的人

I would then be able to get feedback on what I was doing right and wrong　我可以得到我表现好坏的反馈

having a native speaker as my teacher　讲母语的人做我的老师

extremely beneficial　非常有利

in terms of　就……而言

developing a good accent　获得一个好的口音

regarding what equipment I would need to study French　关于我需要什么设备来学法语

more or less the same　差不多相同的

a laptop and a smartphone　一台笔记本电脑和一部智能手机

download various things like podcasts　下载各种资料比如播客

learning materials　学习材料

with regard to what difficulties I think I might encounter　关于我可能会遇见的困难

quite a bit of difficulty with the pronunciation　许多发音方面的困难

it would take an extremely long time to speak it well　会花相当长的时间把(法语)说好

besides the pronunciation　除了发音以外

every language has its own set of grammar rules　每种语言都有它的自身语法规则体系

French is no exception　法语也不例外

16. Describe something healthy you enjoy doing 描述你喜欢做的健康的事情

You should say:

What you do

Where you do it

Who you do it with

And explain why you think doing this is healthy

Sample Answer

Stopping being a late-night sleeper is something healthy that I enjoy doing. Actually I've been a night owl for years, going to sleep anytime between 12 and 3 a.m. on a normal night. I know that staying up late could be toxic to my body for many reasons, but I just can't sleep on time. And I can't remember how many times I've stayed up late studying for an exam while having snacks. So after gaining about 20 pounds, I finally made up my mind to get rid of this bad habit.

Honestly, it was not that easy at the very beginning, because I always lost track of time easily, but I established a strict bedtime and honored it. I mean, I forced myself to go to sleep without carrying any kinds of devices nearby. And if I had a problem falling asleep, counting sheep was the first and only choice. And you know what, 4 weeks later, I developed good sleeping habits and lost those 20 pounds gradually.

As to why it keeps me healthy, there's a combination of reasons, one of which could be that sleep helps me maintain a healthy balance of hormones that make me feel hungry or full. When I don't get enough sleep, my level of ghrelin goes up and my level of leptin goes down. This makes me feel hungrier than when I'm well-rested. On top of that, sufficient sleep also supports healthy growth and development, simply because deep sleep triggers the body to release the hormone that promotes normal growth and this hormone boots muscle mass and repair cells. So, that's something I do for health.

词汇和句型

a late-night sleeper 一个晚睡的人

a night owl 夜猫子

staying up late 熬夜

be toxic to my body 对我的身体有毒害

stayed up late studying for an exam while having snacks 边吃东西边熬夜准备考试

made up my mind to get rid of this bad habit 决定改掉这种坏习惯

lost track of time 忘记时间

established a strict bedtime 制定了严格的睡觉时间

forced myself to go to sleep without carrying any kinds of devices nearby 不带任何（电子）设备，强迫自己去睡觉

if I had a problem falling asleep 如果我入睡有问题

developed good sleeping habits 养成了好的睡眠习惯

lost those 20 pounds gradually 逐渐减肥 20 磅

maintain a healthy balance of hormones 维持激素的健康平衡

ghrelin 饥饿激素，胃内产生的一种肽，生长素释放肽

leptin 瘦素，一种由脂肪组织分泌的蛋白质类激素

makes me feel hungrier 使我感觉更加饥饿

well-rested 充分休息

On top of that 除此之外

sufficient sleep 充分睡眠

deep sleep triggers the body to release the hormone that promotes normal growth 深睡眠促使人体释放出一种促进正常生长的激素

boots muscle mass 提升肌肉密度

repair cells 修复细胞

第四章　IELTS Speaking Part 3 Questions and Sample Answers 雅思口语 Part 3 真题和范文

第一节　雅思口语 Part 3 核心技巧

核心技巧 1
回答考官问题时,一定要把答案讲透,要多用理由和例子(但不要用个人例子)。

核心技巧 2
运用雅思写作的方法,通过观点表达和分类阐述方法回答问题。

核心技巧 3
对于自己不熟悉的话题要用生活化的例子去解释,Part 3 也要讲究雅思生活化(但不要用个人例子)。

核心技巧 4
连接词的运用要自然有效,注重递进、因果和转折三方面的有意识表达。

核心技巧 5
充分运用自己准备的素材库。

核心技巧 6
回答问题不能过于抽象,不能过于深入,否则考官会就你回答的继续发问。

核心技巧 7
绝对不要出现冷场情况,否则分数会大幅下降。没有 idea 的时候要多举例(新闻中或者书中看到的例子),也就是充分实践黄金原则 1 和 3。

核心技巧 8
保持一种和考官交流的感觉,充分运用语调和节奏,创造一种自然流畅的交流氛围。这样一来,即使你的语言上有缺陷,但是能够充分交流就能得高分。

第二节 雅思口语 Part 3 高频话题真题及范文

1. Advantages & Disadvantages 优缺点

考试原题和范文

What are the advantages and disadvantages of television?

【Sample Answer】 I suppose it's fair to say that there are a number of pros and cons. For example, television provides us with a lot of entertainment, which is important because people's lives are stressful. And as well as this, I guess another plus is that many programs on TV are educational, so there's a lot of stuff we can learn through watching TV. And regarding the drawbacks, I guess the main one is that watching TV tends to be quite addictive, so it's easy to spend several hours a day watching it, which gives us less time to do other things. But, all in all, I would say that the advantages outweigh the disadvantages.

What are the advantages and disadvantages of travelling alone?

【Sample Answer】 I'd say the good thing about travelling alone is that you get to do whatever you want, without having to ask for anyone else's opinion. So basically, you can be really flexible with your plans. But on the downside, if you're travelling on your own, you might feel lonely at times, especially if you've got no one to talk to.

What are the pros and cons of long-distance travelling?

【Sample Answer】 Looking at the pros, I guess I'd basically say that when you travel far away, you get to see things that you wouldn't normally see where you're from. So for example, if I went to Africa, I'm sure I would get to see a whole new lifestyle, something completely different from what I'm used to here. And as for the cons, first of all, travelling a long way can be quite stressful and exhausting, especially if there are delays involved. And I know from personal experience that long-haul flights tend to be particularly uncomfortable, unless you're in business or first class, you have very little leg space, and it's really difficult to fall asleep. So it's often not a great deal of fun, especially if you're travelling on your own.

What are the advantages of giving money as a gift?

【Sample Answer】 I guess one of the biggest advantages is that the person receiving the money can buy whatever they want with it, so you save yourself the risk of wasting your money on something that the person has no interest in. And as well as this, I guess another advantage is that it saves a lot of time, because you don't have to bother about going out and buying something. So all in all, money makes a pretty good gift.

词汇和句型

a number of pros and cons　很多优缺点

people's lives are stressful　人们的生活压力很大

And as well as this　除此之外

plus　优点

regarding the drawbacks　关于缺点

all in all　总的来说

the advantages outweigh the disadvantages　好处多于坏处

you can be really flexible with your plans　你的计划可以非常灵活

on the downside　从消极的方面来看

at times　有时候

a whole new lifestyle　一种全新的生活方式

as for the cons　关于坏处

long-haul flights　长途飞行

tend to be particularly uncomfortable　往往是非常不舒服的

unless you're in business or first class　除非你坐商务舱或者头等舱

little leg space　很小的腿部空间

it's really difficult to fall asleep　真的很难入睡

if you're travelling on your own　如果你独自旅行

2. Questions about Changes 关于"变化"的问题

考试原题和范文

How has the relationship between neighbors changed between now and the past?

【Sample Answer】　I'd say it's changed a lot，and probably the main change has been that currently people don't really see their neighbors all that often，whereas in the past，they used to do quite a lot of things together. For example，people would often have their neighbors over for lunch or dinner，which doesn't really happen that much anymore.

Have cities changed much in your country in the past few decades?

【Sample Answer】　Yeah，I'd say they definitely have，because they've become a lot more built-up，and there are considerably more high-rise buildings than there used to be. And as well as this，another big change would be the traffic，which has got a lot worse in most cities，simply because there are far more cars on the road than there used to be.

Is it easier or more difficult to get a job today than in the past?

【Sample Answer】　I would say it's definitely more difficult to get a job currently than it was in the past，and one of the reasons for saying this is that in the past，there was generally less competition for jobs，because not that many people went to university，whereas these days，there are millions of graduates looking for jobs，which has made it extremely difficult to find a decent and high-paying job, unless of course you have good personal connections. Another point I should mention is that 20 or 30 years ago, people were actually assigned jobs after completing university, so getting a job was pretty much guaranteed, whereas this is no longer the case.

Is the material that furniture is made from today different to the material that was used in the past?

【Sample Answer】　Yeah, I would say it is, because in the past, furniture used to be made of wood, whereas currently, there's a huge variety of different materials that are used for making furniture, of which a few that come to mind are plastic, leather, and suede. And I think this reflects the fact that people's tastes are diversifying as their standard of living improves.

词汇和句型

whereas in the past　但是在过去

people would often have their neighbors over for lunch or dinner　人们经常会邀请他们的邻居来吃午饭或晚饭

built-up　高楼林立的,建筑物众多的

there are considerably more high-rise buildings　有更多的高层建筑

simply because　主要是因为

one of the reasons for saying this is that ...　这样说的其中一个原因是……

not that many people went to university　不是那么多人去读大学

whereas these days　而如今

there are millions of graduates looking around for jobs　有成百上千万的毕业生求职

made it extremely difficult to find a decent and high-paying job　使得找到一个既体面又高薪的工作极其困难

good personal connections　很好的人脉关系

Another point I should mention is that ...　我想要提一下的另外一个点是……

this is no longer the case　现在情况已经不是这样了

3. Questions about Differences 关于"区别"的问题

考试原题和范文

What are the differences in the music that young and old people listen to?

【Sample Answer】　I suppose there are a handful of differences, one of which would be that young people, on the whole, mainly like listening to pop music, whereas the older generation tend to prefer listening to more traditional music, like folk music, Chinese opera, and even old revolutionary songs. So that's one difference, and I guess another would be that young people often listen to western music as well as Chinese music, whereas in contrast, I think it's fair to say that most elderly people just listen to Chinese music.

What are the differences between living in cities and living in the countryside?

【Sample Answer】 To begin with, one difference would be that living in rural areas is generally a lot more relaxing than living in urban areas, as the pace of life is relatively slower and more laid-back. So that's one thing, and as well as this, I guess another difference would be that in the countryside, there are generally not as many things to do as there are when you are living in cities.

What are the differences between a city center and the suburbs?

【Sample Answer】 It's fair to say that the city center tends to be the most built-up area of the city, and it is where most of the main commercial buildings are situated, like shopping malls and office blocks, whereas the suburbs are generally much more residential. So this is one aspect, and I suppose another thing to mention would be the traffic, because in most cities, the downtown areas, on the whole, tend to get horrendously congested, whereas in the outskirts, the traffic's normally not too bad, which is why I guess more and more people prefer living a little bit further out from the city center — at least this seems to be the case here in Shanghai anyway.

词汇和句型

a handful of differences 一些区别

the older generation 老一代

folk music 民间音乐

I guess another would be that ... 我觉得另外一个(区别)是……

whereas in contrast 但是相对比而言

it's fair to say that ... 说实话……

living in rural areas is generally a lot more relaxing than living in urban areas 住在农村要比住在城市令人放松

the pace of life is relatively slower and more laid-back 生活节奏相对更慢更松弛

in the countryside, there are generally not as many things to do as there are when you are living in cities 在农村不像你在城市里有这么多的事情可以做

the city center tends to be the most built-up area of the city and it is where most of the main commercial buildings are situated 市中心往往是城市中建筑物最密集的地方,也是主要的商业建筑坐落的地方

shopping malls 购物商场

office blocks 办公楼

the suburbs are generally much more residential 郊区总体而言更多是用来居住的

this is one aspect, and I suppose another thing to mention would be ... 这是一方面;我觉得另外一个需要提一下的是……

the downtown areas 市中心区域

get horrendously congested 变得非常拥堵

in the outskirts 在市郊

which is why I guess ... 这就是为什么我认为······

more and more people prefer living a little bit further out from the city center 越来越多的人喜欢住在离市中心稍微远一点的地方

at least this seems to be the case here in Shanghai anyway 至少在上海情况是如此

4. Questions about the Future 关于"将来"的问题

考试原题和范文

What will restaurants be like in the future?

【Sample Answer】 I suppose quite a few things could happen, one of which might be that waiters will be replaced by robots, because by doing this, restaurants will reduce their labour costs. So that's one thing, and on top of this, I imagine it's also quite possible that we will see an increase in the number of high-end restaurants, simply because people's living standards are increasingly higher. Of course other things are bound to happen, but right now this is all that comes to mind.

What websites will be popular in the future?

【Sample Answer】 If we look at what's happened in the last few years, I think most people would agree that social networking sites have become incredibly popular, and I would say this trend is likely to continue into the foreseeable future, simply because people enjoy spending time chatting with their friends, whether it be in person or on the Internet.

How do you think work will change over the next few decades?

【Sample Answer】 That's a good question, and thinking about it, I guess one thing that could happen is that more people might start working from home, simply because it's becoming more and more inconvenient travelling to work due to traffic congestion. So that's one thing, and I guess it's also quite possible that work, in general, will become more internet-based, because the influence of the Internet on people's work has increased incredibly in the last 10 years or so, and I can't see this changing. I mean, more or less everything we do now can more or less be done on the internet, and because it's so convenient, I would say it will play an even bigger role in our lives in years to come.

Do you think that cities will become noisier in the future?

【Sample Answer】 That's a hard question, and I'm really not that sure to be honest with you, but I guess my feeling would be that they probably will get noisier, yeah, basically because if you compare the situation in cities now to what it was like 10 or 15 years ago, then it's obvious that cities have become a lot noisier, mainly of course, due to the increase in traffic on the roads. And I think it's pretty safe to say that the traffic will continue to get worse in cities as more people will be able to afford their own cars, which means that, in all likelihood, urban areas will get even noisier.

Will traffic problems worsen in the future?

【Sample Answer】 If things continue to go the way they're going at the moment, then for sure, it'll get worse. But I reckon it's also quite possible that governments will step up their efforts to reduce congestion, and if they do so, we might see an improvement.

词汇和句型

reduce their labour costs 减少他们的劳动力成本

and on top of this 除此之外

we will see an increase in the number of high-end restaurants 我们将会看到顶级餐厅的数量增加

people's living standards are increasingly higher 人们的生活标准正在不断提高

other things are bound to happen 其他事情也注定会发生

social networking sites 社交网站

become incredibly popular 变得非常流行

this trend is likely to continue into the foreseeable future 这个趋势在可预见的将来将会继续下去

whether it be in person or on the Internet 不论是面对面还是在网上

start working from home 开始在家工作

due to traffic congestion 因为交通拥堵

in the last 10 years or so 在过去的大约十年中

I would say 我觉得

play an even bigger role in our lives 在我们的生活中起到更大的作用

in years to come 在未来的几年内

to be honest with you 跟你说实话

if you compare the situation in cities now to what it was like 10 or 15 years ago 如果你把城市中的现状和大约十年或十五年前相比

due to the increase in traffic on the roads 由于道路上的交通流量增加

more people will be able to afford their own cars 将会有更多人能够买得起私家车

in all likelihood 十有八九，多半

if things continue to go the way they're going at the moment 如果事情按照现在的情况发展下去

I reckon 我认为

step up their efforts 更努力

5. "Why" Questions 关于"为什么"的问题

考试原题和范文

Why do you think we need leisure activities?

【Sample Answer】 If we didn't have them, life would be extremely monotonous. I mean, we would just be working, eating, and sleeping, with nothing in between. So having leisure activities is a good way to break up the day, and it also helps us relax and take our mind off things.

Why are people spending more time on the computer?

【Sample Answer】 I'd say there are a handful of reasons as to why this is the case, one of which is that we are now able to do more and more things on the computer, like watching films and TV series, whereas in the past, we were only able to watch them on TV. And if you watch stuff on your computer, you don't have to sit through all the annoying advertisements which you get on the TV.

Why do some people not like to buy things from other countries?

【Sample Answer】 I guess one reason would be that imported products tend to be more expensive than domestically-made things. And as well as this, I suppose another reason is that a lot of people here aren't that familiar with many of the foreign brands, or indeed products, so they're not exactly sure whether they would be worth buying or not.

Why do we need leaders?

【Sample Answer】 I'd say there are quite a few reasons why we need them, and one would basically be that leaders help teams work together and stay organized. I mean, if we didn't have leaders, just imagine the chaos that everything would be in. For example, companies wouldn't be able to function properly, and on a bigger scale, it would be impossible to govern a country if there were no leaders. So yeah, I think it's extremely important that we have them.

Why do people like to buy expensive things they don't use?

【Sample Answer】 I'm not really that sure to be honest, but one reason might be due to the fact that people tend to want things more when they don't have them, so once they've bought something it often doesn't feel that special anymore. And as well as this, another reason would be that a lot of expensive things go up in value over time, a prime example being flats and houses, so many people buy these things as an investment, rather than something that they will use.

词汇和句型

life would be extremely monotonous　生活将会极其单调
take our mind off things　不再想那些事情
I'd say there are a handful of reasons as to why this is the case　我觉得有一些原因会造成这种情况
do more and more things on the computer　在电脑上做越来越多的事情
whereas in the past　然而在过去
the annoying advertisements　令人讨厌的广告

imported products　进口产品

domestically-made things　国产商品

a lot of people here aren't that familiar with many of the foreign brands，or indeed products　很多人不那么熟悉这么多的外国品牌或者说是产品

they're not exactly sure whether they would be worth buying or not　他们不确定哪些产品是值得买的

leaders help teams work together and stay organized　领导者帮助团队协同工作并且保持组织有序

function properly　正常运作

on a bigger scale　从更大范围来说

extremely important　特别重要

I'm not really that sure to be honest　说实话我不是那么确定

due to the fact that …　因为⋯⋯

a lot of expensive things go up in value over time　很多昂贵的东西会随着时间而升值

a prime example　一个最好的例子

many people buy these things as an investment，rather than something that they will use. 许多人买这些东西是作为投资，而不是作为使用的东西的。

6. Giving Suggestions 关于"给出建议"的问题

考试原题和范文

How could the traffic in cities be improved?

【Sample Answer】　I guess congestion could be reduced in a number of ways. For example，one thing would be to increase the number of car lanes，in so doing，cars would have more space to drive around. So that's one thing，and I suppose another possibility might be to introduce a congestion charge，as by doing this，people would think twice before getting into their cars.

How do you think noise in cities could be reduced?

【Sample Answer】　Thinking about it，I guess there are a number of things that could be done，one of which would be to impose a fine on companies or individuals who make excessive noise，especially construction companies，because I'd say they're，by far，the biggest culprits. And as well as this，maybe another thing might be to ban vehicles from hooting，because it's one of the noisiest sounds in cities，and I'm sure they would become a lot quieter without cars hooting all the time.

How can children be encouraged to play less computer games and more sports?

【Sample Answer】　That's a tough question，because it's practically impossible tearing a child away from a computer screen when they're busy playing a game，but I guess one thing that could be done would be to make sports more appealing by providing more sports facilities. So, in other words, if a child only has to walk five minutes to get to a basketball court, he's much more likely to play basketball than if he had to catch a bus and ride for half an hour.

How should parents educate their children before they start school?
【Sample Answer】 That's a tough question and I'm no expert, but I guess one thing they should do is encourage their children in everything they do, even if they make mistakes, because this'll help build children's confidence and self-esteem. So that's one thing, and I guess another good thing for parents to do would be to read stories, especially ones with good moral values, because all children love stories, and, in this way, they'll be learning things without even realizing it.

词汇和句型
congestion could be reduced in a number of ways 拥堵可以通过各种方法来减少
increase the number of car lanes 提升车道数量
another possibility 另外一个可能的方法
a congestion charge 拥堵费
think twice 三思
impose a fine on companies or individuals who make excessive noise 对于产生大量过分噪声的公司和个人进行罚款
especially construction companies 特别是建筑公司
the biggest culprits 最大的罪魁祸首
And as well as this 除此之外
ban vehicles from hooting 禁止车辆鸣笛
a tough question 一个复杂的问题
it's practically impossible tearing a child away from a computer screen when they're busy playing a game 把一个忙着玩游戏的孩子从电脑屏幕前拽开基本上是一件不可能的事情
make sports more appealing 使体育更有吸引力
sports facilities 体育设施
walk five minutes to get to a basketball court 走路五分钟到一个篮球场
catch a bus and ride for half an hour 坐公共汽车半小时
build children's confidence and self-esteem 建立孩子的信心和自尊
good moral values 良好的道德价值观
learning things without even realizing it 潜移默化地学到东西

7. Family 家庭

考试原题和范文
Why should young people respect old people?
【Sample Answer】 Young people should do so because old people have contributed a lot

to the society. The world in which young people live now is established by their previous generations, so they should show some respect to seniors. Furthermore, elderly people have more life experience and wisdom. They can give young people a lot of good advice, which is also very respectable.

What is the importance of family to people?

【Sample Answer】 Family is the driving force for people. For most people, they work hard so that their family can live a better life. Besides, when people are in trouble, family members are the people they can trust and turn to for help and for comfort.

What is the influence of social network system on family relationship?

【Sample Answer】 The function of social network system is a substitute for family relationships. Since people cannot always rely on their family members, sometimes they need to turn to their friends rather than their family for help. In a society, people can meet and make friends with each other through social networks. For example, children make friends with their classmates and adults know people from work. This kind of friendship is an alternative to family relationships.

词汇和句型

old people have contributed a lot to the society　老年人对社会贡献良多

elderly people　老年人

life experience and wisdom　生活经验和智慧

the driving force　驱动力

live a better life　过更好的生活

turn to ... for help and for comfort　向……寻求帮助和安慰

a substitute　一种替代

an alternative　一种替代

8. Children and Childhood 儿童和童年

考试原题和范文

Why are children often teased to laugh?

【Sample Answer】 I think this is because children are innocent. They have a simple mind, feeling curious about anything new, and are extremely reactive to funny things.

What is the best age for people to get married and have a child in your country?

【Sample Answer】 The common age for people to get married in China, I think, is between 25 to 30, and most people get their first child at around 27 - 32. It is hard to say what the best age is, but I think in big competitive cities where people are usually busy climbing their career ladder, it is better to get married later, maybe around the age of

28 – 30. At this age，young people have generally accumulated some experience and are valued by the company. Even if they get married and have a child，there is a place for them in the company. If you get married and decide to have a baby，say at 25，you still lack experience，and are in a relatively low position. The birth of a baby will take a lot of your attention. You won't make much progress in your career.

What is required for a couple to have child?

【Sample Answer】 I think two factors are important. The first thing is that the couple should have stable jobs with salaries at least able to support a family of three members；second，what I think is more important，is to be prepared to accept a new member in the family，for raising a baby will be very demanding. The young couple may need to completely adjust their lifestyle，abandoning their hobbies，and devoting most of their off-work time to caring for the babies.

Why do people miss their childhood?

【Sample Answer】 I think childhood is mostly a carefree period when children are able to spend a lot of time playing. Of course，the only possible pressure is from study. But compared to adults' problems like finding a respectable job，buying a house，and recovering from being dumped，such pressure can be safely neglected. On the other hand，when we were children，we usually kept a much more positive attitude towards life. We focused more on the bright side，and we were curious about everything new. Thus，we became happy easily. However，as we grow up，we are more likely to notice the negative sides. It is harder for us to be happy. That's why we often miss our childhood.

What is the best stage in people's life?

【Sample Answer】 I think the best stage is the period when you can stay together with your family members. Currently，society is becoming increasingly mobile. And it's common for family members to live and work apart，even in different countries. It's ok when everything goes well. However，if one is ill，or is emotionally hurt，nothing can compare to the support or consolation from family members. So I think people should cherish the time spent with family members and try to create such moments.

词汇和句型

children are innocent 儿童是天真的

big competitive cities 大型的具有竞争力的城市

people are usually busy climbing their career ladder 人们通常忙着在职业上的发展

lack experience 缺乏经验

make much progress in your career 取得职业上的大进步

stable jobs 稳定的工作

raising a baby will be very demanding 养一个孩子会很有挑战的

The young couple　年轻的夫妇

completely adjust their lifestyle　完全调整他们的生活方式

abandoning their hobbies　放弃他们的爱好

devoting most of their off-work time to caring for the babies　把大部分的下班时间花在照顾小孩上

a carefree period　一段无忧无虑的时期

recovering from being dumped　从失恋中恢复

kept a much more positive attitude towards life　对生活保持一种积极的态度

focused more on the bright side　更多的关注好的一面

curious about everything new　对所有的新东西好奇

notice the negative sides　关注负面的东西

miss our childhood　怀念我们的儿童时期

society is becoming increasingly mobile　社会的流动性越来越大

the support or consolation from family members　家庭成员的支持和安慰

cherish the time spent with family members　珍惜和家人共处的时光

9. Politeness 礼貌

考试原题和范文

How do Chinese people show politeness?

【Sample Answer】 We really value politeness and good manners in China，and there are many types of polite behaviour. One of the first things we learn as children is to say "please" and "thank you". As adults，I think we are careful not to be too direct with the language we use. For example，we would never say "Bring me the bill" in a restaurant because this kind of direct instruction would sound rude. It would be more polite to say "Could we have the bill，please?".

Are we less polite with members of our families than with people we don't know?

【Sample Answer】 I suppose it's normal to be a bit more relaxed about politeness with family members. Most people tend to speak in a more informal way at home；in China，we still say "please" and "thanks"，but it's fine to use colloquial language and things like nicknames that you would never use with someone you didn't know.

Is there any difference between etiquette in cities and that in small towns?

【Sample Answer】 Yes，there is a difference. It is very common in small towns that if you see a person in the eye when you are walking down the street or anywhere in a building，to say a friendly phrase，"Hi！How are you doing?" Typically，you smile and then say the phrase. This is a very common way to greet people. Irrespective of if you know the person or not，you always ask the person "How are you doing?" It is a common etiquette in small towns. In cities，people do not say Hi to random people on the street and it is considered as intruding upon someone's personal space.

What kinds of behavior are not polite?

【Sample Answer】 It doesn't matter where you are，but if you're around people，blasting music is rude whether it's from your car，your home stereo，or in your yard. We can all relate to how irritating it is to pull into a gas station where two or more cars are blasting their bass. Cutting lines is another impolite behavior. It happens all the time at the grocery store，at public events，and at amusement parks. No one is amused. Skipping others in line shows that you think you are better than everyone else and that waiting is below you. In reality，everyone has to wait. That's just life.

词汇和句型

value politeness and good manners 重视礼貌

direct instruction would sound rude 直接的指令听起来很粗鲁

in a more informal way 以一种非正式的方式

colloquial language 口语化的语言

Irrespective of if you know the person or not 不管你是否认识这个人

a common etiquette 一个普遍的礼节

random people on the street 街上不认识的路人

intruding upon someone's personal space 侵犯了人们的个人空间

It doesn't matter where you are 不管你在哪里

blasting music 大音量播放音乐

home stereo 家用音响

irritating 令人不快的

a gas station 一个加油站

Cutting lines 插队

another impolite behavior 另外一个不礼貌的行为

grocery store 杂货店

amusement parks 游乐园

Skipping others in line 插队

In reality 实际上

10. Being polite and Being friendly 礼貌和友好

考试原题和范文

What are the differences between being polite and being friendly?

【Sample Answer】 There are several differences between being polite and being friendly. The first difference is that being polite is a passive action，which means that people have to do something in a reluctant way，and they have to pretend to be nice even if when they are facing people they don't like. In contrast，being friendly is an active action, which means that people do something sincerely, without any reluctance. The second difference is that being polite is just a verbal manner. For example, people would say "good morning" to others, even strangers. However, being friendly means people are willing to do something to help others. For example, some people would help their neighbors to move furniture.

Is being friendly important?

【Sample Answer】 Yes, it is very important to be friendly on all occasions. For example, if a visitor gets lost in your city and people give him/her the way to the destination in a friendly manner, that visitor will feel grateful. He or she will be friendly to others next time. Being friendly is a basic standard of civilized society. It is of great importance not only to individuals but also to the society.

Is being friendly important in business?

【Sample Answer】 Yes, it is crucial to be friendly to others in business. When people are doing business, being friendly would make a good impression on potential partners or clients. This will increase the business opportunities. In some cases, being friendly, in the business world, means being initiative. A friendly person is considered to be active, extroverted, and self-confident.

词汇和句型

a passive action 一种被动行为

in a reluctant way 以一种不情愿的方式

they are facing people they don't like 他们在面对他们所不喜欢的人

do something sincerely 真心地去做一些事情

a verbal manner 一种言语方式

on all occasions 在所有的场合下

feel grateful 感到感激

a basic standard of civilized society 文明社会的基本标准

It is of great importance not only to individuals but also to the society 这不仅对个人重要也对整个社会重要

make a good impression on potential partners or clients 对潜在合作伙伴或者客户留下好印象

A friendly person is considered to be active, extroverted and self-confident. 友好的人被看作是主动的、外向的并且有自信的。

11. Clothes 衣服

考试原题和范文

Do Chinese people spend much money on clothes?

【Sample Answer】　Yeah, I'd say they do, at least everyone I know does anyway. And one of the reasons is that clothes are ridiculously expensive. I mean, just for a normal pair of jeans, the price is probably around three to seven hundred RMB, which is quite a sizeable proportion of many people's income. So yeah, I think it's true to say that people here in China spend quite a lot (of money) on clothes.

Do you think you can learn anything about a person from the clothes they wear?
【Sample Answer】　I think you can learn a fair amount, yeah. If you see someone walking down the street in a suit, then I think it's pretty safe to assume that they have an office job of some sort. (Of course that might not be the case, but there's a pretty good chance it is.) And also, if you see someone dressed immaculately, with shiny shoes and no creases on their clothes, then I think you can deduce that that person cares a lot about their appearance and pays a lot of attention to detail, which can't be said for people who walk around in old, dirty clothes.

What are the differences between formal and casual clothes?
【Sample Answer】　I'd say it's what they seek to achieve. So basically what I mean is that, for formal clothes, one's appearance is the most important aspect. In other words, you want to look good and presentable in front of others; whereas for casual clothes, then I'd say comfort is the most important thing, which is why most people wear casual clothes when they're at home. So formal clothes might look better than casual clothes, but they're definitely not as comfortable.

Why do you think fashion seems to be constantly changing?
【Sample Answer】　I think it's pretty obvious. The fashion houses that are instigating the changes are doing it to make more money. I mean, if fashion didn't change so quickly, then people would not feel the need to go out and buy more clothes. But as it is at the moment, people are buying stuff they don't need, just to keep up with the latest trends.

Why do some companies require their employees to wear a uniform?
【Sample Answer】　I suppose one of the reasons is that a uniform puts the staff into a work frame of mind, and thereby helps increase efficiency. So in other words, it has an effect on the mentality of the employees and constantly reminds them that they're at work. And as well as this, I imagine another purpose that a uniform might serve is to create a sense of unity within a company, because everyone will be wearing the same thing. So it could help develop their team spirit.

词汇和句型
ridiculously expensive　贵得离谱
a normal pair of jeans　一条普通的牛仔裤

a sizeable proportion of many people's income　许多人收入的很大一部分

learn a fair amount　了解很多

you see someone walking down the street in a suit　你看到街上有人穿着正装在走路

it's pretty safe to assume that ...　比较确定地认为······

they have an office job of some sort　他们做办公室之类的工作

Of course that might not be the case　当然情况有可能不是这样

there's a pretty good chance it is　很有可能是这样的

you see someone dressed immaculately　你看到某人穿着干净整洁

shiny shoes　擦得很亮的鞋

no creases on their clothes　衣服上没有褶皱

you can deduce that ...　你可以推测······

that person cares a lot about their appearance　那个人很关注外貌

pays a lot of attention to detail　非常关注细节

formal clothes　正式服装

look good and presentable in front of others　在其他人面前看起来不错

casual clothes　休闲服装

comfort is the most important thing　舒适是最重要的因素

which is why ...　这就是为什么······

pretty obvious　非常明显

fashion houses　时装商店,时装品牌

instigating the changes　发起这些变化

make more money　赚更多的钱

people would not feel the need to go out and buy more clothes　人们不会觉得自己需要外出购买衣服

people are buying stuff they don't need　人们买一些他们其实不需要的东西

keep up with the latest trends　跟上最新的潮流

a uniform puts the staff into a work frame of mind　制服使得员工有统一的工作思维模式

increase efficiency　增加效率

has an effect on the mentality of the employees　对员工的心态有作用

constantly reminds them that they're at work　不断提醒他们在工作

create a sense of unity within a company　创造一种公司内部的团结感

develop team spirit　提升团队协作精神

12. Being Famous 成名

考试原题和范文

Why do people want to be famous?

【Sample Answer】 People want to be famous because there are many benefits. The first one is that fame can bring them high social recognition and they can get the feeling of self-satisfaction. More importantly，if people are famous，they will have many business opportunities. For example, many companies would ask famous people to advertise their products. Therefore, most well-known people become millionaires who live in luxury houses and drive extravagant cars.

How do people become famous?

【Sample Answer】 I suppose people become famous mainly from being successful in what they do. For example, if you think of all the most famous film stars, pop stars, and sports stars around the world, then I think it's true to say that they are all incredibly good at what they do, and that's really the main thing that led to them becoming famous.

What types of people become famous in your country?

【Sample Answer】 It's really hard to generalize, because I'd say all kinds of people can become famous. For example, on one end of the scale, you've got people who are super talented and work extremely hard, and then on the other end of the scale, there are people who just do something unusual, a bit out of the ordinary, and end up becoming famous because of it. And there are plenty of examples of such people here in China.

Are there any differences between the people who were famous in the past, and the people who are famous today?

【Sample Answer】 I guess there might be a few differences. I mean, currently it's relatively easier to become famous because of the Internet, which gives everyone the possibility of gaining exposure to a large number of people. So because of this, I'd say that there are a lot of people with normal backgrounds who have been able to become famous, whereas in the past, I imagine this wasn't so much the case, and most people who became famous several decades ago probably received more professional training.

What are the good points about being famous?

【Sample Answer】 First of all, I imagine if you're famous, you're probably welcomed everywhere you go, which must be nice to experience. So that's one thing, and I guess another advantage of being famous is that you get a lot of companies sending you free stuff, like clothes and bags, with hopes that other people will see you with their product and then go and buy it themselves. And I remember once reading an interview with Will Smith, the actor, who said that he hardly needed to buy anything because he got most things for free.

Are there any disadvantages to being famous?

【Sample Answer】 Yeah I'd say there are. And the most obvious one would be a lack of privacy, because most celebrities get followed around everywhere by the paparazzi, even during holidays, which I'm sure they must be sick and tired of. So this would be one disadvantage, and I guess another would be that it might be quite difficult to tell who your real friends are，because it's very likely that a lot of people want to be your friend purely because of your fame. And I guess that's the reason why most celebrities mainly hang out and mingle with other celebrities.

Do you think famous people have much influence on young people?

【Sample Answer】 Yeah，I suppose they do，because I mean young people tend to look up to the celebrities they admire，and find inspiration from them. For example，when I saw sports players being interviewed，a lot them talked about a past champion who was their hero and gave them the inspiration to succeed. And I think this is also the case with other famous people，like popstars and film stars.

词汇和句型

high social recognition 高度的社会认同

the feeling of self-satisfaction 自我满足感

advertise their products 广告代言他们的产品

live in luxury houses 住在豪宅中

drive extravagant cars 开豪车

people become famous mainly from being successful in what they do 人们通过他们所做事情的成功而出名

pop stars 流行音乐明星

are all incredibly good at what they do 都是非常擅长他们所做的事情

It's really hard to generalize 真的很难总结

on one end of the scale 一方面

super talented 非常有才能的

work extremely hard 工作特别勤奋的

on the other end of the scale 另一方面

tell you the truth 说实话

I'm not really all that sure 我不是那么的确定

it's relatively easier to become famous because of the Internet 因为互联网所以出名相对容易些

whereas in the past，I imagine this wasn't so much the case 但是我觉得以前的情况不是这样的

professional training 专业训练

So that's one thing 所以这是一方面

I guess another advantage of being famous is that ... 我觉得出名的另外一个好处是……

a lack of privacy 缺乏隐私

most celebrities get followed around everywhere by the paparazzi 大多数名人被狗仔队到处跟踪

be sick and tired of ... 厌烦……

it might be quite difficult to tell who your real friends are 很难分辨谁是你真正的朋友

it's very likely that ...　很有可能……

I guess that's the reason why most celebrities mainly hang out and mingle with other celebrities.　我觉得这就是为什么大多数名人主要是和其他名人混在一起。

young people tend to look up to the celebrities they admire　年轻人往往会仰慕他们所喜欢的名人

when I listen to sports players being interviewed　当我听运动员的访谈

a past champion　一个以前的冠军

gave them the inspiration to succeed　给了他们获得成功的激励

this is also the case with other famous people　对于其他名人来说也是这样

13. Teamwork & Leadership 团队协作和领导力

考试原题和范文

Do you think teamwork is important?

【Sample Answer】 Yeah，I'd say it's extremely important，because I mean so much of what we do in life involves working together with others. And not only that，but I think it's also true to say that what we can achieve with others is so much more than what we can achieve individually. And I'd say this goes to show just how essential it is to have good teamwork skills.

What qualities do you think a good team member should have?

【Sample Answer】 I guess one important quality would be the willingness to listen to and accept other people's opinions，because it's often the case that people just disregard ideas that are different from their own without really giving them much thought. So that's one thing，and as well as this，I suppose another important quality would be to have an easy-going attitude，which will make it easier to get along with the other members of the team，and in so doing，strengthen the team spirit.

How does a good member of a team contribute to the team?

【Sample Answer】 I guess first of all，the most important thing they do is to carry out their role to the best of their ability. And as well as this，I'd say another thing that good team players do is to help out other members of the team who might be struggling with their work and falling behind. So in other words，they're not just concerned with their own work，but also with that of the whole team.

How do you think a team should be organized?

【Sample Answer】 I suppose the best way would be to delegate roles and responsibilities according to each person's abilities. So for example，if one person has especially good analytical skills，then their job could be to sift through data and draw up conclusions from it，and if another person's especially good at communicating，then their role could be making the presentation for the group. I think if a team's organized in this way, it will be the most effective.

Do you think a team needs to have a leader?

【Sample Answer】 That's a very good question, and to be honest with you, I'm not really all that sure, but my guess would be that it probably depends on the size of the team. So if it's only a team of two, for example, then a leader's probably not all that necessary, but if it's a team of, say, 20, then I think it's fair to say that having a leader would make the group far more organized and effective. So basically I'd say the larger the team, the more necessary it is to have a leader.

How should a team leader do his or her job?

【Sample Answer】 I've never actually been a team leader before, so I can't say for sure, but I suppose the first thing they should do is to make sure everyone in the team is clear about what they are trying to achieve, and then assign roles to each member accordingly. And if any problems arise, then I guess it's the leader's responsibility to solve them.

Can ordinary people be trained to become leaders?

【Sample Answer】 That's a good question and, to be honest, I'm really not that sure, but I guess my general feeling would be that they can, yeah, otherwise companies wouldn't bother spending tons of money on training their staff to become leaders.

Do you think it's always necessary to have a strong team leader?

【Sample Answer】 No, I wouldn't say it is, because if you think about it, if a team was made up of very smart and capable people, then I'm sure they would be able to work together well, regardless of whether or not the leader was strong. But on the other hand, if a team was comprised of relatively incompetent people, then having a strong leader would be much more necessary.

Do you think it's important for children to have experiences doing things in a team?

【Sample Answer】 Yeah, most definitely, because I mean, it's a great way to help children develop their communication and teamwork skills, which will be essential for them later in life.

Do you have any ideas on how to help children learn to cooperate with others and work as a team?

【Sample Answer】 That's a good question, and a tough one to answer, because I don't have any such experience, but thinking about it, I'd say one way of cultivating their teamwork skills would be through games, because after all, every child enjoys playing games. So if they were given games to play which involved working together with other children, then I think this would be a very effective way of developing their sense of teamwork.

What are the qualities of a good leader?

【Sample Answer】 I guess a leader should have a number of qualities, one of which would be being decisive, because if you think about it, one of the most important things that leaders have to do is to make decisions, and more often than not, there's no clear-cut answer to a solution, so if you're not good at making decisions under such circumstances, then you probably won't make a very effective leader. So for me, this would be the main quality, but of course, there are other important ones too, like having respect for others, as well as being able to inspire them, which all the best leaders tend to do.

词汇和句型

extremely important　特别重要

because I mean . . .　因为……

so much of what we do in life involves working together with others　生活中我们所做的事情大多数是要跟其他人合作的

And not only that　不仅如此

what we can achieve with others is so much more than what we can achieve individually　我们跟别人合作所达到的成就要比我们独自完成的成就要大得多

this goes to show just how essential it is to have good teamwork skills　这说明了良好的团队合作技能有多重要

the willingness to listen to and accept other people's opinions　倾听并接受他人观点的意愿

disregard ideas that are different from their own without really giving them much thought　不经过认真思考就不理会和自己观点不一致的想法

an easy-going attitude　随和的态度

get along with the other members of the team　和团队其他成员相处融洽

strengthen the team spirit　加强团队协作精神

carry out their role to the best of their ability　充分运用自身能力发挥角色作用

And as well as this　除此之外

good team players　好的团队成员

help out other members of the team who might be struggling with their work and falling behind　帮助工作上有困难并落后于团队目标的其他成员

So in other words　所以换句话说

they're not just concerned with their own work, but also with that of the whole team　他们不仅关注自己的工作,也关注整个团队的工作

delegate roles and responsibilities according to each person's abilities　根据每个人的能力

授权角色和责任

good analytical skills　良好的分析技能

sift through data　筛选数据

draw up conclusions from it　从中得出结论

it probably depends on the size of the team　这有可能取决于团队的大小

having a leader would make the group far more organized and effective　有一个领导者会使团队组织有序更有效率

the larger the team，the more necessary it is to have a leader　团队越大,越有必要有个领导者

assign roles to each member accordingly　相应地分配角色任务给每个成员

if any problems arise　如果有任何问题出现

otherwise companies wouldn't bother spending tons of money on training their staff to become leaders　否则公司不会去花很多钱培训员工成为领导者

if a team is made up of very smart and capable people　如果这个团队是由非常聪明和有能力的人组成的

work together well　协作良好

regardless of whether or not the leader was strong　不管领导者是否强大

But on the other hand　但是另一方面

if a team was comprised of relatively incompetent people　如果这个团队是由能力不强的人组成的

develop their communication and teamwork skills　提升他们的沟通和团队协作能力

be essential for them later in life　在他们今后的生活中是重要的

a tough one　一个困难的(问题)

one way of cultivating their teamwork skills　培养他们团队协作能力的方式之一

a very effective way of developing their sense of teamwork　一个培养他们团队协作意识的非常有效的方法

being decisive　果断的

make decisions　做决定

more often than not　往往,多半

clear-cut answer　清晰的答案

under such circumstances　在这种情况下

inspire them　激励他们

14. Apology 道歉

考试原题和范文

Is it important to say sorry?

【Sample Answer】　Yes，it is crucial to say sorry in any case. In public areas，for example，when a person accidentally steps on the foot of others，he or she should say sorry. Otherwise，conflict would occur. People might even fight with each other if they don't say sorry. In the business world，people need to cooperate with each other to fulfill the goal. When one person in a team makes a mistake，he or she should say sorry to others and ask for forgiveness as the member has dragged the team behind.

On what occasion do people say sorry?

【Sample Answer】　People say sorry in many cases. A common occasion is when a person makes noise in a quiet place such as a library because he or she disturbs others. Another situation is when a person pushes others without deliberation on a crowded bus or subway train.

Why do some people not want to say sorry?

【Sample Answer】　There are a couple of reasons，one of which is that some people are too shy to communicate with others. When they interrupt others，they are often at loss and do not know what to say. Another reason is that some people are not well educated. When they do something wrong，they do not regard it as an unacceptable behavior and take it for granted.

When do people say "thank you"?

【Sample Answer】　People say "thank you" in many cases. When a person gets help from others，he or she，undoubtedly，says "thank you" even if the assistance is trivial. For example，when a person gets help pushing the luggage to the shelf on the train, he or she will naturally say "thank you". In another case，when people do business，they will always say "thank you". It is a polite phrase in the business world. Even if you don't like your partners or collaborators，you should say "thank you" if they do a good job.

词汇和句型

in any case　在任何情况下

steps on the foot of others　不小心踩到别人的脚

the conflict would occur　会发生矛盾

fulfill the goal　达成目标

ask for forgiveness　请求原谅

dragged the team behind　拖了整个团队的后腿

in many cases　在许多情况下

push others without deliberation　无意间推了别人

in a crowded bus or subway train　在拥挤的公共汽车或者地铁列车上

an unacceptable behavior　一个不可接受的行为

take it for granted　认为理所当然

the assistance is trivial　这个帮助是微不足道的

pushing the luggage to the shelf　把行李推到架子上

your partners or collaborators　你的合伙人或合作者

15. Personality 个性

考试原题和范文

Does people's personality change over time?

【Sample Answer】 Yes，sure. People's personality changes over time. Because of the changing surroundings, people will meet other people who are from different cultural backgrounds and have different religious beliefs, even totally different lifestyles, all of which would, more or less, affect one's personality. For example, if an introverted person went to the US to live for one year, this person would be an extroverted person because most US people are outgoing. That's why I believe personalities change over time.

词汇和句型

People's personality changes over time   人们的个性随着时间而变化

religious beliefs   宗教信仰

more or less   或多或少

an introverted person   一个内向的人

an extroverted person   一个外向的人

16. Creativity 创造力

考试原题和范文

Is creativity important?

【Sample Answer】 Yes，creativity is crucial not only to the economic development of a single country but also to the advancement of human beings. For one thing, innovative ideas could remove a range of financial obstacles. For example, stock market and mortgage problems can be solved by new and effective methods. For another, a variety of problems influencing human beings could be addressed by novel ideas. For instance, global warming can only be solved by innovative measures proposed by the elites in different countries. Therefore, creativity is the most important thing in our daily life.

词汇和句型

For one thing   一方面

innovative ideas   创新的想法

remove a range of financial obstacles   消除各种财政困难

stock market   股市

mortgage problems   抵押权问题

For another   另一方面

a variety of problems influencing human beings could be addressed by novel ideas   各种影响人类的问题可以通过新的想法来解决

17. Jobs 工作

考试原题和范文

What jobs pay the highest salary in your country?

【Sample Answer】 I'm not exactly that sure, but my guess would be that things like banking and real estate are probably the sectors which pay the highest, because I mean, there's so much money invested in property here in China, so the salary's bound to be pretty high if you work in real estate. And as for banking, I think it goes without saying that most jobs related to banking are relatively well-paid, which is one of the main reasons why so many graduates here want to find a job in a bank.

Do you think changing jobs is a positive thing to do?

【Sample Answer】 Yeah, I'd say it's perfectly fine to change jobs. I mean, I can't see any point in doing one job throughout your whole career. So for me I would say the main thing is to be passionate about your job, and if at any point you start to lose enthusiasm in what you're doing, then it might be a good time to consider trying something else.

What age you think is suitable to start work?

【Sample Answer】 It's really hard to generalize, because some people feel ready to start work as soon as they've finished high school, and a lot of people who've done this have ended up quite successful. But I guess it probably also depends on what job you want to do, because highly-skilled jobs, like being a doctor or surgeon, require many years of training, whereas menial jobs, like working behind a till at McDonald's, hardly require any training, so probably any age from 15 onwards would be suitable for that kind of work.

Are qualifications overvalued?

【Sample Answer】 I guess my general feeling would be that they are to some extent, yeah, because from what I've heard and read, it seems that employers tend to put a lot of emphasis on qualifications, without taking too much into account other things like attitude, which, for me, is equally, if not more, important than qualifications.

What types of companies are there in China?

【Sample Answer】 There's a huge range of companies here. I mean, on one end of the scale there are big state-owned enterprises and foreign multinationals, and on the other end you've got smaller private companies, which make up the vast majority.

What is important if you start your own business?

【Sample Answer】 For starters, you obviously need a fair amount of money to get the company up and running. And I guess the other thing would be to have talented people, because when you boil things down，people are a company's most valuable asset，which I'm sure you'd agree with.

How would you define a successful company?

【Sample Answer】 In a nutshell，I'd say that a successful company is basically one that provides decent products or services whilst also being able to operate at a profit. And one example that springs to mind would be Apple，which，as I'm sure you'll agree，makes unbelievably good products.

词汇和句型

I'm not exactly that sure   我不是那么确定

banking and real estate   银行业和房地产业

there's so much money invested in property   有很多钱投资到房地产

it goes without saying that ...   毫无疑问……

be passionate about your job   对你的工作有热情

lose enthusiasm in what you're doing   对你的工作失去热情

I guess it probably also depends on what job you want to do   我觉得这也取决于你想做什么工作

highly-skilled jobs   高技能工作

doctor   医生(尤其指全科医生，提供综合性医疗服务)

surgeon   外科医生(专指外科医生，以手术为主)

whereas   但是

menial jobs   卑微的工作

working behind a till at McDonald's   在麦当劳收银的工作

from what I've heard and read   就我听到的和看到的而言

put a lot of emphasis on qualifications   很重视学历证书

without taking too much into account other things like attitude   不是太关注其他方面比如态度

There's a huge range of companies here.   在这里有各种类型的公司

on one end of the scale   一方面

big state-owned enterprises   大型国有企业

foreign multinationals   外国跨国公司

on the other end   另一方面

make up the vast majority   占到绝大多数

For starters   对于初创公司而言

a fair amount of money   大量资金

get the company up and running   运作这个公司

boil things down   归根到底

most valuable asset   最重要的资产

In a nutshell   简而言之

a successful company is basically one that provides decent products or services whilst also being able to operate at a profit 一个成功的公司是在提供好的产品和服务的同时也能赚钱

And one example that springs to mind would be ... 我马上能想到的一个例子是……

makes unbelievably good products 生产非常好的产品

18. Language Learning 语言学习

考试原题和范文

Do you it is necessary to have a global language for all the countries in the world?

【Sample Answer】 No，I don't think it's necessary because I think a language can reflect culture，which means that a word or a phrase of a language may have some special meaning. If we have a global language，some people may feel that it is unnecessary to learn their mother tongue because they will not use it. As a consequence，we may lose sight of our own culture and lose our cultural identity.

What are differences of learning a new language between children and adults?

【Sample Answer】 I would say children may learn a new language more quickly than adults. The reason is that adults are likely to regard learning a new language as a challenge；however，children enjoy learning a new thing that they are curious about. But I think adults will be more patient than children，as kids are not mature enough and they lack self-discipline.

What are the ways for people to learn a new language?

【Sample Answer】 Attending classes can be a good choice because teachers who have experience can help people to find and fill the knowledge gaps and teach you some tips to learn a new language well. Besides，people can search for some useful materials on the Internet. What's more，people could make new friends with native speakers who can help them improve their pronunciation.

词汇和句型

As a consequence 因此

cultural identity 文化特征

regard learning a new language as a challenge 把学习新语言当作是一种挑战

children enjoy learning a new thing that they are curious about 儿童会享受学习他们所好奇的新东西的过程

they lack self-discipline 他们缺乏自律

Attending classes can be a good choice 参加课程是个好选择

find and fill the knowledge gaps 发现和弥补知识空白

19. Pollution 污染

考试原题和范文

What could individuals do to solve the problem of pollution?

【Sample Answer】 Individuals could do a couple of things to address the problem of pollution. The simplest way is to walk to their companies or schools every day rather than drive private cars if where they live is not far away from where they work or where they study. Another thing ordinary people can do is that they can categorize the garbage according to the chemical properties of the rubbish. For example, they should not throw used batteries into rubbish bins because the chemicals in the batteries are not biodegradable and poisonous to the human body. Instead, what they should do is to take the used batteries to the battery collection place where specialists will deal with these highly-toxic things.

What can the government do about pollution?

【Sample Answer】 I guess they could do a number of things, one of which would be to encourage people to reduce their carbon footprint, in other words, become more environmentally-friendly. And one way of doing this, I suppose, might be to introduce a system whereby people are paid for recycling stuff, such as empty bottles and cans; otherwise they have no incentive.

词汇和句型

address the problem of environment pollution 解决环境污染问题

where they live is not far away from where they work or where they study 他们住的地方离工作或者学习的地方不远

Another thing ordinary people can do is that ... 另外一个普通人能做的事情是……

categorize the garbage according to the chemical properties of the rubbish 根据垃圾的化学属性分类垃圾

they should not throw used batteries into rubbish bins 他们不应该把用过的电池扔进垃圾桶

the chemicals in the batteries are not biodegradable and poisonous to the human body 电池中的化学物质不可降解而且对人体有害

what people should do is to take the used batteries to the battery collection place where specialists will deal with these highly-toxic things 人们应该做的是把用过的电池带去电池收集站,在那里有专业人员处理这些剧毒的东西

carbon footprint 碳足迹,是指企业机构、活动、产品或个人通过交通运输、食品生产和消费以及各类生产过程等引起的温室气体排放的集合。它描述了一个人的能源意识和行为对自然界产生的影响,号召人们从自我做起。

become more environmentally-friendly 变得更加环保

whereby 凭借

empty bottles and cans 空瓶子和罐子
no incentive 没有动力

20. Relaxation 放松

词汇和范文
How do people do to relax in China?
【Sample Answer】 In China different people have different ways to relax. Old people practice tai-chi or dance in the square, while young people like playing video games and going to parties. Other people like to rest in a cafe or just chill out at home and watch TV.

What should employers do to relax their employees?
【Sample Answer】 I think employers should try to make their employees feel less nervous about their work by hiring more people, reducing the work hours, and giving a pay rise. Improving the work environment can also help to reduce employees' pressure. For example, they can rent a bigger and brighter workplace and put some green plants in the office.

Why is it hard for students to relax?
【Sample Answer】 One reason is that there is too much pressure in schools. Students have to study very hard to avoid being punished by their teachers. So many students are afraid of not getting good exam scores. They do a lot of homework every day and don't have any time to rest. Also, the competition among students is fierce and some students cannot bear it. Therefore, they are always worried and anxious.

词汇和句型
practice tai-chi 打太极拳
dance in the square 跳广场舞
chill out at home and watch TV 在家看电视放松
reducing the work hours 减少工作时间
giving a pay rise 给予加薪
Improving the work environment 改善工作环境
reduce employees' pressure 减少员工的压力
the competition among students is fierce 学生间的竞争是激烈的
they are always worried and anxious 他们总是担忧和焦虑

21. Colors 色彩

考试原题和范文
What colors are the least popular in your country?
【Sample Answer】 That's an interesting question, and I've never actually thought about

it before. I suppose it depends on what you're talking about. So I mean, for clothes, I don't see that many people wearing orange. So that's not really a very popular color in terms of clothes. And for things like cars, orange is also not such a popular color. I can't remember even seeing an orange car around. So yeah, I guess that's probably the least popular color here.

Might this color become popular in the future?

【Sample Answer】 Sure. I mean, no one can look into the future, right? I think it's highly likely that at some stage in the future unpopular colors like orange are going to come into fashion. Things are always coming in and out of fashion, and I guess color's no different. But when exactly this might happen is anyone's guess.

What was the most popular color last year?

【Sample Answer】 It's hard for me to say, because I don't really follow fashion that closely. I don't pay that much attention to the latest trends, but off the top of my head I would say red seems to have been quite popular in the last year. Quite a lot of people seem to have been wearing red as well as black and white, which I think are actually popular every year, simply because they go well with most other colors. So yeah, I'd say it's a toss-up among those three — red, white, and black.

How do colors affect people's mood?

【Sample Answer】 I guess some colors tend to have a positive effect on people's mood. For example, warm colors like red and yellow make people feel relaxed. And bright, and striking colors like pink might give you an energetic feel. And in terms of dark colors, they might have a somber effect on people. If you walk into a dark room, it might somewhat dampen your mood somewhat. So yeah, I think colors can, to some extent, subconsciously affect all of us.

What colors are mostly seen on buildings?

【Sample Answer】 I guess it's generally light colors like grey and white, which are not really exciting. But I've noticed that in some of the smaller cities, there are quite a few other colors of buildings, like pink and yellow, but grey and white, I'd say, are definitely the predominant colors.

What color is suitable for offices?

【Sample Answer】 That's a good question. I suppose a color that would make people feel attentive and focused on their work, and also give people a happy feeling when they walk into the office. So, for me I'd say a bright color could help create such a positive effect. For example, I think yellow would be good — not too bright a yellow, but a kind of light yellow, or maybe a light grey or green. I think all these kinds of colors could have a positive effect.

How differently do men and women look at the same color?

【Sample Answer】 My initial thought would be not all that differently. Because I mean, if you take pink, for example, then both men and women see it as a feminine color, and the same goes for purple. So I think they see colors in pretty much the same way. Having said that, though, I suppose there are instances when women might pay more attention to a color, for example when choosing clothes. I mean, men, on the whole, don't ponder a lot over the color, whereas women tend to do so quite often. For instance, they might see black as a color that makes them look slim, while white may have the opposite effect. And men definitely don't think about that kind of stuff when they're choosing what color to wear. They're much more laid-back about it.

What colors are suitable for formal occasions?

【Sample Answer】 It's hard to generalize because it really depends on what the formal occasion is, but I suppose, on the whole, colors that don't stand out too much, like grey, white, black, and brown, would be suitable, unless, of course, you really want to make an impression, in which case you might want to go for something bold and striking, like bright red.

Do business people need to wear dark clothes?

【Sample Answer】 No, I'd say most definitely not. It seems to be an outdated concept, that they should wear dark clothes. And I mean, a lot of the most successful business people are young Internet whizzes, and they turn up to press conferences in all kinds of casual wear, like jeans and T-shirts. So wearing dark colors is definitely not a "must". Looking presentable is really the main thing.

词汇和句型

that's not really a very popular color in terms of clothes　就衣服的颜色而言,那个颜色确实不太受欢迎

the least popular color　最不受欢迎的颜色

it's highly likely that ...　很有可能……

at some stage in the future　在未来的某个阶段

unpopular colors like orange are going to come into fashion　诸如橘色这种不受欢迎的颜色会成为时尚

when exactly this might happen is anyone's guess　究竟会在什么发生,每个人的猜测都各有不同

I don't really follow fashion that closely　我不是那么紧跟时尚

I don't pay that much attention to the latest trends　我不是那么关注最新的潮流

Quite a lot of people seem to have been wearing red　许多人都穿过红色的衣服

they go well with most other colors　它们和其他颜色很好搭配

it's a toss-up among those three — red, white, and black　只能掷硬币来决定哪个颜色最

流行——红色、白色还是黑色

some colors tend to have a positive effect on people's mood　有些颜色会对人的情绪产生积极影响

an energetic feel　一种有活力的感觉

dark colors　深色

have a somber effect on people　对人产生一种忧郁的影响

somewhat dampen your mood somewhat　有点抑制你的情绪

colors can, to some extent, subconsciously affect all of us　颜色会从不同程度上潜移默化地地影响着我们

light colors　浅色

the predominant colors　主要颜色

a color that would make people feel attentive and focused on their work　一种让人感到可以集中注意力并关注工作的颜色

a bright color　一个鲜艳的颜色

create such a positive effect　创造出这种积极作用

not too bright a yellow　不是太鲜艳的那种黄色

light yellow　浅黄色

My initial thought would be ...　我一开始的想法是……

a feminine color　一个女性化的颜色

the same goes for purple　紫色也是如此

Having said that, though, I suppose ...　尽管话虽如此,但是我觉得……

on the whole　总的来说

a color that makes them look slim　会让自己看起来更苗条的颜色

have the opposite effect　有相反的效果

more laid-back　更加懒散

colors that don't stand out too much　不那么显眼的颜色

make an impression　给人留下印象

something bold and striking　大胆和引人注目的东西

bright red　鲜红色

an outdated concept　一个过时的概念

young Internet whizzes　年轻的因特网专家

turn up to press conferences　出现在记者招待会上

casual wear　休闲装

looking presentable is really the main thing　看起来得体是最重要的

22. Cafes and Restaurants 咖啡馆和餐厅

考试原题和范文

What are the differences between a cafe and a restaurant?

【Sample Answer】　A cafe generally offers people a light and casual environment to sip on beverages and eat lunch or snacks. However, a restaurant is a dining establishment that usually offers much more varied service, a formal environment, and is designed around the idea of the "meal", usually dinner. There is a greater variety of foods in a restaurant than in a cafe. In some restaurants, alcoholic beverages are also served. Additionally, tipping a waiter is common in restaurants while it is optional in cafes.

Why do some people like having dinner with friends in a cafe or restaurant?
【Sample Answer】 Eating out at a cafe isn't limited to couples and dates. You can also dine out with colleagues, family, and friends. It's always a memorable event. You remember the people you spend the time with, the laughter, the smiles, and the endless conversations. That's why parties, social events, and business meetings are usually done at cafes or restaurants. It adds to the whole aura of an event and sets the mood of the occasion.

Is it important to have dinner with friends at home?
【Sample Answer】 Yes, it's very important to have dinner with friends at home. Conversations during the meal provide opportunities for the friends to bond, plan, connect, and learn from one another. It's a chance to share information and news from the day. Having meals with friends at home fosters feelings of warmth and security, as well as a sense of belonging. Additionally, meals prepared and eaten at home are usually more nutritious and healthy. They contain more fruits, vegetables, and dairy products along with additional nutrients such as fiber, calcium, vitamins A and C, and folate. Home-cooked meals are usually not fried or highly salted. Also, soda and sweetened beverage consumption is usually lower at the dinner table at home.

词汇和句型
a light and casual environment 一个轻松休闲的环境
sip on beverages 喝喝饮料
alcoholic beverages 酒精饮料
tipping a waiter 给服务员小费
dine out 在外面吃饭
a memorable event 一个难忘的事件
the endless conversations 说不完的话
adds to the whole aura 增添气氛
share information and news 分享信息和新闻
a sense of belonging 归属感
meals prepared and eaten at home are usually more nutritious and healthy 在家自己做饭吃更有营养更健康
dairy products 乳制品
additional nutrients 额外的营养物质

fiber，calcium，vitamins A and C，and folate　纤维素、钙、维生素 A 和 C 以及叶酸
Home-cooked meals　家里自己做的饭
are usually not fried or highly salted　通常不会油炸或高盐的
soda and sweetened beverage consumption　苏打水和含糖饮料的摄入

23. Working in a Foreign Country 在外国工作

考试原题和范文

What are the advantages and disadvantages of working in a foreign country?

【Sample Answer】　The most obvious advantage is that people can learn more skills related to their jobs. For example，people in developing countries would go to the developed countries to work for one year to get trained. After coming back to their own country，they could make full use of the skills they have mastered to work for their companies and for their own country. So that's one thing. Another benefit of working in a foreign country is that people would be working in an unfamiliar environment so they would be curious about the things and people around them during work，which means that they would have more motivation to work. However，as to the drawbacks of working in foreign countries，I would say that people，in most cases，cannot adapt to the local culture and customs. Therefore，they would feel frustrated because they are unable to communicate well with their colleagues and other locals. Also，they would miss their families if they were sent to work in a foreign country. Homesickness is a common sentiment for people working in foreign countries.

词汇和句型

people can learn more skills related to their jobs　人们可以学习更多和他们工作相关的技能
make full use of the skills they have mastered　充分运用他们所掌握的技能
have more motivation to work　有很多的工作动力
adapt to the local culture and customs　适应当地的文化和习俗
homesickness is a common sentiment for people working in foreign countries　想家是在国外工作的人们普遍的情绪

24. Buildings 建筑

考试原题和范文

What do you think of the buildings that are similar everywhere?

【Sample Answer】　It is not a good development for buildings to have similar appearances and styles all over the world. In urban areas，some skyscrapers are built to meet the increasingly high demands of business. But at the same time，some cultural identities are lost. In large cities，such as Los Angeles，Shanghai，New York，and Tokyo，buildings are so identical that people would have no idea where they actually are. It is pathetic to be architecturally uniform. I suppose that some unique and traditional architectural styles should be maintained to keep the cultural diversity.

What kind of buildings do young people like?

【Sample Answer】 Young people like modern and multifunctional buildings, particularly the malls. Young people are curious about new things and malls can satisfy their curiosity. On weekends, young people go shopping in the mall to buy clothes and bags they like. If they get tired, they grab some snacks in the fast food chains, which are commonly seen in malls. Malls also provide entertainment for young people, such as movie theaters and gyms. Young people definitely love malls.

Why do some people like old buildings?

【Sample Answer】 There are several reasons why people like old buildings. The first one is that old buildings reflect the traditional culture of a city or a country. People could know what happened in history from the appearance and internal decoration of a building. Another reason is that some ancient buildings can be regarded as works of art. Many old people like to research the building materials and architectural styles.

Why do some old buildings get demolished?

【Sample Answer】 I guess one reason would be that they might not be safe to live in anymore. For example, the walls of an old building may start cracking. And I suppose another reason why a lot of old buildings get knocked down is that the government has decided that it would be better to put up a new building in its place, which would be especially the case if it's occupying a prime piece of real estate in the city center.

Do you think tourists prefer to see old buildings or new buildings?

【Sample Answer】 Without a doubt, I'd say tourists definitely prefer to see old buildings. The main reason is that old buildings have a lot more history and culture attached to them. So when you visit them, they give you a glimpse into the history of a place, as well as the local lifestyle, which you don't really get from looking at a new building.

Do you think historic buildings should be preserved?

【Sample Answer】 Yeah, most definitely, because I mean, there's a lot of culture which is embedded in historical buildings, and if they weren't preserved, then a lot of culture would be lost, which would be a terrible shame. So that's one thing, and as well as this, I think it's also true to say that if it wasn't for historical buildings, then most cities would look pretty much the same. And if you think about all the famous landmarks around the world, like the Big Ben in London and the Temple of Heaven in Beijing, a lot of them are historic buildings, so they actually play a very strong role in giving a city its identity.

Do you think the style of a building's design is important?

【Sample Answer】 Yeah, I'd say it is, because essentially the style should accord with the purpose of the building. So if you take an office building as an example, then the style should be as practical as possible, which is why most of them tend to be rectangular shaped. And as for residential buildings, I guess the style affects a lot of things, like living space and the general level of comfort. So for me, I'd say the architectural design of a building is absolutely crucial.

Do young people feel that history is very important?

【Sample Answer】 Probably not, no, because I think a lot of young people currently don't really feel that history has a direct impact on their own lives, which I guess is reflected in the fact that not many students choose History as their major at university, at least compared to other subjects like Accounting or Finance. So I think this is a good indicator that many young people don't see history as being that important to them.

What is the value of learning about history?

【Sample Answer】 I'd say there's a lot of value in learning it, and one of the main reasons would be that history quite often repeats itself, so if we've learnt history well, we should be able to avoid making the same mistakes as we did in the past. And as well as this, I guess another important aspect is that history plays a big part in helping us understand how things came into being. So for example, through learning history, we get to understand things like why we speak the language we do, and how our country developed the way it did. And in a way, I think this helps us better appreciate everything we have around us, instead of just taking it for granted.

Do you think old buildings play an important role in preserving history?

【Sample Answer】 Yeah, I'd say they do, without a doubt, because if you think about it, old buildings are a visual reminder of our past; so without them, it would be all too easy to forget about the history of a place, which would be a great pity. Of course there are other things that also preserve history, like antiques, but most of the time they're hidden away somewhere or kept in a museum, so I think they play a far smaller role than old buildings, which are in full view of everyone to see, thereby serving as a greater reminder of our history. So yeah, that's basically what I reckon.

词汇和句型
some skyscrapers are built to meet the increasingly high demands of business 摩天大楼被建造起来以满足不断增长的商业需求
cultural identities 文化特性

architecturally uniform　建筑上的一致性

unique and traditional architectural styles　独特和传统的建筑风格

the cultural diversity　文化多样性

multifunctional buildings　多功能建筑

satisfy their curiosity　满足他们的好奇心

movie theaters and gyms　电影院和健身房

old buildings reflect traditional culture　旧建筑反映传统文化

the appearance and internal decoration of a building　一个建筑的外观和内部装饰

ancient buildings　古代建筑

works of art　艺术品

building materials and architectural styles　建筑材料和建筑风格

the walls of an old building may start cracking　旧建筑的墙可能会开始开裂

old buildings get knocked down　旧建筑被拆掉

it's occupying a prime piece of real estate in the city center　它占据了市中心房地产的黄金地段

Without a doubt　毫无疑问

there's a lot of culture which is embedded in historical buildings　有很多文化已经植入了历史建筑

the famous landmarks　著名的地标

the Big Ben in London　伦敦大本钟

the Temple of Heaven in Beijing　北京天坛

historic buildings　历史建筑

the style should accord with the purpose of the building　建筑风格应该和建筑目的一致

an office building　一座办公楼

the style should be as practical as possible　款式尽可能实用

which is why ...　这就是为什么……

rectangular shaped　长方形的

residential buildings　居民楼

living space　生活空间

the general level of comfort　总体的舒适程度

architectural design　建筑设计

history has a direct impact on their own lives　历史对他们自己的生活有直接影响

many young people don't see history as being that important to them　许多年轻人认为历史对他们不是那么重要

avoid making the same mistakes as we did in the past　避免犯以前犯过的相同的错误

history plays a big part in helping us understand how things came into being　历史在帮助我们理解事情发生的原因的方面起到重要作用

taking it for granted　认为这是理所当然的

old buildings are a visual reminder of our past　旧建筑从视觉方面让我们想起过去

antiques　古董

25. Reading Books 看书

考试原题和范文

What are the books people like reading?

【Sample Answer】 The classic literature works are popular among people at different ages. Meanwhile, reading books written by sports stars and entertainment stars, including autobiographies, is a new trend, because people are curious about the life of celebrities.

Do you think women would like to read some books about finance?

【Sample Answer】 I don't think finance is a very attractive subject for most women, because generally speaking, women are not sensitive to numbers. However, some of them do read finance books if necessary. I mean, they would do that when they are looking for some pieces of financial advice.

How could reading books change people?

【Sample Answer】 It is said that reading books makes people wiser. Books are a kind of traditional media though which people get information and acquire knowledge. Unlike other media, such as television, books are more likely to be about serious issues.

Do you think people would like to read more paper books or more electronic books in the future?

【Sample Answer】 The major trend is that people read more electronic books on their smart phone or iPad, which is convenient because they don't need to bring a book with them any more. Many electronic books are free and easy to get. However, I don't think traditional paper books will disappear because many people feel more comfortable and concentrated reading the paper ones.

Do you think the way people read books will change in the future?

【Sample Answer】 Yes. The media change is one aspect, I mean, the increasing popularity of electronic books. Another point is that people will be more interested in less serious topics in the future. Many people will read books just for entertainment, so they would not go to the library or even be at the desk when they are reading; instead, they will read books during the snack time or on the subway.

What are the differences between books and magazines?

【Sample Answer】 Magazines are about the latest issues, which means that they are mainly focused on what is happening now, which is not necessarily the case for books. On the other hand, books usually don't include lots of colorful pictures, but magazines do.

词汇和句型

The classic literature works 经典文学作品

are curious about 对……好奇

reading books makes people wiser 看书使人更睿智

get information 获取信息

acquire knowledge 学习知识

feel more comfortable and concentrated 感到更舒服更能集中注意力

the increasing popularity of electronic books 电子书的日益普及

one aspect 一方面

they are mainly focused on what is happening now （杂志）主要关注现在正在发生的事情

lots of colorful pictures 许多彩色的图片

26. Gifts 礼物

考试原题和范文

What gifts do people give in China?

【Sample Answer】 It depends on who you intend to give the gift to. For parents, people usually give healthcare products like vitamin supplements or ginseng or some massage equipment. For young kids, people often buy toys or new clothes. Among young lovers or couples, it's common for males to buy flowers, gold accessories and females to give leather wallets or ties or belts. The most typical gift in China would be "hongbao", a red packet full of a certain amount of money. It can be given during the Spring Festival, weddings, occasions of moving to a new house, etc.

What gifts do people give to people they are not familiar with?

【Sample Answer】 In this case, personal belongings would not be a good choice. People tend to buy things that would generally be accepted. For example, if you visit a person for the first time, you may bring wine, fruit, or some healthcare products if the person you visit is senior.

When do people give gifts in your country?

【Sample Answer】 People give gifts on a lot of occasions in China, such as on special days like the Spring Festival, weddings, and even funerals in some places. Besides, when you visit someone's home, you need to bring gifts like food and wine. If you visit a new home, you may give the owners some practical household appliances or home decorations as gifts. Also, when people go on a trip, they will buy souvenirs for their family members, friends, and colleagues.

Is it easy choosing gifts for others?

【Sample Answer】 Choosing a gift is not difficult, but choosing a satisfying gift is. To buy a satisfying gift, you need to know the potential gift receiver's needs and interests, and balance it against your financial ability. If he is your family member or close friend, he, for the sake of you, may not want you to spend money on him and thus won't tell you what he really needs. Then you may have to guess. On the other hand, if he is a person you are not familiar with, it will be harder for you to find out what he actually likes.

Who are more likely to give gifts, men or women?

【Sample Answer】 I think women are more likely to give gifts, because they are more careful about any special days, like family members' birthdays and wedding anniversaries. And they are more patient when choosing a gift. In contrast, men are in nature careless or in reality more devoted to work. Thus, they tend to forget some important days. They would rather be told when they have to give a gift and what to give.

What are the differences between men and women when they are choosing gifts?

【Sample Answer】 It is similar to buying other goods. Men tend to be quicker in deciding what to buy, while women usually spend more time in comparing the appearances, designs, and prices of the gifts.

Do people in your country give books as gifts to children?

【Sample Answer】 Yes, people in China give books as gifts to children. New clothes, toys, and money are the most popular gifts for children in China. Books are not the mainstream gift, but giving books is a rising trend. I suppose it is due to the change of young people's opinions. Young parents are paying more attention to having their children develop good reading habits. On the other hand, a lot of online book stores are emerging, making it easier to buy children books. So, I believe more and more book gifts will be given to children in the future.

Why do people give gifts to others on festivals?

【Sample Answer】 One reason is that gifts normally contain some emotional value and can reflect your best wishes to others. For example, people always send flowers to their mom on Mother's Day, because we are moved by their mother's love and we want them to have a comfortable life. Another reason is that sending gifts on festivals is a good way to show our respect. Giving gifts to teachers on Teacher's Day is a typical example of this.

Is it time-costing to make some gifts by hand?

【Sample Answer】 Yes, it is. Those delicate handcrafts are really time-consuming, and some gifts even take a couple of years to finish. But I think these time-costing gifts are more valuable than ordinary gifts; I mean these gifts are normally given to people who are really important to you，so it is worthwhile to make a gift for them.

Who are good at making gifts by hand，men or women？
【Sample Answer】 I think women may be better than men in terms of making handcrafts. You may agree that men are likely to be interested in machines but women are generally fond of making things by hand from an early age. It is true that many girls like to make dresses for their dolls.

词汇和句型

It depends on who you intend to give the gift to 这取决于你想要给谁礼物

healthcare products 保健品

vitamin supplements 维生素补充剂

ginseng 人参

massage equipment 按摩仪

gold accessories 黄金饰品

leather wallets or ties or belts 皮夹、领带或腰带

The most typical gift 最典型的礼物

moving to a new house 搬家

personal belongings 个人物品

the person you visit is senior 你去拜访的是老年人

on a lot of occasions 在各种场合

practical household appliances 实用的家用电器

home decorations 家用装饰品

buy souvenirs 购买纪念品

Choosing a gift is not difficult，but choosing a satisfying gift is. 买一件礼物不难，但是买一件令人满意的礼物就不简单了。

the potential gift receiver's needs and interests 可能收礼物的人的需求和兴趣

financial ability 财力

close friend 好朋友

for the sake of you 为了你考虑

if he is a person you are not familiar with 如果他是一个你不熟悉的人

it will be harder for you to find out what he actually likes 你更难知道他真正喜欢什么

wedding anniversaries 结婚纪念日

in nature 本质上

in reality 事实上

Men tend to be quicker in deciding what to buy 男性往往会很快决定买什么

women usually spend more time in comparing the appearances，designs and prices of the gifts 女性通常会花更多时间比较礼物的外观、设计以及价格

the mainstream gift 主流的礼物

due to the change of young people's opinion 因为年轻人观点的变化

Young parents are paying more attention to having their children develop good reading habits 年轻的父母越来越关注培养孩子的良好阅读习惯

emotional value 情感价值

reflect your best wishes to others 表达你对别人的美好祝愿

show our respect 表达我们的敬意

delicate handcrafts 精致的手工艺品

really time-consuming 真的很耗时

ordinary gifts 普通礼物

it is worthwhile to make a gift for them 值得为他们制作一个礼物

women are generally fond of making things by hand 女性总的来说更喜欢手工制作东西

many girls like to make dresses for their dolls 许多女孩喜欢为她们的洋娃娃做衣服

27. Technology 技术

考试原题和范文

Why are children interested in technology?

【Sample Answer】 Children are curious about the things around them and technology is one of those things they would like to explore. For example, they would wonder why they can see people who live thousands of miles away through video chat. Then they will ask their parents how video chat works. In other words, children are interested in technology because they don't understand how the products of modern technology work and they want to figure it out.

What are disadvantages of relying too much on home appliances?

【Sample Answer】 If people depend heavily on electrical appliances, they would be lazier than before. For example, they don't need to wash clothes themselves because they could throw the clothes into the washing machine and lie in the couch watching TV. Besides, some manual skills would be lost if they rely too much machines. Take the microwave as an example. In the past, people cooked food by using different cooking techniques; but at present, people just cook everything by means of microwaves so the tastes are awful. If people continue doing this, some traditional cooking skills would disappear.

词汇和句型

they want to figure it out 他们想要弄明白

electrical appliances 家用电器

manual skills 动手能力

the microwave 微波炉

cooking techniques 烹饪方法

the tastes are awful 味道很差

28. Art 艺术

考试原题和范文

Do people in China like works of art?

【Sample Answer】 Yes，but I would say only a small percentage of people in China like works of art. For example，there aren't that many art collectors in China and even though the museums are free，people don't really go to them to see works of art.

Is learning art important for children?

【Sample Answer】 Yes. Children are still building their vocabulary and can't really express their feeling verbally and art is another way of knowing what is in children's minds. For example，if the pictures depict a lot of joyful moments，then we could know that the child is happy. Also learning how to draw can be another way to discover a child's talents.

Is learning art important for adults?

【Sample Answer】 No，not really. Adults are busy and learning more practical skills is more important such as learning money management，cooking，and even how to raise children.

What are the popular works of art in China?

【Sample Answer】 Most of the important works of art would be ceramics from a long time ago such as vases，bowls，and cups. Also there are a lot of famous paintings that are popular and people will line up to see them if there is an art expo showing these works of art.

词汇和句型

a small percentage of people 一小部分人
affect people in different ways 从不同方面影响人们
express their feeling verbally 口头表达他们的感觉
depict a lot of joyful moments 描绘很多欢乐时刻
ceramics from a long time ago 很早以前的陶瓷器
line up to see them 排队看它们
an art expo showing these works of art 一个展示这些艺术作品的艺术展

29. Photograph 照片

考试原题和范文

In your opinion, what makes a good photograph?

【Sample Answer】 I guess it basically depends on what kind of photograph it is. So for example，for pictures of scenery，I would say a good photo is one which really captures the beauty of a place，and I also find that landscape photos which have contrasting shades of light and dark tend to look better，probably because it makes the photo more visually appealing. And as for pictures of people，I'd say the best ones are those which capture the natural facial expressions of the people in the photo，because I'm sure you would agree that facial expressions are，by far，the most interesting part of the photo.

Do you think people need to be trained in order to take good photographs?

【Sample Answer】 I think it depends on how good a photographer you want to be，because I'd say most people are perfectly capable of taking relatively good photos without any training，but if you want to take photos of professional quality on a consistent basis，then I guess a bit of training would be necessary.

词汇和句型

pictures of scenery 风景照片

really captures the beauty of a place 真正捕捉到一个地方的美

landscape photos 风景照片

contrasting shades of light and dark 明暗对比阴影

visually appealing 视觉上更吸引人

pictures of people 人物照片

the natural facial expressions 自然的脸部表情

by far 到目前为止

most people are perfectly capable of taking relatively good photos without any training 大多数人不需要任何培训就完全有能力拍出相对较好的照片了

take photos of professional quality on a consistent basis 一直拍出专业水准的照片

30. Furniture 家具

考试原题和范文

In your country, where do people buy the furniture for their homes?

【Sample Answer】 I would say the vast majority of people tend to go to big furniture superstores for their furniture. The main reason is that these places have，by far，the best variety of choices.

For a married couple, who usually makes the decisions about what furniture to buy, the husband or the wife?

【Sample Answer】 I guess in most cases，it would be a joint decision between both the husband and wife，and if it happens to be that they can't agree on something，then the wife probably has the final say，because women usually tend to be the boss when it comes to household matters.

What factors do people need to consider when buying furniture for the home?

【Sample Answer】　Obviously things like style，quality，and price should to be taken into consideration. And as well as this，I'd say another important factor to consider is size，because if you have a big living room，then a small sofa would look a little out of place，and vice versa.

Do you think the style of furniture is important?

【Sample Answer】　Yes，I guess it is，because I mean，we've all been to houses where the furniture is hideous，and it ruins the whole home，whereas if you get the style right，then you can make your home look really nice and cozy. So I guess the point I'm trying to make is that the style of furniture，to a large extent，determines the whole feel of the home，and that's what makes it so important.

Is there much difference between home furniture and office furniture?

【Sample Answer】　Yes，for sure there is. For example，home furniture tends to come in a much greater variety of styles than office furniture，simply because，I guess，most people want their homes to look unique，whereas for offices，the most important thing is functionality，so in other words，the practicality and comfort of the furniture are far more important than the style，and I guess that's the reason why most offices tend to have pretty much the same kinds of desks and chairs in them.

Is the material that furniture is made from today different to the material that was used in the past for furniture?

【Sample Answer】　Yes，I would say it is，because in the past，furniture mostly used to be made of wood，whereas currently，there's a huge variety of different materials that are used for making furniture，of which a few that come to mind are plastic，leather，and suede. And I think this reflects the fact that people's tastes are diversifying as their standard of living improves.

词汇和句型
the vast majority of people　大多数人
the best variety of choices　选择面最广
in most cases　在大多数情况下
a joint decision　一个共同的决定
if it happens to be that they can't agree on something　如果碰巧他们无法达成一致
then the wife probably has the final say　那么妻子可能有最终的决定权
women usually tend to be the boss when it comes to household matters　谈到家庭事务的时候，通常是女性说了算
style，quality，and price　款式、质量和价格
should to be taken into consideration　应该被考虑进去

look a little out of place　有点不合适

and vice versa　反之亦然

the furniture is hideous　家具很不好看

ruins the whole home　破坏了整个家

the point I'm trying to make is that ...　我想要表达的重点是······

the style of furniture，to a large extent，determines the whole feel of the home　从很大程度上，家具的款式决定了整个家的感觉

a much greater variety of styles　款式更加多样化

functionality　功能性，实用性

the practicality and comfort of the furniture　家具的实用性和舒适性

a huge variety of different materials　各种不同的材料

a few that come to mind are ...　我能想到的其中一些有······

plastic，leather，and suede　塑料、皮革和绒面

people's tastes are diversifying as their standard of living improves　随着生活标准的提高，人们的品位更加多样化

31. Shopping 购物

考试原题和范文

Why do people like shopping?

【Sample Answer】　There are a couple of reasons why people，especially females，prefer shopping in their spare time. The most obvious one is that purchasing things could help relieve stress from daily lives. When people shop in supermarkets or department stores，they see arrays of products，which have different shapes and colors. This way，they can forget about the annoying things in their lives. Another reason is that some people do not like being alone；instead，they like crowded places and communicating with others. That is why some of them like shopping in open markets，where buyers can negotiate prices with sellers.

What are the differences between shopping online and shopping in the stores?

【Sample Answer】　The first difference is that the prices of the products in the online stores are much lower than those in the department stores and supermarkets. Because online shops do not rent places to sell the products，the costs of products are relatively low. Another difference is that people cannot try the products such as clothes and food if they purchase things online，while in the stores，people can see and even try the products in person. The third difference is that the authenticity cannot be guaranteed if people buy online products，but the quality of products in shopping malls and supermarkets are supervised.

词汇和句型

a couple of reasons　两个原因

in their spare time 在他们的业余时间

purchasing things could help relieve stress 购物可以帮助减压

the annoying things in their lives 生活中的令人烦恼的事情

buyers can negotiate prices with the sellers 买家和卖家可以讨价还价

the online stores 在线商店

try the products in person 亲自试一下产品

the authenticity cannot be guaranteed 真伪无法保证

32. Growing Plants 种植植物

考试原题和范文

Do people in your country like growing plants?

【Sample Answer】 Yes，they do. It can range from keeping a low light solitary flowering plant in the home to planning and designing elaborate schemes on vast lands and properties. It is incredibly gratifying to see flowers and fruits. Flowers provide visual beauty，intoxicating scents，and remind people to take a few minutes regularly to indulge in the potency of nature.

Why do people grow plants?

【Sample Answer】 Cultivating plants is very important for a couple of reasons. First，daily gardening chores are a great way to augment an exercise regimen. Granted，most of the time gardening is not a substitute for focused cardio and strength training，but it combines low-impact exercise with other benefits we can't find at the gym. In addition，vegetable gardening gives us positive feelings of self-sufficiency.

Do you think people will grow vegetables to eat by themselves in the future?

【Sample Answer】 Yes，I suppose people will grow their own vegetables in the future because there are obvious benefits. First，eating more fresh fruits and vegetables is one of the most important things you and your family can do to stay healthy. When people are growing vegetables in the backyard，they will naturally consume more of these nutritious goods that are high in vitamin content. What's more，growing vegetables organically，without pesticides and herbicides，can help avoid unnecessary air and water pollution. People can also reduce the use of fossil fuels and the resulting pollution that comes from the transport of fresh produce（in planes and refrigerated trucks）to the supermarket.

What do you think is the most important plant in your country?

【Sample Answer】 Rice plant is the most important plant in China because rice is a staple food. People in China eat rice at least twice a day，so rice plant is crucial to people's survival. Therefore，rice plant is by far the most important plant in China.

词汇和句型

a low light solitary flowering plant　微光单株开花植物

planning and designing elaborate schemes　规划和设计复杂的项目

incredibly gratifying　非常令人高兴的

intoxicating scents　醉人的香味

indulge in the potency of nature　沉浸于大自然

daily gardening chores　日常的园艺工作

augment an exercise regimen　加强运动训练

Granted　的确

focused cardio and strength training　集中的有氧和无氧训练

it combines low-impact exercise with other benefits we can't find at the gym　它把低强度的训练和其他在健身房无法获得的好处结合在了一起

vegetable gardening　种蔬菜

self-sufficiency　自给自足

stay healthy　保持健康

in the backyard　在后院

vitamin content　维生素含量

What's more　此外

pesticides and herbicides　杀虫剂和除草剂

the transport of fresh produce　新鲜农产品的运输

refrigerated trucks　冷藏车

rice plant　水稻

a staple food　一种主食

rice plant is crucial to people's survival　水稻对人们的生存很重要

by far　到目前为止

33. Vacation 假期

考试原题和范文

Why do people buy souvenirs when they are on vacation?

【Sample Answer】　The main reason people want to buy souvenirs is probably that souvenirs are usually pretty, special and are something they can't find in the place they come from. They may want to give the souvenir to their friends to share the happiness, or keep it as a reminder of the good time they had during the vacation. Some souvenirs, such as bookmarks or caps, have practical functions and others can serve as decorations.

What are the advantages and disadvantages of taking photos when people go traveling?

【Sample Answer】　It is a lot of fun taking photos of the beautiful scenes and some travelers may even create masterpieces. People may want to record an exciting moment during the trip, so that they can have something to remember it by. However, some people tend to spend too much time and energy on taking photos, and they forget to enjoy the trip itself.

词汇和句型

share the happiness　分享快乐
keep it as a reminder of the good time they had during the vacation　保留(纪念品)作为一种度假时期所享受的美好时光的回忆
practical functions　实用功能
serve as decorations　起到装饰的作用
some travelers may even create masterpieces　一些旅游者可能还会拍摄出伟大的(摄影)作品

34. Cell Phones 手机

考试原题和范文

What are the advantages and disadvantages of cell phones?

【Sample Answer】　The first advantage is that people can communicate with their friends with ease. In fact, as smart phones are getting popular, people can make use of various Apps, such as Skype, Facebook, and Twitter to keep in touch with their friends every moment. The second benefit is that if there is an emergency, people can call the police or ambulance for help immediately. In contrast, the disadvantage is that people are indifferent to each other because they are always using their smart phones on the subway, at school, or at home.

Is it good for children to use cell phones?

【Sample Answer】　No. It is not good for children to use cell phones. Instead, it is harmful for children. The electronic touch screen display hurt children's eyes. In fact, most school-age children are short-sighted because they often play with cell phones. In addition, if they rely too much on cell phones, or smart phones to be exact, children would become addicted to cell phones. They would not study academic subjects or do outdoor sports.

What are the differences between the cell phones now and the cell phones 10 years ago?

【Sample Answer】　There are two differences. The first one is that cell phones now are implemented with computer functions, so those cell phones are actually small portable computers while the cell phone 10 years ago did not have this system so the only functions were texting messages and calling others. The second difference is that the screen of modern cell phones is much larger than that of cell phones a decade ago.

What do you think of the future development of cell phones?

【Sample Answer】　I think the future development of cell phones lies in the following aspects. The first development is that the screen size will be larger in the future so that the words and pictures can be seen clearly, even for the senior citizens. The second development is that cell phones will be smarter. Some cell phones will be used to control cars or home appliances in the near future.

How have communication technologies changed people's lives?

【Sample Answer】　Communication technologies have significantly changed people's lives. People in different countries or different continents can communicate with one another with ease by means of Facetime or Skype. In addition, people can buy things online conveniently. For example, people can get on Ebay or Amazon to buy whatever they want. They don't need to go to supermarkets or shopping malls to purchase things.

Are cell phones popular in your country?

【Sample Answer】　Yes. Cell phones are extremely popular in my country. Almost everybody has a cell phone, no matter how old he or she is. Most people use cell phones to keep in touch with their friends and businessmen use smart phones to send or receive emails. But for some children and senior citizens, they use cell phone mainly for fun.

Is it hard for elderly people to use cell phones?

【Sample Answer】　Yes. It is pretty hard for elderly people to use cell phones because most of the cell phones are smart phones so that there are many Apps that should be downloaded and applied. Some old people are not accustomed to this kind of operation. So cell phones, especially smart phones, are difficult for elderly people to use.

When do parents buy cell phones for their children?

【Sample Answer】　When their children start schools, parents would buy cell phones for them because it is necessary for parents to keep contact with their children in case of emergencies. But parents should tell their children not to play with games downloaded from the App store.

词汇和句型

communicate with their friends with ease　很容易地和朋友沟通
keep in touch with friends every moment　每时每刻和朋友保持联系
people are indifferent to each other　人与人之间互相很冷漠
electronic touch screen　电子触摸屏
become addicted to cell phones　对手机上瘾
do outdoor sports　做户外运动
cell phones now are implemented with computer functions　手机植入了电脑功能
texting messages　发短信
the screen of modern cell phones is much larger than that of cell phones a decade ago　现

在手机的屏幕比十年前大很多

the senior citizens　老年人

home appliances　家用电器

Communication technologies have significantly changed people's lives　通信技术极大地改变了人们的生活

extremely popular　特别流行

they use cell phone mainly for fun　他们用手机主要是为了玩

are not accustomed to this kind of operation　不习惯这种操作

in case of emergencies　以防万一

35. Goals 目标

考试原题和范文

Should parents choose the goals for their children?

【Sample Answer】 No，they shouldn't because no one should choose goals for others. It will cause a lot of problems if parents choose the goals for their children. For example，in current society，many parents think their children should be doctors or lawyers in the future. But their children want to be pop stars or sports stars when they grow up，and they won't feel happy if they really become doctors or lawyers. In this case，parents shouldn't make the decision for their children. In a word，it is the children's right to set goals for themselves，and parent shouldn't deprive their children of the right to do so.

When should young children have their own goals?

【Sample Answer】 Young children should have their own goals as early as possible. If people，including young children，don't have any goals，they will waste their precious time. So when children reach the age of 3 - 4，they can try setting goals for themselves under their parents' guidance and supervision，such as completing an art craft or learning a new song. With their own goals，young children can spend their time in a meaningful way.

词汇和句型

in current society　在现代社会

In this case　因此

make the decision for their children　为他们的孩子做决定

In a word　简而言之

set goals　设定目标

deprive their children of the right　剥夺他们的孩子这种权利

precious time　宝贵的时间

under their parents' guidance and supervision　在父母的指导和监督下

36. Mistakes 错误

考试原题和范文

Why do people make mistakes?

【Sample Answer】 People make mistakes when they are doing things they are not familiar with because they lack experience. For example, statistics shows that experienced drivers make less mistakes than new drivers. So the lack of experience should be the main reason for making mistakes.

What measures can be taken to avoid mistakes?

【Sample Answer】 One way to avoid mistakes is to learn from one's experience and make sure that the mistake will not be repeated again. For example, some people forget to set the alarm clock and oversleep. As a result, they are late for work. They can learn from their own mistake and be careful to never forget to set the alarm clock.

词汇和句型

make mistakes 犯错
lack experience 缺乏经验
the lack of experience 经验的缺乏
set the alarm clock 设定闹钟
oversleep 睡过头

37. Imagination 想象力

考试原题和范文

What kinds of job need imagination?

【Sample Answer】 Many types of jobs need imagination. The architect is a kind of job that requires rich imagination. In the process of designing a building, the architect has to use his or her creativity to visualize the height and shape of it. Another kind of job would be the CG (Computer Graphics) designer. In most science-fiction movies, CG designers' work is to make unrealistic things come true. Additionally, fashion designers need much imagination as well.

What needs more imagination, reading novels or watching movies?

【Sample Answer】 Reading novels needs more imagination because people have to transform texts into real scenarios, but watching movies is a relatively simple activity. What people need to do is to follow the plot and watch the main characters' actions. So, in my view, seeing movies doesn't really need any imagination. In contrast, when reading novels, people have to focus on the description of the people and sceneries and relate these things with their own life experience. Therefore, imagination plays a key role in reading novels.

What games do children play that involve imagination?
【Sample Answer】 One game is Hide and Seek. Kids have to guess where other children might hide. In this case, imagination is an important tool for them to use to find people. So that's one game. Another game that is probably connected with imagination is the car-racing video game. In X-box games, the car-racing game is very popular with children. But the picture of the video game is not so realistic. So kids need to imagine that they are driving on a real road. These are two games that involve imagination.

词汇和句型
rich imagination　丰富的想象力
visualize the height and shape of it　想象出它的高度和形状
science-fiction movies　科幻电影
fashion designers　时装设计师
transform texts into real scenarios　把文本转换为现实的场景
focus on the description of the people and sceneries and relate these things with their own life experience　关注对人物和场景的描绘并把这些和他们自己的生活经历关联起来
Hide and Seek　捉迷藏
car-racing video game　赛车游戏

38. Skills 技能

考试原题和范文
What skills are important in people's life?
【Sample Answer】 There are many crucial skills for people. For example, cooking skills, computer skills, and the ability to drive a car are all necessary for adults. However, the ability to communicate with people is one of the most important skills of people in modern society. Because people have to deal with others all the time and they cannot avoid talking with others, it is important for people to grasp good communication skills.

What should be considered when people learn new skills?
【Sample Answer】 A lot of factors should be considered when people learn new skills. First, people should figure out how important the new skill is to them and how difficult it is. Then, they can decide how much time and energy they should spend on learning it. It is important for people to make a practical plan so that they can learn the new skill systematically. Finding a good teacher and adopting an efficient learning method are important things to consider as well.

词汇和句型
crucial skills　重要技能
grasp good communication skills　掌握良好的沟通技能

make a practical plan　制定一个切实的计划
adopting an efficient learning method　采用有效率的学习方法

39. Season, Weather, and the Environment 季节、天气和环境

考试原题和范文

What's the difference between "season" and "weather"?

【Sample Answer】 The difference is basically that seasons are a time of the year, whereas weather refers to atmospheric conditions, such as wind, rain, snow, and sun. So it's a pretty big difference.

Please briefly describe the different seasons in China.

【Sample Answer】 Ok, I'll give it a try, but it's not as easy as it might sound. The reason is that China's such a huge country, so different parts of the country experience different weather conditions. But to put it simply, spring in most parts of the country is a pretty pleasant time of year, because the temperature is relatively mild, and it doesn't get too hot or cold. As for summer, in most areas it's extremely hot, and just to give you an example, here in Shanghai, the temperature goes up to about 39 degrees centigrade or so. Then in autumn, the temperature drops quite a bit, but when winter arrives, it can get really cold, especially up in the north of China, where I think the temperature gets as low as minus 30 degree centigrade.

In general, do you think people prefer to live in very hot places or very cold places?

【Sample Answer】 That's a good question, and I'm not all that sure, but I suppose most people probably prefer to live in very hot places, because for example, if you compare the number of people living in the far north of the country, where it gets extremely cold, to the southernmost part of the country, where it gets really hot, a lot more people live down south, at least as far as I know anyway. So I think this shows that most people would rather choose a very hot place to live in as opposed to a cold place.

In the future, what do you think will be some of the effects of global warming?

【Sample Answer】 From what I've seen and read, I think one of the likely effects will be a rise in sea-levels, due to the melting of the polar ice caps. So that's one thing, and as well as this, I think what will also happen is that more rivers and lakes will dry up as a result of global warming, and this has already started happening in many parts of the world. So unfortunately, it looks like the effects will all be pretty adverse.

For Chinese people, how important is protecting the environment?

【Sample Answer】 I'd say it's extremely important for most Chinese people. I think it's fair to say that most people in the country are aware of the need to look after and protect the environment，because it's become clear that if we don't，we will all be affected by the negative consequences，such as water and air pollution.

词汇和句型

whereas　然而，但是

atmospheric conditions　大气条件，气候条件

give it a try　试试看

weather conditions　天气条件

to put it simply　简单地说

a pretty pleasant time of year　一年中一段非常舒服的时间

the temperature is relatively mild　气温相对舒适

extremely hot　非常热

39 degrees centigrade or so　大约摄氏 39 度

really cold　非常冷

minus 30 degrees centigrade　零下 30 摄氏度

the far north of the country　这个国家的最北面

the southernmost part of the country　这个国家的最南面

at least as far as I know anyway　最起码据我所知是这样的

as opposed to　相对……而言

one of the likely effects　可能的结果之一

a rise in sea-levels　海平面的上升

due to the melting of the polar ice caps　由于极地冰帽的融化

global warming　全球变暖

the effects will all be pretty adverse　结果将会是非常负面的

most people in the country are aware of the need to look after and protect the environment
这个国家中的大多数人意识到了照料和保护环境的需求

the negative consequences　负面结果

40. Food 食物

考试原题和范文

Do you think food has changed much in your country in the past ten years?
【Sample Answer】　Yes. Food has changed a lot in my country in the last decade. The first aspect is that western food has influenced Chinese market so most children prefer to eat hamburgers and fried food. For adults，they like eating pizza and steak. In contrast，another change is that some people，especially in large cities，have become health conscious. These people will choose to eat more vegetables in order to live a healthy life. And for the food itself，more types of fruits and vegetables have been grown because of the scientific advance in agriculture.

Do you think that food is important in your culture?

【Sample Answer】 Yes. Food is the very important in my culture. In China，there are more than ten traditional festivals during a year. Food is closely related to all of these festivals. For example，during the Spring Festival，family members gather together to eat dumplings to celebrate. In the Mid-autumn festival，the majority of people eat mooncakes，and if they don't，most people would not think that they have not celebrated that festival yet. That's why I would say that food is a key element in my culture.

What types of food will Chinese people be eating?

【Sample Answer】 I guess Chinese people will be eating new types of vegetables in the future. I mean vegetables that combine nutrition with good flavor. Broccoli is a popular vegetable but it does not taste good. So I think people would choose new types of good-tasting vegetables. Another trend is that people would try new types of staple foods such as oat because it contains more fiber，which is the most important element for physical health.

Do you think it would be a good job to work in a restaurant?

【Sample Answer】 No，I don't think it's a good option. Most employees working in the restaurants have to work two or three shifts per day，which means that they don't have much time to rest. It's a demanding job so it's not a healthy lifestyle. Besides，the waste smoke emitted by the cooking process is harmful to people. If a person works in a restaurant for more than a year，he or she will get lung diseases. So it's definitely not a good job.

What skills would it take to be a good cook?

【Sample Answer】 The first skill is patience. Cooking is a complicated process. Something unexpected always occurs. So a good cook should be extremely patient in order to successfully make an appealing dish. Another skill is to know how to use the tools including cookware and control the fire level. If a cook is able to use these tools skillfully and flexibly，they can cook dishes with different flavors. The use of sauces is another important skill for a good cook.

Do you think that it is good if people can cook?

【Sample Answer】 Sure. If a person can cook，he or she doesn't need to eat out in restaurants. This can save time and provide people with the healthier food. They can control the use of salt，sugar，and oil as well. It can prevent people from getting diseases such as heart attack and diabetes.

Who does most of the cooking in your culture, men or women?

【Sample Answer】 Women do the most of the cooking in my culture. In Chinese culture，women do the most of the domestic tasks including cooking. And women are more patient and careful than men so they are more suitable than men to cook. But with the increasing equality between men and women, women are also working in the daytime, so men do the cooking as well.

What are the differences between eating in a restaurant and eating at home?

【Sample Answer】 There are a couple of differences between eating in a restaurant and eating at home. The first one is that eating in a restaurant is more expensive than eating at home. Because of the service and high operation costs of restaurants, it is much more expensive than eating at home. Another difference is the kind of food you could choose. At home, it is impossible for people to cook all popular kinds of food in the world. But in restaurants, people can try Italian food, Japanese food, and French food. People have more opportunities to try food from other cultures.

Is it important to have a healthy diet?

【Sample Answer】 Yes. It is crucial to have a healthy diet. If people have healthy diets every day, they would not be sick and they will always be energetic. However, if people eat too much meat, they will gain weight and get sick. For example, they could get diabetes, hypertension, and heart attack. So it is strongly recommended to eat healthy diet every day.

Are there problems with junk food in your country?

【Sample Answer】 Yes. Junk food is currently popular with young people especially teenagers. As a result, overweight people are commonly seen in China. This problem is serious because in the long term there will be an increasing number of unhealthy people in China. Consequently, the economic development of a country would suffer. So this trend should be reversed.

How can we improve some people's diet do you think?

【Sample Answer】 There are a couple of methods. The first one is that governments should recommend healthy diets to citizens. For example, they can print some brochures to hand out to the public. In these brochures, healthy vegetables could be listed so the public will know what to eat. Another useful way is that primary schools could set up courses about nutrition intake and how to maintain a balanced diet. So children could develop a good habit of eating healthy diets from childhood.

词汇和句型
in the last decade 在过去的十年中
The first aspect is that ... 第一个方面是……
fried food 油炸食品
pizza and steak 比萨和牛排
In contrast 相对而言
health conscious 具有健康意识

live a healthy life　过一种健康的生活

the scientific advance in agriculture　农业方面的科技进步

the majority of people　大多数人

a key element　一个重要因素

broccoli　花椰菜,西兰花

staple foods　主食

oat　燕麦

the physical health　身体健康

It's a demanding job　这是个很高要求的工作

a healthy lifestyle　健康的生活方式

lung diseases　肺部疾病

a complicated process　一个复杂的过程

Something unexpected always occurs　意外的事情总是会发生

a good cook　一个好厨师

extremely patient　非常耐心

make an appealing dish　制作一道吸引人的菜

cookware　烹饪器具

fire level　火候

use these tools skillfully and flexibly　有技巧地灵活使用这些工具

eat out in restaurants　在餐厅吃饭

heart attack and diabetes　心脏病和糖尿病

domestic tasks　家务活儿

a couple of differences　两个区别

a healthy diet　健康饮食

gain weight　增肥

get sick　生病

diabetes，hypertension and heart attack　糖尿病、高血压和心脏病

overweight people　超重的人

in the long term　长期而言

So this trend should be reversed　因此,这个趋势应该被逆转

print some brochures to hand out to the public　印刷一些小册子分发给公众

nutrition intake　营养摄入

balanced diet　均衡饮食

develop a good habit of eating healthy diets from childhood　从小养成健康饮食的好习惯

41. Sky 天空

考试原题和范文

What is the sky like in the eyes of children?

【**Sample Answer**】　For most children，the sky is a mysterious place with some beings living there, and this is due to the influence of sci-fi movies or traditional Chinese fairy tales. They have loads of questions about it, like how the sky came into being, how far the distance between the earth and the sun is, and whether or not they can get to the moon one day. Besides, they admire everything flying in the sky. That's why they are always excited about taking a plane.

Is it necessary for children to learn astronomy?

【Sample Answer】 No, it isn't. I think being curious about space is one thing, while learning astronomy is another. Astronomy is too hard for children to learn, because it requires a solid knowledge base and deals with high technology. Learning astronomy would pose great difficulty for children and is likely to damage their natural curiosity about space. Of course, learning basic knowledge about astronomy in forms of comics or cartoons or visiting museums would be welcome.

What is the effect of watching sky on people's creativity?

【Sample Answer】 People usually look into the sky for clouds in the daytime and for stars at night. Clouds move and change shapes, which makes people imagine what they look like. Dots of stars are also connected in people's minds to resemble things familiar to them. This kind of association produces positive effects on creativity. On the other hand, when one is full of worry or drained of ideas, he can look into the sky. This tends to clear their messy mind and help them regain creativity.

What technology can help people see the stars and other planets?

【Sample Answer】 Observatories are the ideal place to observe stars and planets. They are usually built on top of a hill to ensure nothing blocks the observers' vision field. They house sophisticated equipment like optical telescopes, through which people see remote stars. However, some stars are not visible, but their radio waves can be detected. So another kind of equipment is radio telescopes.

Is it wasting money to research space?

【Sample Answer】 I think it depends. If the country is wealthy enough and people's needs for basic life have already been satisfied, then it's important to spend money on space exploration, because resources on earth will inevitably deplete one day. I believe some planets have untapped resources. Thus, exploring space can provide future human beings with better survival possibilities. On the other hand, if this is a country whose people are still living in poverty, then I think the priority would be to help them. Long-term plans like researching space are a waste of money, and should give way.

Do people in your country believe in aliens?

【Sample Answer】 I don't think people believe in aliens. A creature's existence is based on enough water, air, and light. Until now, only earth provides these elements. The closest planets to earth are Venus and Mars. Venus is too close to the sun, so most of the gas evaporates and the temperature is too high for a being to survive. By contrast, Mars is too cold to live on. And other planets have worse environments.

词汇和句型

a mysterious place　一个神秘的地方

sci-fi movies　科幻电影

fairy tales　童话,神话故事

how the sky came into being　天空是如何形成的

being curious about space　对太空感兴趣

solid knowledge base　扎实的知识基础

pose great difficulty for children　对儿童造成巨大困难

comics or cartoons　漫画或卡通

look into the sky　仰望天空

produces positive effects on creativity　对创造力产生积极影响

clear their messy mind　清理他们的混乱思维

observatories　天文台

ensure nothing blocks the observers' vision field　确保没有东西挡住观察者的视野

They house sophisticated equipment　(天文台)配备了复杂的设备

optical telescopes　光学望远镜

radio waves　无线电波

radio telescopes　射电望远镜,无线电天文望远镜

space exploration　太空探索

resources on earth will inevitably deplete one day　有一天地球上的资源将会不可避免地耗尽

untapped resources　尚未开采的资源

people are still living in poverty　人们仍然生活在贫困中

Long-term plans　长期计划

give way　让路,退让

Venus and Mars　金星和火星

42. Making Decisions 做决定

考试原题和范文

What do you think are the most important decision that people make in their lives?

【Sample Answer】 Off the top of my head, I guess it would be decisions like who you want to marry and spend your life with, how many children you want to have, and what kind of job you want to pursue, because these are things which will have a huge effect on your whole life.

What skills are necessary when making decisions?
【Sample Answer】 I suppose one skill that's necessary in making decisions is analytical skills, because this will help you weigh up each choice you face, and therefore guide you to make a good decision. And as well as this, I think that having the ability to make decisions quickly without pondering too much is also necessary, because we often have to make decisions without full knowledge of something.

How can people improve their decision-making skills?
【Sample Answer】 I suppose one thing people could do would be to trust their gut instinct more. And by that I mean they should attach more importance to how they are feeling deep down, because I think we have a sixth sense in knowing what the right thing to do is.

Do you think that parents should make important decisions for their children?
【Sample Answer】 On the whole, I'd say they shouldn't, no, because what parents think is best for their children isn't always necessarily the best thing. So as far as I'm concerned, I think whenever possible, parents should let their children make their own decisions, because after all, it's their child's life, not theirs. And even if the child doesn't make a good decision, they will still end up learning from it.

How can older people help young people make their own decisions wisely?
【Sample Answer】 I'd say probably the main thing they can do is to help younger people understand what the most important things to take into consideration are before they make a decision. Older people have experienced more in life, and so they're generally more aware of what's important and what things should be prioritized. So I think there's a lot that young people can learn from them.

词汇和句型
Off the top of my head　不假思索马上能想到的是
these are things which will have a huge effect on your whole life　这些是对你的生活会有巨大影响的事情
analytical skills　分析能力
weigh up each choice you face　衡量你面临的选择
guide you to make a good decision　指导你做出一个好决定
the ability to make decisions quickly without pondering too much　不纠结快速做决定的能力
make decisions without full knowledge of something　在没有完全具备某方面知识的情况下做决定
trust their gut instinct more　更相信他们的直觉
by that I mean ...　我的意思是……

attach more importance to how they are feeling deep down　更重视他们内心深处的感觉

a sixth sense　第六感

On the whole　总的来说

what parents think is best for their children isn't always necessarily the best thing　父母认为对他们孩子来说最好的东西不一定是最好的

they will still end up learning from it　他们最终会从中吸取教训的

the main thing they can do is to help younger people understand what the most important things to take into consideration are　他们能做的主要是帮助年轻人理解需要考虑的最重要的事情是什么

they're generally more aware of what's important and what things should be prioritized　他们总体上更清楚哪些事情是重要的以及应该优先处理哪些事情

43. Movies 电影

考试原题和范文

What factors contribute to a good movie?

【Sample Answer】 I think a good story is the main factor that contributes to a good movie，because most people focus on the plot of a film. A good screenplay can draw more people's attention. Another factor is the actors and actresses. It is true that some fans go to the cinema just to see their favorite movie stars.

What are the differences between the movies that young people like and the movies that old people like?

【Sample Answer】 There are several differences between the movies that young people like and the movies that old people like. The first difference is the movie type. Young people like action movies or horror movies because young people like stimulating things. And they can adjust themselves when they see some exciting or horrible scenes in the movie. However，old people have cardiovascular diseases so they would like to choose some "gentle and mild" movies such as comedies and love stories，which are good for their physical and mental health. The second difference is the country in which the movies are produced. For young people，they like to watch foreign movies because they are curious about the foreign culture and they have mastered some foreign languages. In contrast，old people are more traditional so they would like to see movies from their own country. And language would not be a barrier if they watch a movie produced in their home country.

词汇和句型

focus on the plot of a film　关注一部电影的情节

A good screenplay　一个好的电影剧本

action movies　动作电影

horror movies　恐怖电影
stimulating things　刺激的东西
cardiovascular diseases　心血管疾病
comedies and love stories　喜剧和爱情故事
physical and mental health　身体和心理健康

44. Rules 规则

考试原题和范文

Are the rules in school beneficial to children?

【Sample Answer】　Yes，they are. School rules are supposed to guide and help young students. For example，the rule that students should not throw litter on campus lets students understand that they should be responsible for the environment they live in. Through the rule that asks students to say "please" and "thank you" to the faculty，students learn the importance of being polite and grateful.

When companies make rules, should they consider the opinions of the employees?

【Sample Answer】　Yes，they should. A company should know how the employees think in any case，including when they are making rules. If decision makers ignore the employees' thoughts，it is probable that the rules they make will fail. For example，if the employees love their jobs very much and the employer decides to cut their salary by，say 5%，most of the employees will accept that and not complain too much. However，supposing that the employer reduces the same percentage of the income of the employees who are already unsatisfied with their work，then there will be a great possibility that these angry employees will quit. Therefore，it is crucial for a company to take the employees' opinions into consideration.

词汇和句型

guide and help young students　指导和帮助年轻学生
throw litter on campus　把垃圾扔在校园里
they should be responsible for the environment they live in　他们应该为他们所生活的环境负责
say "please" and "thank you" to the faculty　对教职员工说"请"和"谢谢"
learn the importance of being polite and grateful　了解礼貌和感激的重要性
decision makers　决策者
supposing that ...　假设……
there will be a great possibility that ...　很有可能……
take the employees' opinions into consideration　考虑员工的观点

45. Rewards 奖赏

考试原题和范文

What rewards should be given to children?

【Sample Answer】 In most cases, less expensive rewards are more appropriate for kids in case they become spoiled. Choices range from stationeries, such as notebooks, pens, and school bags, to sports equipment like a basketball or a pair of badminton bats. Non-material rewards are also a good option to reward and educate the kids, such as a field trip or a tour to the museum.

What should children do to get the rewards?

【Sample Answer】 First of all, they should behave themselves and stop doing inappropriate things. Then, efforts should be made in various aspects, including studying harder, helping people in need, trying to clean their own bedrooms, and respecting their teachers, classmates, and themselves.

What are some of the disadvantages if parents give pressure to their children to get some rewards?

【Sample Answer】 Kids can be unhappy if their parents force them to do things they are reluctant to do even if there is a reward. It is possible that those young children only do as their parents ask to get the prize but neglect the meaning of doing it. For example, a kid is promised a reward if he respects the elderly and he may do so to get the reward, but he never truly understands why he should respect senior citizens. Then, when the kid grows up, he will not show respect anymore.

What rewards should be given to employees to encourage them to work harder in companies?

【Sample Answer】 It depends on what the employees really want, which is usually a pay raise, a promotion, or a paid vacation. On-the-job trainings and relevant seminars, lectures or conferences are good rewards for those who want to learn and be experts in the industry. Other people will be satisfied with better working environment like a separate office. Anyway, if employees are happy about their rewards, they will dedicate more to their work.

What are the benefits to companies if they give rewards to employees?

【Sample Answer】 Employees work harder if they know there is a reward, and this improves the productivity and creates more profit. What's more, a company is often seen as a generous one if it rewards its staff, and it will enjoy a high reputation in the job market, which can attract more talents.

词汇和句型

in case they become spoiled　免得他们被宠坏了

stationeries 文具

a pair of badminton bats 一对羽毛球拍

Non-material rewards 非物质奖赏

a good option 一个好选择

reward and educate the kids at the same time 同时奖励和教育孩子

a field trip 一次实地考察旅行

a tour to the museum 一次博物馆之旅

they should behave themselves 他们应该举止得体

their parents force them to do things they are reluctant to do 他们的父母强迫他们做他们所不愿意做的事情

neglect the meaning of doing it 忽略这样做的意义

senior citizens 老年人

a pay raise 一次提薪

a promotion 一次升职

a paid vacation 一次带薪假期

On-the-job trainings 岗位培训

a separate office 一个单独的办公室

they will dedicate more to their work 他们会更投入工作

creates more profit 创造更多的利润

enjoy a high reputation 享有很高的声望

attract more talents 吸引更多的人才

46. Playing 游玩

考试原题和范文

Is it safe for children to play outside their home?

【Sample Answer】 No，it is not safe for children to play outside their home，especially in China. The first reason is that the traffic problem is terrible. There are many rude and impatient drivers who have just finished the driving courses. So it is extremely dangerous for children to do sports or play hide-and-seek in heavy-traffic areas. The second reason is that the environment is getting worse in China，especially the air quality. If children play with their friends outside，they might develop respiratory diseases. Therefore，it is not safe for children to play outside their home.

What games do children play currently?

【Sample Answer】 There are a variety of games that children play in present society. The most popular one is definitely basketball game. Most primary school and secondary school children play basketball games after school every day. Another popular game among children is the football game（or we call it soccer ball）. While Chinese people are not good at playing football，kids like playing football with their friends to boost teamwork spirit and improve their physical health.

What are the benefits of playing games for children?

【Sample Answer】 There are several benefits of playing games. The first advantage is that children could develop their intelligence if they play intelligence-boosting games. Another upside is that if they play sports games，they will have a sense of teamwork and responsibility. When the children grow up，they will get along with other people.

What are the advantages and disadvantages of using the iPad for children?

【Sample Answer】 The first benefit of using iPad is that there are numerous Apps designed for iPad. If children could make full use of the educational Apps，they could learn a lot and achieve good academic performance. The second advantage is that iPad is a good entertainment tool. Kids can watch animation movies or play electronic games on the iPad. However，there are some disadvantages as well. The most obvious flaw of using the iPad is that children would waste a huge amount of time on playing iPad games，which are very addictive. The second disadvantage is that their eyesight would get hurt if they spend a long time on playing with their iPad.

词汇和句型

rude and impatient drivers　粗鲁无礼的司机
the driving courses　驾驶课程
extremely dangerous　特别危险
hide-and-seek　捉迷藏
in heavy-traffic areas　在车流量大的区域
respiratory diseases　呼吸系统疾病
boost teamwork spirit　提升团队协作精神
improve their physical health　提高他们的身体健康
develop their intelligence　提高他们的智力
intelligence-boosting games　益智游戏
make full use of the educational Apps　充分利用教育类应用软件
good academic performance　良好的学习成绩
animation movies　动画电影

47. Learning Science 学习科学

考试原题和范文

How important is it to learn science for children?

【Sample Answer】 It is highly important for kids to learn science because they could develop the skills of logical thinking by learning courses such as math. Even if these kids will not become mathematicians in the future，they will be able to do things in a logical manner，which is the most crucial factor for success. Also，science is the basic subject for all the other fields such as finance，logistics，and international trade. So it is strongly recommended for children to learn science.

What could be done to learn science well?

【Sample Answer】　A couple of things could be done to learn science well. The most effective one is to learn from a good teacher，which is the decisive factor to learn anything well. A good teacher could give students motivation to study the course on their own. If the students are willing to learn science，they would，without a doubt，achieve high scores in the test. In addition to the teachers' effort，students could make use of the Internet to get to know more aspects of science. For example，they could watch videos on YouTube about the latest science. In this way，students can have a range of perspectives about science. These are two means for the students to learn science well.

词汇和句型

highly important　非常重要

logical thinking　逻辑思维

do things in a logical manner　有逻辑地做事情

the decisive factor　决定性因素

give students motivation to study the course on their own　激励学生独立地学习这门课程

a range of perspectives about science　各种对于科学的见解

two means　两个方法

48. Advertisements 广告

考试原题和范文

In general，what are the pros and cons of advertisement?

【Sample Answer】　Looking at the advantages，I'd say that the main one is that it can help increase the awareness of a product or service，and in a lot of cases，you can reach a very wide target market through advertisement，such as TV and Internet ads. And as for the drawbacks，I suppose the most obvious one is the cost，because advertisements aren't cheap，and you have to pay for it up front，before you can start enjoying the benefits. So，in other words，there's quite a big element of risk to it，because you could end up losing quite a lot of money if your advertisement campaign isn't successful.

Do you think there's too much advertisement in our daily lives?

【Sample Answer】　Yeah，I'd say there is，because it seems that wherever we look，there's something being advertised. It's almost impossible going anywhere without seeing an advertisement. So it feels like we're being constantly bombarded with information. And for the most part，people don't have the desire to see any of it. So yeah，I think there's way too much advertisement at the moment.

What are the different ways that products and services are advertised in society today?

【Sample Answer】 I'd say there's a large number of ways, such as TV, radio, newspaper, and Internet, just to name a few. And then on top of that, there are also more indirect ways that companies advertise, like product placement, which seems to be happening a lot now in films and TV programs. So yeah, I mean there are countless ways to advertise.

What's the most frequently used method of advertisement?

【Sample Answer】 I'd say it's probably online advertisement, because people are spending so much time on the Internet. And companies have basically latched on to this fact, because almost every website you go on now has an advertisement of some sort on it.

Which do you think is the most effective means of advertisement?

【Sample Answer】 I'm no expert, but I suppose it depends on the product you're trying to sell. So for example, if it's a mass-market product like shampoo, then I guess TV advertisements would be the most effective, as it reaches the widest audience, and also uses moving images and sounds, unlike newspaper ads, which just use still images. But if, on the other hand, it's a niche product which only has a very small target customer group, then I'd say you're better off using a more focused means of advertisement, such as putting ads on websites which are related to that particular product or service, because that way, the ad will only be viewed by people who might actually be interested in it, and it will also be a lot more cost-effective than using other ways to advertise.

Do you think the number of advertisements will increase in the future?

【Sample Answer】 Yes, I imagine it's very likely that it will, because I mean, it's already increased considerably since 20 years ago. It seems that everywhere you look now, you can see advertisements, such as in lifts and on the street, and so I can't see any reason why it won't go on increasing, especially seeing as commercialism in society seems to be getting more and more prevalent, which, I think you would agree, goes hand in hand with advertisement.

Do you think there should be some controls or restrictions placed on the advertisement industry?

【Sample Answer】 Yeah, I think it's fair to say that there should be, because otherwise, there would be no limit to the amount of advertisements we're subject to. For example, if there were no restrictions on where advertisements could be placed, then I think everywhere would just get filled up with them, which might not be so bad in a city, but in the countryside it would really spoil the natural scenery. So that's one thing, and I suppose another aspect that should be controlled to some extent is the content of advertisements. The reason is that a lot of companies at the moment seem to make their products look better than they really are. One example that comes to mind is the instant noodle ads where they show all these lovely freshly-cooked vegetables being added into the noodles, and it looks really tasty, but in fact the vegetables you get are dried and shriveled, and most likely have lost all of their nutritional value. So I think something should be done about this kind of thing, as it's just not right.

What impact on people does music in advertisements have?

【Sample Answer】 I suppose one impact it has is that it makes advertisements more memorable. So in other words, if an advertisement has a catchy tune to it, it tends to stay in the mind longer.

What effects can advertisements have on young children?

【Sample Answer】 I guess they can have both positive and negative effects on children. For example, looking on the positive side, I think it's possible that some advertisements can help give children a better understanding of the things they see and use in their daily life. But I would say it's more often the case that advertisements can have a negative effect, because a lot of the things which are advertised aren't suitable for young children, such as alcoholic drinks, and a lot of advertisements which target young children are for things like sweets and chocolate biscuits, which aren't all that good for kids, but seeing such advertisements will make them pester their parents to buy these things for them, which I know because this is exactly what I did when I was younger.

词汇和句型

increase the awareness of a product or service　增加(人们对)一个产品或服务的认识

in a lot of cases　在很多情况下

reach a very wide target market through advertisement　通过广告达到非常广阔的目标市场

And as for the drawbacks　说到缺点

pay for it up front　预先付款

quite a big element of risk　很大的风险因素

you could end up losing quite a lot of money　你可能最终损失很多钱

advertisement campaign　广告活动,广告攻势

an advertisement　一则广告

it feels like ...　好像是……,似乎是……

we're being constantly bombarded with information　我们一直在被信息轰炸

there's way too much advertisement at the moment　现在广告实在是太多了

just to name a few　不胜枚举,仅举几例

on top of that　除此之外

product placement　（电影、电视中的）产品植入

countless ways　很多方法

companies have basically latched on to this fact　很多公司已经了解了这个事实

it reaches the widest audience　（电视广告）覆盖最广泛的观众群体

a mass-market product　一个大众市场产品

still images　静止图片

a niche product　一个小众产品

a very small target customer group　很小的目标顾客群体

a more focused means of advertisement　一个更加集中的广告方式

the ad will only be viewed by people who might actually be interested in it　这个广告只会被对它真正感兴趣的人看到

more cost-effective　更有成本效益的，更划算的

it's very likely that ...　很有可能……

already increased considerably　已经大幅增长

commercialism in society seems to be getting more and more prevalent　社会中的商业主义越来越普遍

goes hand in hand with　和……紧密相连

there would be no limit to the amount of advertisements we're subject to　对我们所接触到的广告的数量会没有限制

everywhere would just get filled up with them　任何地方都会充斥着(广告)

in the countryside　在农村

spoil the natural scenery　破坏自然风景

So that's one thing，and I suppose another aspect that should be controlled to some extent is ...　所以这是一方面,我觉得另外一个需要从某种程度上被控制的是……

the content of advertisements　广告的内容

a lot of companies at the moment　现在的许多公司

the instant noodle ads　方便面广告

freshly-cooked vegetables　新鲜烹制的蔬菜

dried and shriveled　干枯的

nutritional value　营养价值

it makes adverts more memorable　（音乐）使广告更容易让人记住

an advert has a catchy tune to it　一个广告配有吸引人的旋律

stay in the mind　铭记在心

have both positive and negative effects on children　对儿童既有积极影响也有消极影响

give children a better understanding of the things they see and use in their daily life　使儿童很好地理解他们日常生活中所看到的和所使用的东西

it's more often the case that ...　情况往往是……

a lot of the things which are advertised aren't suitable for young children　很多做广告的商品不适合小孩子

alcoholic drinks　酒精饮料

a lot of advertisements which target young children 许多目标群体是儿童的广告
sweets and chocolate biscuits 糖果和巧克力饼干
pester their parents to buy these things 缠着他们的父母买这些东西

49. Health 健康

考试原题和范文

What do most people do to keep fit in your country?

【Sample Answer】 I guess most Chinese people prefer to keep healthy by doing all kinds of physical exercises, like badminton and table tennis, mainly because these sports burn our extra fat effectively. On top of that, having a balanced diet is what we do for health as well. I mean, in my country, we eat a lot of fresh fish and vegetables every day. And that is a good way for us to obtain the necessary nutrients.

What do you think influence most on health? Food, physical exercise, or other factors?

【Sample Answer】 I think whether you are healthy or not is determined by plenty of factors and each one of them is equally important. To be more precise, food provides us with nutrients. Physical exercise is beneficial to body-building while sufficient sleep means our bodies can get a good rest after a long day of work. So, all of these factors join hands to guarantee a healthy state.

What are the methods that schools can use to improve students' mental health?

【Sample Answer】 I guess the most effective way is to include an hour of exercise in the daily curriculum, basically because physical activity improves mental health, especially aerobic exercise for it reduces stress, improves attention, and buoys the mood. Besides, offering mental health screening is another way. By saying that I mean, schools can test for emotional well-being to identify troubled kids early on.

词汇和句型

burn our extra fat effectively 有效燃烧额外脂肪
On top of that 除此之外
a balanced diet 均衡饮食
a lot of fresh fish and vegetables 很多的新鲜鱼类和蔬菜
obtain the necessary nutrients 获得必要的营养物质
plenty of factors 许多因素
equally important 同等重要
To be more precise 具体来说
sufficient sleep 充分的睡眠
all of these factors join hands to guarantee a healthy state 所有这些因素结合在一起确保一个健康的状态

in the daily curriculum　在每天的课程中

physical activity improves mental health　体力活动促进心理健康

aerobic exercise　有氧运动

reduces stress，improves attention，and buoys the mood　减少压力、提高注意力以及振作精神

mental health screening　心理健康筛查

By saying that，I mean ...　我的意思是……

emotional well-being　情感健康

第五章　IELTS Speaking Vocabulary
雅思口语分类话题词汇

1. Types of Music 音乐类型

General 总体类型
- children's music（including nursery rhymes）儿童音乐（包括儿歌）
- Latin Dance music（e.g.，Flamenco，Tango）拉丁舞音乐（如弗拉门科民歌，探戈）
- electronic（Digital）music 电子（数字）音乐
- ethnic and national music（including traditional Chinese music，Chinese opera，folk songs）民族音乐（包括传统中国音乐、中国戏曲、民歌）
- film music 电影音乐

Classical European Music 欧洲古典乐
- baroque music 巴洛克音乐
- chamber music 室内乐
- orchestral music（such as composed by Mozart，Beethoven，etc.）管弦乐（如莫扎特、贝多芬等创作的作品）
- opera 歌剧
- ballet music 芭蕾音乐

Modern Popular Music 流行音乐
- bluegrass 蓝草音乐
- blues 布鲁斯音乐
- country and western music 西部乡村乐
- disco music（techno，trance ...）迪斯科音乐（高科技舞曲、迷幻舞曲……）
- hip-hop 嘻哈；美国街头说唱
- jazz（e.g.，big band，ragtime）爵士乐（如爵士乐团、雷格泰姆旋律）
- pop songs 流行歌曲
- rap music 说唱音乐
- reggae 雷鬼乐
- rhythm and blues 节奏布鲁斯
- rock "n" roll（including rockabilly，heavy metal）摇滚乐（包括乡村摇滚乐、重金属摇滚乐）

2. **Types of Movies** 电影类型

- action and adventure 动作冒险
- animated cartoons 动画片
- comedy 喜剧
- drama 戏剧
- horror 恐怖片
- martial arts 武术
- musicals 音乐片,歌舞片
- romance 爱情片
- romantic comedy 浪漫喜剧
- science fiction 科幻
- silent movies 无声电影
- (suspense) thrillers (悬疑)惊悚片
- teen movies 青少年电影
- war movies 战争电影
- westerns 西部片
- documentary films 纪录片

3. **Types of TV Shows** 电视节目类型

- cartoons 卡通
- children's shows 儿童节目
- documentary programs 纪录片节目
- drama (e.g., police dramas) 戏剧(如警匪片)
- game shows 娱乐节目
- made-for-TV movies (including mini-series) 电视电影(包括中篇剧集)
- musical video shows (e.g., MTV) 音乐视频节目 (如音乐电视)
- reality TV 真实电视,真人秀
- situational comedies (sitcoms) 情景喜剧
- comedy shows 喜剧影片
- sports programs (e.g., live broadcasts of sports events) 体育节目(如运动项目的现场直播)
- Talk Shows 谈话节目
- The News 新闻
- news programs (stress on first word) 新闻节目(第一个单词重读)
- current affairs and news analysis (including interviews) 时事新闻分析(包括采访)
- variety shows (e.g., The Chinese New Year family entertainment program) 综艺节目(如新年家庭娱乐节目)
- pop music videos 流行音乐录像片

- advertisements（Make sure you can understand the British pronunciation of this word when you hear it）广告（请确保在听到该单词的英式发音时能明白）

4. Types of Advertising 广告类型

- TV and radio advertisements（= TV and radio commercials）电视广播广告
- newspaper and magazine ads（including the classified ads）报纸杂志广告（包括分类广告）
- billboards（next to main roads，railway lines，on subway station walls etc.）广告牌（主要道路，铁路，地铁站墙壁上的广告等）
- cell-phone text messages 手机短信
- flyers and handouts（e.g.，on the street，put into letterboxes etc.）宣传单和小册子（如在街上发的，或投递到信箱中的等）
- Internet advertisements（e.g.，pop-up ads）网络广告（如进入某网站时，会自动弹出的广告）
- posters（e.g. wall posters，bus stop posters）海报（如墙上贴的海报，公交车站的海报）

Visible Logos 可见商标
- on professional athletes' clothing 在职业运动员的服装上
- on signs in front of shops etc. 在商店前的招牌上
- on T-shirts，hats，jackets and other clothing 在 T 恤，帽子，夹克衫和其他服装上
- on handbags and other accessories 在手提包和其他配件上
- on Formula 1 cars 在 F1 赛车上
- on racing yachts 在赛艇上
- on hot-air balloons 在热气球上

Advertisements in Other Prominent Places 其他显著位子的广告
- on the side of buses and trains 在汽车和火车的侧面
- cinema advertising 电影院广告
- sports stadium advertising 体育馆广告

5. Things to Read 读物

For News 新闻
- newspapers 报纸
- news magazines 新闻杂志
- company and organization newsletters 公司和机构的新闻刊物、时事通讯

Magazines 杂志
- fashion magazines 时尚杂志

- movie magazines 电影杂志
- computer magazines 计算机杂志
- news magazines 新闻杂志
- sports magazines 体育杂志
- hobbyist magazines 业余爱好者杂志
- technical and professional journals 专业技术杂志
- art magazines 艺术杂志
- home decoration magazines 家居装潢杂志
- women's magazines 女性杂志

Literature 文学
- autobiographies 自传
- biographies 传记
- novels（historical novels，thrillers，mystery stories，romance novels，detective stories，science fiction）小说（历史小说、惊悚小说、怪诞小说、爱情小说、侦探小说、科幻小说）
- poetry 诗歌
- plays 戏剧
- short stories 短篇小说
- essays 随笔
- literary criticism 文艺评论，文学批评

Education 教育
- textbooks 教科书
- reference books 参考书
- encyclopaedias 百科全书
- self-help books 励志书籍（心灵鸡汤和成功方法等）

Entertainment 娱乐
- comic books 漫画书
- puzzle books 益智书

Personal Correspondence 私人信函
- letters 书信
- emails 电子邮件
- postcards 明信片
- cell-phone text messages 手机短信

The Internet 网络
The Internet now includes most of the examples above

现今网络包括了以上提到的大多数内容

6. Types of Clothing 服装类型

Casual Wear 便装
- a pair of jeans 牛仔裤
- a pair of slacks 宽松裤
- a T-shirt T恤
- a sweater 运动衫,毛线衫
- a pair of shorts 短裤
- a cardigan 开襟羊毛衫

Formal Wear 正装
- a business suit 西装
- a vest 背心,马甲
- a tie 领带
- a bow tie 领结
- a wedding gown 结婚礼服
- a ballroom gown 宴会礼服
- a tuxedo 无尾礼服
- an overcoat 外套大衣
- a fur coat 裘皮大衣

Both Formal and Casual Wear 正式休闲皆可
- a pair of trousers（Br.）= a pair of pants（U.S.）长裤
- a shirt 衬衫
- a skirt 裙子
- a dress 服装,连衣裙
- a blouse 女式衬衫
- a coat 外套
- a jacket 短上衣,夹克衫

Sportswear 运动装
- a tracksuit 运动服
- clothes for football, basketball etc. 足球,篮球服装
- ski clothes（a ski vest, a pair of ski pants, a ski jacket）滑雪服（滑雪背心、滑雪裤、滑雪上衣）
- a pair of swimming costumes = a swimsuit 游泳衣
- golf clothes 高尔夫服装
- sports fishing clothes 钓鱼服装

Work clothes 工作服

- a pair of protective overalls 防护性工作服
- a doctor's gown 医生的长袍
- a lab coat 实验工作服
- an apron 围裙

Uniforms 制服

For the following groups：为以下群体设计：

- school children 学生
- police 警察
- security guards 保安,警卫
- the military ＝ the armed forces（army，navy，air-force）军队(陆军,海军,空军)
- mailmen ＝ postmen 邮递员
- some company and factory employees 一些公司和工厂的员工
- airline pilots and flight attendants 飞行员和乘务员
- railway and bus-line employees 铁路和公交站线的员工
- nurses 护士
- waiters and waitresses 服务员
- sports teams 运动队
- marching band members 军乐队成员

Footwear 鞋类

- shoes 鞋子
- dress shoes（＝ formal shoes）盛装鞋
- sandals 凉鞋
- house slippers 家居拖鞋
- thongs（U.S. ＝ "flip-flops"）夹脚凉鞋
- gym boots（sneakers）旅游鞋,运动鞋
- dancing shoes 跳舞鞋
- martial arts slippers 武术鞋
- sports shoes — football，golf，track and field 运动鞋——足球,高尔夫,田径
- work boots 工作鞋
- rain boots 雨靴
- fur-lined winter boots 毛皮衬里的冬季靴子
- high-heels 高跟鞋
- platform shoes 女士厚底鞋

Hats 帽子

- baseball caps 棒球帽
- cowboy hats 牛仔帽

- straw hats 草帽
- berets 贝雷帽
- fur hats 毛皮帽
- hard hats（safety hats）安全帽
- motorcycle helmets 摩托车头盔

Other 其他
- baby clothes 婴儿服
- underwear 内衣
- pyjamas（U.S. ＝ pajamas）睡衣裤
- a dressing gown 晨衣,浴衣
- a raincoat 雨衣

7. **Electrical and Electronic Appliances** 电器和电子仪器

Home Appliances 家用电器
- refrigerator 冰箱
- microwave oven 微波炉
- electric stove 电炉
- rice cooker 电饭煲
- blender/food mixer 食物搅拌器
- washing machine 洗衣机
- clothes dryer 干衣机
- air conditioner 空调
- electric heater（radiator）电暖气
- humidifier 加湿器
- electric fan 电扇
- kitchen exhaust fan（above the stove）厨房抽油烟机（在炉子上方）
- vacuum cleaner 真空吸尘器
- electric shaver 电动剃须刀
- electric toothbrush 电动牙刷
- hairdryer 吹风机
- reading lamp 台灯,阅读灯
- electric drill 电钻

Computer Appliances 计算机设备
- computer（including laptop computer ＝ notebook computer）计算机（包括笔记本电脑）
- monitor 显示器
- scanner 扫描仪
- printer 打印机

Office 办公室

- fax machine 传真机
- photocopy machine (photocopier) 复印机

8. Methods of Storing Memories 存储记忆方法

- photographs (in a photo album) 照片(存储于相册中)
- photographs (stored as digital photos on a computer or an electronic storage device) 照片(以电子相片的形式储存在计算机或电子存储装置中)
- diaries 日记
- videos 视频
- keeping old letters 保留旧的信件
- storing emails 储存电子邮件
- keeping souvenirs and mementos 保留纪念品

9. Things That Some People Collect 人们所收集的东西

- stamps 邮票
- coins 硬币
- sports cards 运动卡
- rocks 岩石
- shells 贝壳
- butterflies/Insects 蝴蝶/昆虫
- antiques 古董
- art (paintings, calligraphy etc.) 艺术(绘画,书法等等)
- comics，magazines，old books 漫画,杂志,旧书
- postcards 明信片
- dolls 娃娃
- models (model cars，model trains，model ships，model planes etc.) 模型(汽车模型、火车模型、船模型、飞机模型等等)
- matchboxes 火柴盒
- cigarette packs 香烟盒
- beer cans 啤酒罐
- telephone cards 电话卡

10. Environmental Problems 环境问题

The Problems 问题

- pollution：air pollution, water pollution (including oceanic pollution)，soil pollution, noise pollution 污染：空气污染、水污染(包括海洋污染)。土壤污染、噪声污染

- global warming 全球变暖
- species loss 物种灭绝
- deforestation 森林采伐
- desertification 沙漠化
- soil salinification 土壤盐化
- ozone depletion in the upper atmosphere 高层大气的臭氧层破坏
- waste disposal 废物处理
- water shortage 水资源短缺

Other Related Vocabulary 其他相关词汇

Pollution 污染

- fertilizer 化肥
- factory waste 工厂废料
- rivers and streams 河流和溪流
- heavy metals 重金属

Global Warming 全球变暖

- melting of the glaciers and the polar icecaps 冰川和极地冰盖的融化
- extremes of weather 极端恶劣的天气
- the El Nino phenomenon 厄尔尼诺现象
- the greenhouse effect 温室效应
- carbon dioxide，sulphur dioxide 二氧化碳,二氧化硫
- man-made causes，possible natural causes 人为原因,可能的自然原因
- fuel 燃料
- fossil fuels 化石燃料(如煤和石油)
- hydrogen 氢
- wind power，solar power，solar cells 风能,太阳能,太阳能电池
- vehicle exhaust 车辆废气
- power station 发电站

Waste Disposal 水处理

- recycling 循环利用

Desertification 沙漠化

- sand storms（dust storms）沙尘暴
- overgrazing 过度放牧
- grasslands 草原
- reforestation 重新造林
- land regeneration 土地再生

<u>Species Loss</u> 物种消失

- habitat loss 栖息地的消失
- ecological balance 生态平衡
- genetic diversity 遗传多样性
- genes; genetic engineering 基因,基因工程

<u>Soil Salinification</u> 土壤盐化

- the water table 地下水位

11. <u>Housework</u> 家务活

- washing the dishes 洗盘子
- sweeping (the floor) 扫地
- mopping (the floor) 拖地
- making the beds 铺床
- preparing meals 做饭
- washing vegetables 洗菜
- cooking 烹饪
- tidying 清洁
- ironing 熨烫
- dusting 打扫
- taking out the garbage 倒垃圾
- doing the laundry (washing clothes) 洗衣服

12. <u>Secondary School</u> 中学

("Secondary School" is rather formal; "high school" is usually used.)

- physics 物理
- chemistry 化学
- geography 地理
- politics 政治
- mathematics [math (U.S.); maths (Br.)] 数学
- P.E. (Physical Education) (This is not normally called a "school subject".) 体育

13. <u>Leisure Time and Relaxing</u> 休闲时间和放松

- to relax (Don't add "myself" or any variation of "self" after this word.) 放松
- to "wind down" 放松
- to "take it easy" 慢慢来,不紧张

- to take a stroll; to take/have a walk 散步
- to meditate 深思，沉思
- holidays（Br.）= vacation（U.S.）假期
- holiday［A "holiday" usually refers to a public holiday, i.e., a day or small number of days when most people take time off work.］假期
- weekend 周末
- go on a trip 旅行
- take a trip 旅行
- to travel 旅行
- to go sightseeing 观光
- a hobby 业余爱好
- an interest 兴趣
- a pastime 消遣，娱乐
- to pass the time（Do not say, "to kill time" except when you are talking about situations when time seems to be moving particularly slowly because you have nothing to do such as waiting for two hours at the train station to catch your train.）消磨时间

14. Rain 雨

- humid 潮湿的
- sticky 湿热的
- uncomfortable 不舒服的
- refreshing 提神的，新鲜宜人的
- cooling 凉快的
- a storm 暴风雨
- a thunderstorm 雷电交加的暴风雨
- thunder 雷声
- lightning 闪电
- a deluge 暴雨
- to pour 倾盆而下
- to "rain cats and dogs"= to rain very heavily 下倾盆大雨
- a flood 洪水
- an underpass 地下通道
- to inundate 淹没
- the rainy season 雨季
- the monsoon season 季风季节
- the tropics 热带地区
- a drought 干旱
- parched 炎热的
- to sprinkle 洒

- a drop 雨滴
- not a drop 一滴也没有
- a dry spell 不下雨,干旱

15. Restaurants and Food 餐厅和食物

- menu 菜单
- hotpot 火锅,土豆炖肉
- seafood 海鲜
- Cantonese style food 粤菜
- Sichuan style food 川菜
- American-style fast food 美式快餐
- pizza 比萨
- vegetarian 素食者
- take-away food（U.S. = food to go）外卖食物
- hot = spicy 辣的
- salty 咸的
- sour 酸的
- sweet 甜的
- a cafe（this is a small restaurant，not a coffee shop such as Starbucks）咖啡馆(特指小餐馆)
- a restaurant 餐厅
- a cafeteria（this is usually a self-serve eating place such as in a school or factory）学校或者工厂的自助餐厅
- a snack bar 小吃店
- instant noodles 方便面

16. Letters 信件

- business letters 商务信函
- personal letters 个人信函
- postcards 明信片
- love letters 情书
- spam 垃圾邮件
- an attachment 附件
- to download 下载
- a computer virus 电脑病毒
- to keep in touch with someone 和某人保持联系
- to hear from someone 收到某人的来信

17. **Daily Routine** 日常生活

- usually(通常)，always(总是)，often(经常)，frequently(常常,频繁地)，sometimes(有时)，rarely(很少地,罕有地)，seldom(很少,不常)，never(从未)
- alert(警惕的,提防的)
- fresh(新鲜的)
- tired(疲劳的)，tiring(累人的,引起疲劳的)
- to take a break（休息一会儿）
- to go online(上网)
- to check my email（查看电子邮件）
- warmed-up(加热了的,热身过了的)
- in the evening(s)(在晚上)
- in the afternoon(s)（在下午）
- in the morning(s)（在早晨）
- in the middle of the night（在半夜）
- during the day（在白天）
- during working hours(在上班时间)

18. **Animals** 动物

Major Biological Classifications of Animals 主要的生物分类动物
- mammals(哺乳动物)
- reptiles(爬行动物)
- amphibians(两栖动物)
- birds(鸟类)
- fish(鱼类)
- insects（昆虫）

Domesticated Animals 驯服的动物
a）Pets 宠物
Dogs 狗
- Pekinese(小狮子狗,叭儿狗)
- Chihuahua（奇瓦瓦狗）
- poodle(狮子狗)
- cocker spaniel(可卡犬)
- chow（中国狗）
- pug（哈巴狗）
- beagle(毕尔格猎犬)
- collie（柯利狗）
- bull-dog(牛头犬)

- bull-terrier(叭喇狗)
- German shepherd(德国牧羊犬)
- Labrador(拉布拉多猎狗)
- golden retriever(金毛猎犬)

young dog ＝ a puppy(小狗)

Cats 猫
- long-haired cats（长毛猫）
- short-haired cats（短毛猫）
- Siamese cats(暹罗猫)
- Burmese cats（缅甸猫）
- tabby cats(虎斑猫)
- alley cats(流浪猫)(feral cats 野猫，street cats 流浪猫)
- a tom cat（雄猫）

young cat ＝ a kitten(小猫)

Birds 鸟
- the Asian mynah bird（亚洲八哥鸟）
- the canary（金丝雀）
- the budgie (＝ the parakeet ＝ the budgerigar)(相思鹦鹉)
- the parrot（鹦鹉）
- the finch(雀类)
- the pigeon(鸽子)

bird food：birdseed(鸟饵)

Fish 鱼
- goldfish(金鱼)
- tropical fish（热带鱼）

Other Pets 其他宠物
- Rabbits(兔子)
- guinea pigs（豚鼠）
- hamsters（仓鼠）
- gerbils(沙鼠)
- rats（田鼠）
- ferrets（雪貂）
- tortoises（龟）

b) Farmed animals 养殖动物
- chickens(鸡)
- ducks(鸭)
- geese(鹅)
- pigs（= hogs)(猪)
- sheep(羊)
- beef cattle(肉牛)
- dairy cows（奶牛）
- goats（山羊）

c) Work Animals 役畜
- water buffalo（水牛）
- horses(马)
- donkeys(驴子)
- mules(骡子)
- camels（骆驼）
- elephants(大象)
- yaks（牦牛）
- goats(山羊)
- dogs(狗)

Wild Animals 野生动物
a) Endangered Animals of China 中国濒危动物
- the panda(熊猫)
- the tiger(老虎)
- the black bear(黑熊)
- the wolf(狼)
- the Mongolian wild horse(蒙古野马)
- the elephant(大象)

b) Other Wild Animals in China 中国其他野生动物
- rats and mice（老鼠）
- snakes（蛇）
- yaks(牦牛)
- foxes（狐狸）
- deer（鹿）
- wild horses（野马）
- monkeys(猴子)

c) <u>Wild Animals in the Cities of China</u>(中国的城市野生动物)

The following wild animals are seen in some parts of some cities.

- squirrels(松鼠)
- ferrets(雪貂)
- rats and mice (老鼠)
- possums (负鼠)
- bats(蝙蝠)
- birds (sparrows 麻雀,magpies 鹊,seagulls 海鸥,swallows 燕子 crows/ravens 乌鸦)
- feral cats(野猫)

19. **Parks** 公园

- the entrance(入口)
- an entrance fee(入场费)
- a statue(雕像)
- sculptures(雕塑品)
- a fountain(喷泉)
- a pool(水池)
- a lake(湖)
- a pond(池塘)
- a river(河)
- a bridge(桥)
- a rockery(假山)
- a bamboo grove(竹林)
- a fish pond(鱼塘)
- lawns(草坪)
- gardens(花园)
- flowers(花)
- trees(树)
- vines(攀爬植物,藤,蔓)
- bamboo (竹子)
- a park bench = a park seat(公园的长椅)
- in the shade(荫凉处)
- in the sun(阳光下)
- a pathway = a path(小路)
- to stroll(漫步)
- to walk(散步)
- to jog (慢跑)
- to do exercises(做运动)

- to do stretching exercises(做伸展运动)
- to do aerobics(做有氧运动)
- to do tai ji ＝ to practice tai ji(练太极)
- to chat(聊天)
- to dance(跳舞)
- to play a musical instrument(玩乐器)
- to perform(表演)
- to sing(唱歌)
- to play chess(下象棋)

20. Describing People 描述人

The adjectives below could be used in the following sentence:"She's very _____." Or, "She's a very _____ person." Or, "She's a very _____ type of person." Of course, instead of "*very*" you can also use other words such as:"*quite*"(十分,完全), "*rather*"(相当), "*somewhat*"(稍微,有点) and "*extremely*".(极端地,非常地)

- friendly(友好的)
- easy-going(随和的)
- relaxed(不拘束的)
- mellow(老练的)
- open(坦率的,开放的)
- natural(自然的)
- warm-hearted (热心的)
- generous(慷慨的,大方的)
- humourous (富有幽默感的)
- funny(有趣的,好笑的)
- interesting(有趣味的)
- unique(唯一的,独特的)
- special(特殊的)
- impressive(给人印象深刻的)
- kind(和蔼的,仁慈的)
- honest (诚实的,正直的)
- considerate (考虑周到的)
- selfless 无私的(the opposite is, "selfish"自私的)
- down-to-earth (实际的)
- extroverted (外向的)
- outgoing(外向的)
- gregarious(爱社交的)
- sociable (好交际的)

- spontaneous(自发的,自然产生的)
- introverted 内向的,含蓄的（This means, "usually focused on one's own thoughts", such as a research scientist or an author.）
- shy 害羞的(This means, "a little fearful" of other people)
- traditional(传统的)
- conservative(保守的,守旧的)
- old-fashioned(过时的)
- fashionable(时髦的,流行的)
- fashion-conscious（赶时髦的）
- stylish(时髦的,漂亮的)
- well-groomed(穿着考究的)
- well-dressed(穿着考究的)
- attractive(吸引人的,有魅力的)
- good-looking(漂亮的)
- handsome(英俊的)
- beautiful(美丽的)
- pretty(可爱的,漂亮的)
- elegant(端庄的,文雅的)
- graceful(优美的)
- gentle(温和的,文雅的)
- statuesque 雕像般的,轮廓清晰的,体态优美的(usually for tall women)
- well-mannered(有礼貌的)
- cultured(有教养的,有修养的)
- sophisticated(世故的,老练的)
- open-minded（思想开明的）
- confident（自信的）
- competitive(爱竞争的)
- fearless(大胆的,无畏的,勇敢的)
- independent(独立的)
- adventurous(喜欢冒险的,敢作敢为的)
- persistent（坚持不懈的）
- industrious ＝ hard-working(勤勉的,刻苦的)
- motivated（有积极性的）
- single-minded(专一的,坚定的)
- goal-oriented(目标明确的)
- determined(坚决的)
- ambitious(野心勃勃的)
- strong-willed(意志坚强的)
- passionate(充满热情的)
- enthusiastic(充满热情的)

- positive（积极的）
- healthy（健康的）
- fit（＝ healthy）（健康的）
- health-conscious（重视健康的，注意健康的）
- athletic（运动的）
- talented（有才能的）
- intelligent（聪明的，伶俐的）
- bright（聪明的，伶俐的）
- analytical（善于分析的）
- erudite ＝ well-read（usually for older people）博学的
- well-educated（受过良好教育的）
- skilled（熟练的，有技能的）
- professional（专业的）
- careful（小心的，仔细的）
- neat（整洁的，灵巧的）
- precise（精确的，准确的）
- meticulous（小心翼翼的）
- reliable（可靠的，可信赖的）
- punctual（准时的，守时的）
- knowledgeable（知识渊博的，有见识的）
- curious（好奇的）
- far-sighted（有远见的）
- insightful（富有洞察力的）
- wise（明智的，睿智的）
- mature（成熟的）
- responsible（有责任感的）
- intuitive（有直觉力的）
- imaginative（有想象力的）
- creative（创造性的）
- playful 顽皮的（usually children）
- energetic（精力充沛的）
- adorable（可爱的）
- cute（可爱的）
- loveable（可爱的，惹人爱的）
- lovely（可爱的）

21. The Sections of a Newspaper 报纸的各个版块

The following are the main sections that typical newspapers have.

- The Local News Section(当地新闻版)
- The International News Section(国际新闻版)
- The Editorial Section(社论版)
- Letters to the Editor(写给编辑的信)
- The Business Section(经济版)
- The Entertainment Section(娱乐版)
- The Sports Section(体育版)
- The Classified Advertisements Section(分类广告区)
- The Comics (Comic Strips)(漫画区,连环漫画)

22. Types of Magazines 杂志类型

There are magazines for almost every topic of interest，whether a sport，hobby，general interest or a career interest.

杂志的主题包括了几乎所有的兴趣类型,不论是体育、业余爱好、大众化兴趣或是与职业有关的兴趣。

- **sports** magazines (e.g. basketball，football，golf magazines)体育杂志(如篮球、足球、高尔夫杂志)
- **tabloid** magazines (Sensationalized and often exaggerated or untrue articles and gossip about celebrities. This magazine genre also includes magazines with unusual or sensationalized human-interest stories.)八卦杂志(常常被炒作和夸大,或是虚假的关于名人的文章和小道消息。一些包含不寻常的、炒作的及能引起读者共鸣或同情的报道的杂志也属于这一类型。)
- **movie** magazines (Stories and reviews about the latest films)电影杂志(关于最新电影的影评和故事)
- **music and entertainment** magazines（Articles about pop music and movies and entertainment celebrities)音乐娱乐杂志(关于流行音乐、电影和娱乐明星的文章)
- **news and current events** magazines (News，news analysis and opinion pieces)时事新闻杂志(新闻,新闻分析和评论)
- **women's** magazines（Topics of general interest to women，including parenting，family，home，health，beauty and fashion，career and relationship advice，and short stories.)女性杂志(女性感兴趣的话题,包括养育子女、家庭、住宅、健康、美容时尚、对职业生涯和人际关系的建议,以及短篇故事)
- **beauty and fashion** magazines (e.g. Vogue. Articles and many photographs on fashion and beauty for women)美容时尚杂志(如 Vogue 杂志,其中有许多关于女性时尚及美容的文章和图片)
- **teen** magazines（Usually for teenage girls-general interest magazines for teenagers with topics such as romantic short stories，romance advice，fashion and beauty

advice，entertainment etc.）青少年杂志（对象一般为少女，包括青少年感兴趣的话题，如浪漫短篇小说、情感建议、美容时尚建议及娱乐等）

- **men's** magazines（Short stories and articles of interest to（usually）young men，including pictures of pretty girls）男性杂志（一般为年轻男士感兴趣的短篇小说和文章，也包括漂亮女孩的图片）
- **home and gardening** magazines（Articles about buying a home，home decoration，home maintenance，gardening etc.）家居园艺杂志（关于购房、家居装潢、家居保养、园艺等的一些文章）
- **car** magazines 汽车杂志
- **military** magazines（Articles and stories about military history，military equipment and weaponry）军事杂志（关于军事历史、军事装备和武器的文章及故事）
- **hobbyist** magazines（e.g. stamp collecting，antiques，photography，different arts and crafts，pets，different games）爱好者杂志（如集邮、古董、摄影、各种工艺美术、宠物，及各种游戏杂志）
- **computer** magazines（Articles about new developments and products in the world of computers）计算机杂志（关于计算机界的最新发展和产品的文章）
- **computer game** magazines 电脑游戏杂志
- **business and money** magazines（Articles about personal money management，investing，the stock market etc.）商务理财杂志（有关个人理财、投资及股票市场等）
- **puzzle** magazines（With puzzles to solve）益智杂志（解谜）
- **humor** magazines（Jokes，funny cartoons，and humorous short stories）幽默杂志（笑话、趣味卡通以及一些诙谐的短篇故事）
- **travel** magazines（Articles about interesting places to visit）旅游杂志（包含令人感兴趣的旅游景点）
- **science and nature** magazines（e.g.，National Geographic）《科学》与《自然》杂志（如《国家地理》杂志）
- **health and fitness** magazines 健康杂志
- **popular psychology** magazines（Self-help articles and articles on "pop psychology" topics）大众心理学杂志（关于励志和现代心理学主题的文章）
- **literary** magazines（Short stories，poetry，reviews of new books，etc.）文学杂志（短篇小说、诗歌、最新书评等）
- **short story** magazines（Various short stories to read. Different genres exist，e.g.，mystery stories，romance stories，crime stories，science fiction stories）短篇故事杂志（包含各种各样的短篇故事。包括了不同的文学流派，如怪诞小说、爱情小说、犯罪小说、科幻小说等）
- **political** magazines（Usually political analysis and opinion rather than objective political news）政治杂志（通常包含政治分析和主张，而不是客观的政治新闻）
- **scholarly** magazines（Specialized magazines for academics in different subjects）学术杂志（关于不同学术科目的专业杂志）

23. Law 法律

- to commit a crime ＝ to break the law(犯罪,违法)
- to disregard the law，to violate the law(藐视法律,犯法)
- to obey the law ＝ to abide by the law(遵守法律)
- a law-abiding citizen(奉公守法的市民)
- a crime ＝ an infraction of the law ＝ an offence(犯罪,违反法律)
- violent crime(暴力犯罪)
- economic crime(经济犯罪)
- a crime of passion(情杀罪,冲动犯罪)
- criminal negligence(过失犯罪)
- a criminal ＝ a law breaker(罪犯,犯法的人)
- a juvenile delinquent(少年犯)
- be required by the law(依法的,法定的)
- against the law ＝ illegal(违法的)
- within the law ＝ legal，lawful(合法的,法律许可的)
- to "be above the law"(凌驾于法律之上,不受法律限制)
- to "turn to crime"，to "be driven to crime"(走上犯罪道路)
- organized crime(有组织的犯罪,集团犯罪)
- a criminal gang(犯罪集团,犯罪团伙)
- to prohibit(禁止,阻止)
- to ban(禁止,取缔)
- a felony(重罪)
- a misdemeanor(轻罪)
- murder(谋杀)
- manslaughter(杀人,过失杀人罪)
- theft (a thief) 偷窃(小偷)
- robbery (a robber) 抢夺(强盗)
- burglary (a burglar) 夜盗行为(夜贼)
- rape (a rapist) 强奸(强奸犯)
- kidnapping(绑架)
- fraud(欺诈)
- blackmail(勒索)
- bribery(行贿)
- graft(贪污,受贿)
- corruption(腐败,贪污)
- extortion(勒索,敲诈)
- slander(诽谤)
- to defame(诽谤)
- smuggling(走私)

- piracy(盗版)
- forgery(伪造)
- fake，counterfeit(伪造，假冒)
- drug trafficking(毒品走私)
- arson(纵火)
- insurance fraud (保险诈骗)
- bigamy(重婚罪)
- vandalism(故意毁坏文物的行为)
- gambling(赌博)
- a petty crime(轻度犯罪)
- a victim(受害者)
- compensation(补偿，赔偿)
- insider trading(内幕交易)
- prison（Br.）＝ jail（U.S. but also used in Britain and Australia)(监狱)
- punishment ＝ a penalty (处罚，惩罚)
- capital punishment ＝ the death penalty(死刑)
- a sentence，to sentence，to pass sentence(宣判)
- a fine(罚款)
- a criminal record(前科，犯罪记录)
- a regulation，to regulate(规则)
- a harsh law，a harsh sentence(苛刻的法律，重判)
- a lenient sentence，a light sentence(轻判)
- to arrest someone(拘捕某人)
- innocent，guilty(清白的，有罪的)
- the police，the police force(警察部门，警察机关)
- a policeman，a policewoman，a police officer (U.S.)(警察，女警，警官)
- a police station，a police car，a police dog (警察局，警车，警犬)
- traffic police(交警)
- a detective(侦探)
- forensic science (司法科学)
- law enforcement，to enforce the law ＝ to uphold the law(法律实施，执行法律)
- crime prevention(犯罪预防)
- a deterrence(制止，威慑)
- a crackdown on crime(对犯罪进行制裁)
- to combat crime，to fight crime(打击犯罪)
- to prosecute，to defend(起诉，辩护)
- to be convicted of a crime(宣告有罪)
- evidence，proof(证据)
- a witness(证人，目击者)
- a law court ＝ a court of law(法院，法庭)

- a trial(审判)
- a judge(法官)
- a magistrate(地方法官,地方官员)
- a lawyer = an attorney (U.S.), a barrister (Br.), a solicitor (Br.)(律师)
- to practice law(从事法律工作)
- a law firm(律师事务所)
- a law suit, to sue somebody(提出诉讼)
- a license, a business license, a driver's license(执照,营业执照,驾照)
- to enact a law, to institute a law, to adopt a law(制定法律,采用法律)
- to annul a law, to repeal a law(废除法律)

24. Water 水

Water Usage 用水
- domestic uses (= household uses)(生活用水,家庭用水)
- watering public lawns and gardens(灌溉公共草坪和花园)
- taking/having a bath(洗澡)
- taking/having a shower(淋浴)
- cleaning/brushing your (my) teeth(刷牙)
- flushing the toilet(冲厕)
- washing the dishes(洗餐具)
- washing the car(洗车)
- turn off/turn on(关/开)
- a tap (U.S. = a faucet)(水龙头)
- a running tap(流淌着水的龙头)

25. Games 游戏

Adult games 成年人玩的游戏
- chess(国际象棋)
- mahjong(麻将)
- weiqi(围棋)
- card games (e.g. poker)卡片游戏(如扑克)
- billiards, snooker(桌球,斯诺克)
- computer games(电脑游戏)
- drinking games(饮酒游戏)

Children's Games 儿童玩的游戏
- marbles(弹珠)
- "hide and seek"(捉迷藏)

- hopscotch(跳房子游戏)
- "scissors，rock and paper"(剪刀石头布)

26. Playgrounds 游乐场

Basic List(基本列表)
- a swing(秋千)
- a slide ＝ a slippery dip(滑梯)
- a carousel(旋转木马)
- a see-saw(跷跷板)

27. Sports Facilities 体育设施

The information here was written especially to help people answer the questions，*"What sports facilities are there near where you live*?" and，*"What sports facilities are there at your university*?"

- The word "facility" includes the two ideas of *a place* and the *special equipment* in that place，to be used for a certain activity. When speaking of "sports facilities"，you can replace the idea of "equipment" with the idea of "something special about that place". For example，a running track has no "equipment" but it is especially designed，with lines on the ground representing the running lanes.

- For the question，*"What sports facilities are there near where you live*?"，the meaning is facilities that the general public can use. This includes：facilities that people can use free of cost；facilities that people must pay to use；and it also includes such facilities as private sports clubs that you，as a member of the public，can join if you want.

Maybe there's a private school in your community that has a swimming pool and several tennis courts. If you，a non-student at the school，are not allowed to enter and use these facilities（even when you offer to pay），then it is not suitable to include the school's sports facilities as examples of sports facilities near where you live. Of course，you could mention these facts to the examiner and explain how these facilities exist but are not available for the public to use，and that would be suitable for a Part 3 answer but a little unsuitable for Part 1 unless you *firstly* address the question of facilities available to the public. Anyway，in Part 1 you probably won't have time to give such an extended and detailed example.

- What is "sport"? A sport is a physical activity that is done for exercise and amusement （although some sports involve very little exercise and focus more on physical skills. ）

Some sports are done mostly for competition, such as football, basketball, or tennis. This is the main group of activities that people think of when using the word, "sport". These competitive sports have set rules and special areas where the activity is done.

A broader definition of "sport" includes some physical activities that are done purely for recreation, not competition, such as hunting, fishing, or horseback riding. Most of the water sports such as scuba-diving, snorkeling, water skiing, and surfing (surfboard riding) are non-competitive, although water skiing and surfing competitions are held sometimes.

The "extreme sports" are also usually non-competitive. These sports really involve competing against oneself or against nature. Examples of these are: "sky diving", "white water rafting" down a fast-moving river or mountain climbing (rock climbing), such as climbing Mt. Everest.

Some sports don't require much physical exertion but do require physical skills, for example pistol shooting. Similarly, games such as snooker which are games of physical skill rather than physical exertion are usually also classified as "sports".

- Make sure you know the difference between "sport" and simple "exercise". A sport usually involves *physical skills* but exercise is simply the *physical activity* of "moving the body" — walking up the stairs to your 4th-floor apartment is a form of exercise but it's not sport. A "*walking* path" in a public park might be used by a lot of people for exercise, but it is unsuitable to describe that as a, "sports facility".

Sometimes there is a "fine line" (= an unclear dividing line) between what is exercise and what is sport. For example, if you go to the swimming pool three times a week and swim ten laps each time, can you say that you do a sports activity? Personally, I would call it a form of exercise, not a sport. (Certainly you cannot say that is "playing a sport" because you can only "play" a game and swimming, even in competition, is not a "game".) On the other hand, if you hit a ping-pong ball across a ping-pong table with your friend for an hour, without keeping score, then I would say you are *playing a sport*, even though you are not actually playing a formal, competitive game of ping-pong.

However, even though I think swimming laps in a swimming pool is not sport, and even though very few Chinese people swim *as a competitive sport*, it is still suitable to call a swimming pool a "sports facility" because in other parts of the world, a swimming pool is a place that is often used for sporting competitions. For example, in Australia, every public swimming pool has a swimming club where the members hold swimming competitions against each other and against other swimming clubs.

I also would not call "a gymnasium" a sports facility, where "gymnasium" here simply means "an exercise room" with weights and exercise machines. But it's probably ok to use that example in your answer, provided you communicate to the examiner the idea that, "*it's not really a sports facility but more an exercise facility*".

The word，"gymnasium" can also be used to mean "an indoor sports arena" where sporting competitions are held — that certainly is a sports facility.

Below are some common examples of sports facilities that are found in a town/city or school/university. Of course，there are others. And of course，for some of these，using the plural might be more appropriate，for example，"*some basketball courts*" and "*some ping-pong tables*".

Most of these examples are compound nouns. To speak these，the *first word* is spoken with more stress than the second word. "More stress" simply means "a little louder". The stressed part of the compound nouns are shown with heavier print，such as "*table* tennis"，where the word "table" is spoken a little louder than the word，"tennis".

- a swimming pool（游泳池）
- a basketball court（篮球场）
- a badminton court（羽毛球场）
- a tennis court（网球场）
- a squash court（壁球场）
- a volleyball court（排球场）
- a football field（足球场）
- a baseball field（棒球场）
- a hockey field（曲棍球场）
- an athletics field（田径场）
- a running track（跑道）
- a cycling track（自行车道）
- a golf course（高尔夫球场）
- a golf driving range（高尔夫球练习场）
- an archery range（射箭场）
- a shooting range（射击场）
- a shooting gallery（射击场）
- a gymnasium（ = a room for exercising，weightlifting，etc. This item is suitable if you add the fact that it's really an exercise facility rather than a sports facility.）（健身房）
- a bowling alley（for ten-pin bowling）（保龄球馆）
- an ice-skating rink / a roller-skating rink / a skating rink（溜冰场）
- a ski slope / a ski run / a ski resort（滑雪场）
- ping-pong tables（ = table tennis tables）（乒乓球台）
- a skateboarding park（滑板公园）
- a mountain bike track = a mountain bike competition ground（山地自行车赛道）

Exercise Facilities

The following examples are <u>not</u> suitable to use if the question is，"What *sports* facilities are there near where you live?" As noted above，"exercise" and "sport" are not exactly the same in meaning. However, it is possible to include these examples in your answer to that question, if you communicate to the examiner that you know the difference between "exercise facilities" and "sports facilities" and you are giving an extended answer to the question. This is especially true if either of the two questions about sports facilities are used in Part 3. You are unlikely to have enough time in Part 1 for such an extended answer.

"*exercise* machines in an exercise area"(= "*exercise* equipment" in public parks or public exercise areas)(运动机械)

a gymnasium / an *exercise* room(健身房)

a *walking* path in a public park(公园里的散步道路)

a *jogging* track(慢跑道路)

a *yoga* class (Yoga is classified as a form of exercise or a form of physical training rather than "a sport".)(瑜伽课)

an *aerobics* class (or, an *aerobics* group)(有氧健身课程)

a "jazz *dancing*" class or group (which some women join as a form of exercise)(爵士舞课程)

a *hiking* club; a mountain *trail* for hiking(徒步健身俱乐部)

28. Time Management 时间管理

- punctual(准时的,守时的)
- punctuality(准时,守时)
- to plan ahead(提前计划)
- on time(准时的)
- on schedule(准时的)
- a deadline(最后期限)
- a "rush job"("紧急的工作")
- at short notice(临时通知)
- to be behind time(延迟,迟到)
- to delay(延迟)
- to put off doing something (延迟做某事)
- to leave something till the last moment(拖到最后一分钟才做)
- to procrastinate(拖延)
- to postpone(推迟,延迟)
- overdue(超时,过期)
- the due time(交货时间)
- the due date(交货日期)
- prompt(快速的,迅速的)
- to fall behind(落后)
- to be behind(落后)

- to rush(赶快)
- to hurry(赶快)
- urgent(紧急的)
- to cram (for an exam)(仓促备考)
- to be pressed for time(赶工)
- a crash study program(速成的学习项目)
- a timetable(时间表)
- a schedule(时间表)
- to fritter away one's time(浪费某人的时间)
- a short-term goal(短期目标)
- a long-term goal(长期目标)
- goal-setting(目标制定)
- a priority(优先权)
- high priority(高优先级)
- low priority(低优先级)
- efficient，inefficient(有效率的,无效率的)
- flexible（灵活的）

29. Bags 包

- a handbag (The bag that most women carry)（女士用的手提包）
- a purse（Usually a purse is a small bag that a woman uses to hold her money and she keeps it in her handbag when she is carrying her handbag. But sometimes，especially in American English，"a purse" is used to mean "a handbag".）（女士钱包）
- a shoulder bag(单肩包)
- a backpack（A "rucksack" and a "haversack" are words for a bigger type of backpack that people use when they are hiking and camping，although we also can call those bigger bags "backpacks".）（双肩包）
- a book bag（A book bag can be a shoulder bag or a small backpack that school children use.）（书包）
- a briefcase（Carried by businesspeople and also by some older students.）（公文包）
- a laptop computer bag（Some people use this to carry things other than their laptop computer. Or some people always carry this with them wherever they go because they take their laptop computer with them everywhere. It can hold a few extra small things besides the laptop computer.）（笔记本电脑包）
- a shopping bag（A bag that is usually carried by a woman，especially an older woman，when she goes shopping.）（女士的购物包）

附录：雅思口语真题题库话题分类总结

Part 1 真题题库话题分类

个人信息类

1. name & info
2. home
3. hometown
4. house or flat/apartment
5. first day (study & work)
6. major
7. job & university choice
8. place where you live
9. the area you live in
10. studies and education
11. schools
12. high school
13. science class

日常生活类

14. shopping
15. clothes
16. shoes
17. bags
18. hats
19. sunglasses
20. advertisements
21. birthday
22. cooking
23. city & countryside

24. flowers

25. chocolate

26. ice cream

27. fast food

28. nearby shops

29. neighbors

30. colors

31. emails & letters

32. handwriting

33. housework

34. mobile phones

35. Applications（Apps）

36. newspaper

37. magazines

38. online social networking

39. outdoor activities

40. parks and gardens

41. sleeping

42. snacks

43. sports

44. water sports

45. street markets

46. sunny days

47. sunshine

48. rainy days

49. weekends

50. week

51. weather & season

52. primary schools

53. mirrors

54. jewelry

55. daily routine

56. feeling tired

57. makeup

58. tea or coffee

59. cakes

60. garbage

61. perfume

62. jeans

63. T-shirts

64. hairstyle

65. haircut

66. visiting relatives

67. making lists

68. furniture

69. text messages

70. recycling

71. staying up late

72. special costumes

73. barbecue

74. fixing things

75. keys

76. happy things

77. library

78. social media

79. meeting places

80. cinemas

81. websites

82. lost and found

83. bargaining

84. drinking water

85. decoration

86. new year

87. pen or pencil

兴趣爱好类

88. collecting things

89. dancing

90. music

91. movies

92. computers

93. reading

94. painting（art）

95. handwork

96. museums

97. photos

98. relaxation

99. singing

100. swimming

101. morning & evening study

102. take a break
103. TV
104. video games
105. outside activities
106. amusement parks
107. movie stars
108. telling jokes
109. fishing
110. picnic
111. puzzles
112. farm
113. number
114. walking
115. running
116. bikes(cycling)
117. health

旅游交通类
118. bus & taxi
119. bicycles
120. camping
121. holidays
122. public holidays
123. public transportation
124. traveling by car
125. train
126. boat
127. space travel
128. island
129. forest
130. crowded places
131. getting lost
132. seats preference in a car
133. day off
134. old buildings
135. islands

动植物类
136. animals/pets
137. while animals

138. fruits and vegetables

139. trees

140. plants

141. insects

142. zoos

心理及行为类

143. being alone

144. being polite

145. being punctual

146. being bored

147. concentration

148. helping others

149. being in a hurry

150. time management

151. remember things

152. trust

153. smile

154. discussion

155. sharing things

156. borrowing things

157. being patient

158. being tidy

159. boring things

160. memory

161. laughing

人物类

162. celebrities（famous people）

163. friends

164. teachers

165. teenagers

166. pop stars

物品类

167. children's books

168. dictionaries

169. gifts

170. maps

171. toys

172. watches
173. wallets/purses
174. headphones

抽象类

175. history
176. math
177. nature
178. noise
179. science
180. sky and stars
181. outer space and stars
182. teamwork
183. water
184. age
185. changes
186. window view
187. protecting environment
188. dream and ambition
189. small businesses
190. geography
191. talents
192. environmental protection
193. languages

Part 2 & 3 真题题库话题分类

人物类

1. Describe a child who makes you laugh
2. Describe a comic actor (or cartoon character) who is popular in your country
3. Describe a popular comic actor or actress in your country
4. Describe a creative person you admire
5. Describe a creative person whose work you admire
6. Describe a famous foreign person who you would like to meet
7. Describe a famous person you knew from news
8. Describe a famous person you are interested in
9. Describe a foreign person who you have heard or known that you think is interesting
10. Describe a famous sports star or singer you like
11. Describe a popular/well-known person in your country

12. Describe a friend who always travels by air

13. Describe a person who often travels by plane

14. Describe a friend who is a good leader

15. Describe a person who is a good leader

16. Describe a friend you haven't been in contact with for a long time but you would like to see again

17. Describe a leader you admire

18. Describe a neighbor you helped

19. Describe a person who apologized to you

20. Describe a person who does well in work

21. Describe a person who dresses well

22. Describe a person who is beautiful or handsome

23. Describe a person who is fashionable in clothes

24. Describe a person who is fashionable

25. Describe a person who is good at a foreign language

26. Describe a person who is good at cooking

27. Describe a person who just moved home

28. Describe a person you do not like but have to be friendly to

29. Describe a person you knew and wanted to be similar to when you were a teenager

30. Describe a person you know who has a useful job to society

31. Describe a person you know who has an important job

32. Describe a person you met recently and would like to know more about

33. Describe a person you were surprised to meet

34. Describe a singer or band you like

35. Describe a singer you like

36. Describe an intelligent person you know

37. Describe an old person you respect who is important to you

38. Describe an interesting old person you have met

39. Describe one of your best friends

40. Describe a friend you like to talk with

41. Describe someone who has an interesting job

42. Describe your best friend at school

43. Describe two people you know from the same family

44. Describe a polite person you met

45. Describe a couple you know who have a happy marriage

46. Describe someone who is a good parent

47. Describe a businessman you admire

48. Describe a person who gave a clever solution to a problem

49. Describe an interesting person from another country

50. Describe a popular person you know

51. Describe a childhood friend of yours
52. Describe a famous athlete
53. Describe a person you know who likes to talk a lot
54. Describe a talkative person
55. Describe a visitor to you home
56. Describe a person who does something to help protect the environment
57. Describe a teenager you know
58. Describe an interesting person you would like to meet
59. Describe a female leader you would like to meet
60. Describe an interesting neighbor
61. Describe an energetic person that you know
62. Describe a person you are happy to know
63. Describe a person who you have lived with before
64. Describe a person you want to be familiar with
65. Describe a foreign celebrity you want to meet in person
66. Describe someone you like to visit but you don't want to live with
67. Describe a person who wears unusual clothes
68. Describe someone you know who often helps others
69. Describe someone you know who has recently moved to a new place
70. Describe a film character played by an actor or actress you admire
71. Describe a character from a film
72. Describe a person you have met who you want to work/study with
73. Describe a person you met at a party who you enjoyed talking with
74. Describe a person you know who loves to grow plants (e. g. vegetables, fruits, flowers etc.)
75. Describe a person who inspired you to do something interesting
76. Describe a person you know who is from a different culture
77. Describe a person who you follow on social media
78. Describe a person whose work is useful to the society
79. Describe a person you only met once and want to know more about
80. Describe someone you really like to spend time with
81. Describe an old friend that you got in contact again

地点类
82. Describe a beautiful place where you want to have a home
83. Describe a city you visited
84. Describe a beautiful city you visited
85. Describe a country you would like to visit for the first time
86. Describe a foreign country you would like to visit
87. Describe a foreign country you would like to work in for a short period of time

88. Describe a foreign country you would like to know more about

89. Describe a historic building that you have visited

90. Describe a historical place you went to

91. Describe a part of the city

92. Describe a place far away from home

93. Describe a place for people to relax

94. Describe a place near water

95. Describe a place that was full of colors you remember going to

96. Describe a place where you can read and write (not your home)

97. Describe a place you visited that has been affected by pollution

98. Describe a place you visited to learn about its culture

99. Describe a school you studied in when you were a child

100. Describe a seaside place you like

101. Describe a stadium in your city

102. Describe a street that you know well

103. Describe a tall building you like or dislike

104. Describe a tall building in your city you like or dislike

105. Describe an important building in your city

106. Describe an interesting public place that you like

107. Describe an unusual building in your country

108. Describe your favorite park or garden

109. Describe a shop recently opened in your hometown

110. Describe a quiet place you visited

111. Describe a quiet place you like to go

112. Describe a quiet place you like to spend your time in

113. Describe a café you like to visit

114. Describe a café you have been to

115. Describe a popular place where people go swimming

116. Describe a place you know where people go to listen to music (such as a theater or a music hall)

117. Describe an interesting place that few people know

118. Describe a city or a country you want to live or work in the future

119. Describe a public place that you think needs improvement

120. Describe an important river, a lake, or an area of water in your country/in your hometown

121. Describe a leisure facility (cinema, theater, or sports center) you would like to have in your hometown

122. Describe a place you often visit with your friends or family

123. Describe a building where you enjoy the time

124. Describe a new public building

125. Describe a city you once went to with your family
126. Describe a crowded place you have visited
127. Describe a city where you want to live in the future
128. Describe a city that you think is interesting
129. Describe a street market or an outdoor market you've been to
130. Describe a place you have been to where there were lots of people
131. Describe a place you plan to travel to that is far away from your home in the future
132. Describe a new shop that has recently opened in your city/town
133. Describe a place you visited where the air was polluted
134. Describe your favorite place in your house where you can relax
135. Describe a noisy place you have been to
136. Describe another city you would like to stay for a short time
137. Describe a place in your country that you would like to recommend to visitors/travelers
138. Describe the home of someone you know well and that you often visit
139. Describe a place in a village that you visited
140. Describe a person who impressed you most when you were in primary school
141. Describe a place you visited on vacation

物品类
142. Describe a book you recently read that you would like to read again
143. Describe an exciting book you read recently
144. Describe an exciting book that you enjoy reading
145. Describe a book that you have read many times
146. Describe a magazine you like to read
147. Describe a gift that took you a long time to choose
148. Describe a gift that took you a lot of time to prepare
149. Describe a gift you made by hand for your friend
150. Describe a gift you gave someone recently
151. Describe a gift you would like to buy for your friend
152. Describe a thing you took with you when you went traveling
153. Describe a machine or electronic device you would like to buy
154. Describe a painting or a work of art in your school
155. Describe a painting or a work of art
156. Describe a photo of yourself you like
157. Describe a photograph you took that you like
158. Describe a photo you took that you are proud of
159. Describe a piece of broken equipment
160. Describe something that was broken in your home and then repaired
161. Describe a piece of clothing that someone gave to you
162. Describe a piece of clothing you enjoy wearing

163. Describe an item of clothing that someone gave you

164. Describe a piece of equipment which you found hard to use for the first time

165. Describe a piece of equipment you use at home

166. Describe a piece of equipment you want to have in the future

167. Describe a product you bought that made you happy

168. Describe a toy you played with in your childhood

169. Describe an important letter that you received

170. Describe an old object that your family has kept for a long time

171. Describe something special that you saved money to buy

172. Describe something special you brought home from a holiday

173. Describe something useful you borrowed from others

174. Describe something you bought but did not use for a long time

175. Describe something you shared with other people

176. Describe something you had to share with others

177. Describe something you want to buy in the future

178. Describe your first mobile phone (cell phone)

179. Describe your favorite piece of clothing

180. Describe an important plant in your country (such as fruits, flowers, or vegetables) that you like

181. Describe an impressive work of art (such as painting or sculpture) you saw

182. Describe a piece of furniture in your home

183. Describe a traditional product in your country

184. Describe something you bought recently that made you feel happy

185. Describe a thing you own that you want to replace

186. Describe something important that you lost

187. Describe something lost by others but found by you

188. Describe a product or application which is based on artificial intelligence

189. Describe an important technological product you bought

190. Describe a souvenir you bought

191. Describe a picture/photograph in your home

192. Describe a uniform (in a school or company) you wear

193. Describe a handicraft you made

194. Describe a piece of equipment that is important in your home

195. Describe an expensive gift that you would like to give someone when you save a lot of money

196. Describe an object that you think is beautiful

197. Describe a special cake you received from others

198. Describe something that you can't live without (not a computer or phone)

199. Describe something you received for free

200. Describe an item on which you spent more than expected

201. Describe your favorite curtain
202. Describe a kind of bag you want to own
203. Describe something important that has been kept in your family for a long time

事件类

204. Describe a mistake you once made
205. Describe a positive change that you have made to your life
206. Describe a positive experience in your teenage time or childhood
207. Describe a change that will improve your local area
208. Describe a way/change that helps you save a lot of time
209. Describe a project or assignment you did
210. Describe a public activity that keeps you healthy
211. Describe an expensive activity that you enjoy doing occasionally
212. Describe a recent happy event
213. Describe a situation that made you angry
214. Describe a time when you borrowed something from others
215. Describe a time when you decided to wait for someone
216. Describe a time when you decided to wait for something
217. Describe a time when you experienced a traffic jam
218. Describe a time when you were stuck in a traffic jam
219. Describe a sports event that you took part in or watched
220. Describe a time when you planned for a happy event
221. Describe a time when you organized a happy event successfully
222. Describe a time when you watched the sky
223. Describe a time when you were friendly to someone who you disliked
224. Describe a success in your life
225. Describe a surprise that made you happy
226. Describe a team project that you worked on
227. Describe a thing which your friend did and made you proud of him/her
228. Describe something you did that made you feel proud
229. Describe a thing you enjoy doing with the elderly people at home
230. Describe a time when you helped others
231. Describe a time when someone took a photo of you
232. Describe a time when the weather changed your plan
233. Describe a time when you and your friend had a disagreement
234. Describe a time when you felt surprised to meet someone
235. Describe a time when you got up early in the morning
236. Describe a time when you missed an appointment
237. Describe a time when you needed to use imagination
238. Describe a time when you saw an interesting animal

239. Describe a time when you were away from home

240. Describe a time when you were very busy

241. Describe a time when you helped a stranger

242. Describe a time when you lost your way

243. Describe a wedding you attended

244. Describe an age or stage which was enjoyable in your life

245. Describe an art or craft activity you did when you were at school

246. Describe an indoor game you played in your childhood

247. Describe a game (not a sport) you enjoyed when you were a child

248. Describe the game you enjoyed playing when you were younger

249. Describe a computer/ phone game you have enjoyed playing since your childhood

250. Describe an activity you enjoyed in your free time when you were young

251. Describe an outdoor activity you did in a new place recently

252. Describe an activity that you do after school/work

253. Describe a time when someone did not tell you the truth

254. Describe a time when you ate a kind of food for the first time

255. Describe a time when you told a lie

256. Describe a time when someone or something made noise

257. Describe a time when you met your old friend

258. Describe one thing your friend did successfully

259. Describe something important to keep you healthy and fit

260. Describe something you do to keep fit and healthy

261. Describe something you did which was a waste of time

262. Describe something you once forgot to do

263. Describe the first time when you used a foreign language to communicate

264. Describe what you would do if you were given a day off work or college

265. Describe a plan you have for the future (but not related to work or study)

266. Describe a holiday you would like to have in the future

267. Describe an interesting or unusual thing you did recently in your free time

268. Describe a time when you disagreed with a decision that others made

269. Describe a time when a home appliance broke down or stopped working

270. Describe an important event in the history of your country

271. Describe a time when you waited for something special

272. Describe an enjoyable experience you had in the countryside

273. Describe a time when you were not allowed to use your mobile phone

274. Describe a time when something made you laugh

275. Describe something you did with a group of people

276. Describe a time when you moved to a new home or school

277. Describe a time when you went to a crowded place

278. Describe an important change that happened to your life recently

279. Describe a time when you arrived at a place early
280. Describe a leisure activity on or near sea you want to try
281. Describe a leisure activity on/near the sea
282. Describe a time when you had a conversation with a stranger
283. Describe a time when you saw lots of people smiling
284. Describe a time when you taught a friend or a relative
285. Describe a time when other people gave positive comments on what you did
286. Describe a time when you had to be polite
287. Describe a time when you wore a type of clothes on a special occasion
288. Describe a time when you helped someone
289. Describe a special day when you went out but it didn't cost you much
290. Describe a special day that made you happy
291. Describe important event that you celebrated with others
292. Describe a time when you saved money for something
293. Describe the time when you received your first cellphone
294. Describe a time when you changed your plan
295. Describe something interesting that your friend has done but you haven't
296. Describe something you do to keep you concentrated
297. Describe a time when you made a complaint and were satisfied with the result
298. Describe a time when you looked for information on the Internet
299. Describe an activity you do when you are alone in your free time
300. Describe a time when someone gave you money as a gift
301. Describe a time when you taught an old person something new
302. Describe a time when you taught something new to a younger person
303. Describe a time when you had to dress up (wear your best clothes)
304. Describe a time when you decided not to tell the truth to your friend
305. Describe a time when you did not tell a friend the truth
306. Describe a time when you had to keep awake but you were really tired
307. Describe a time when you visited a friend
308. Describe a time when you wasted your time
309. Describe an activity you usually do that wastes your time
310. Describe a time when you saw children behave badly in public
311. Describe an event you experienced in which you did not like the music played
312. Describe a time when you got bored when you were with others
313. Describe a volunteer experience you have had
314. Describe a time when a family member asked you for help
315. Describe a time when someone visited you
316. Describe an unusual experience of traveling
317. Describe a time when you heard a stranger talking on the phone in the public place
318. Describe a time when you spent a lot of money on something

319. Describe a time when you got incorrect information

320. Describe a time when the vehicle you took broke down in your travel

321. Describe a time you enjoyed a day off from work or school

322. Describe a time when you played an indoor game with others

323. Describe a time when you were sleepy but had to stay awake

324. Describe a time when you had to change your plan

325. Describe a time when you met someone for the first time

326. Describe a time when an important flight was delayed

327. Describe a time when you lost something and then got it back

328. Describe an occasion that you lost something

329. Describe a time when you had to take medicine

330. Describe a time when you were scared by someone

331. Describe something interesting that happened when you were in high school

332. Describe something you find interesting on social media

333. Describe a time when you shared something with other people

334. Describe an occasion when you spent (quite some) time with a young child

335. Describe an occasion when you got incorrect information

336. Describe a time when someone gave you something that you really wanted

337. Describe a time when you missed or were late for an important meeting/event

338. Describe a time when you taught a friend/relative something

339. Describe a happy experience from your childhood that you remember

340. Describe a talk you gave to a group of people

341. Describe an exciting adventure you would like to take in the future

342. Describe something that you did with someone/a group of people

343. Describe a daily routine that you enjoy

344. Describe a time when you overcame difficulties in doing something and succeeded

345. Describe a time when you saw a lot of plastic waste (e.g. in a park，on the beach etc.)

346. Describe a time when you needed to search for information

347. Describe a time you used your smartphone/cellphone to do something important

348. Describe an occasion when someone gave you positive advice or suggestions about your work/study

349. Describe a time when you helped a child

350. Describe something that surprised you

351. Describe a time you visited a new place

352. Describe a time you saw something interesting on social media

353. Describe a time when you visited a farm

354. Describe a time when you ate something for the first time

355. Describe your experience at a gym

356. Describe a time when your computer had a problem

357. Describe a time when you made a promise to someone

358. Describe the time when you talked in a foreign language for the first time

359. Describe a time when you received good news

360. Describe an occasion when you forgot something important

361. Describe a time when someone helped you

商业类

362. Describe a big company you are interested in

363. Describe a café (or restaurant) that you know in your hometown

364. Describe a small business that you think is successful

365. Describe a small business you would like to own

366. Describe a successful family business you know

367. Describe an advertisement you like

368. Describe an advertisement you remember well

369. Describe an advertisement you don't like

370. Describe a company that employs a lot of people

工作学习类

371. Describe a course you have attended

372. Describe a well-paid job you would like to do in the future

373. Describe an interesting job that you want to have in the future

374. Describe an important job in your country

375. Describe a job you would not like to do in the future

376. Describe a perfect job for you

377. Describe a new skill you would like to learn

378. Describe an important skill you learned when you were a child

379. Describe a skill that took you a long time to learn

380. Describe a skill that you can learn from older people

381. Describe a skill that was difficult for you to learn

382. Describe a paid work you would like to do

383. Describe an interesting subject that you studied

384. Describe a subject you attended in university or evening classes

385. Describe a subject you did not enjoy in your high school

386. Describe a subject you did not like but you are interested in now

387. Describe an educational trip you went on

388. Describe an educational TV program you like

389. Describe a TV series or drama you enjoy watching

390. Describe an interesting thing you learned from the Internet

391. Describe another language (not English) that you would like to learn

392. Describe something that you don't know how to do but would like to learn

393. Describe something you want to learn but cannot do now

394. Describe an area of science you studied that you are interested in, such as medicine, physics, or mathematics

395. Describe an area of science (physics, biology, psychology, etc.) that interests you

396. Describe an English lesson you enjoyed

397. Describe a rule in your school that you agree or disagree with

398. Describe some useful skills you learned in a math class of your primary or high school

399. Describe an important skill which cannot be learned at school

400. Describe a piece of software you often use

401. Describe an app on your computer or mobile

402. Describe a practical skill you learned

403. Describe a skill that is difficult for you to learn

404. Describe your first day at school that you remember

405. Describe something you would like to learn in the future

406. Describe an important thing you learned (not at school or college)

407. Describe an impressive English lesson you had and enjoyed

408. Describe something you do that can help you concentrate on work/study

409. Describe a lesson you remember

410. Describe a thing you did to learn another language

生活类

411. Describe a meal that you invited others to your home or restaurants to have

412. Describe an unusual meal you had with your friends (in someone's home or in a restaurant)

413. Describe an unusual meal you had

414. Describe a dinner you had with your friends

415. Describe a dinner you really enjoyed

416. Describe a good habit which your friend has and you want to develop

417. Describe a journey you would like to go on by car

418. Describe a bicycle/motorcycle/car trip you would like to go

419. Describe a kind of music you liked in your childhood

420. Describe a long journey by car

421. Describe a long journey you had

422. Describe a short journey you disliked

423. Describe a short trip you have been on and would like to go on again

424. Describe a long walk you enjoyed

425. Describe a long walk you ever had

426. Describe a car or vehicle you would like to have in the future

427. Describe a method that helps you to save money

428. Describe a film you like

429. Describe a foreign film you enjoyed

430. Describe a movie that you dislike

431. Describe a movie you have watched recently and would like to watch again

432. Describe a movie that you want to recommend to others

433. Describe a movie you watched recently that you felt disappointed about

434. Describe a movie that made you think

435. Describe a film that made you laugh

436. Describe a season you like

437. Describe a song you heard when you were a child

438. Describe an interesting song you like

439. Describe a special trip you would like to take

440. Describe a sport you have learned for the first time

441. Describe a sport you like

442. Describe a water sport you would like to try in the future

443. Describe a story or novel that was particularly interesting to you

444. Describe a story someone told you and you remember

445. Describe an activity or a sport you do that is a little expensive

446. Describe an article you read from magazines or Internet about healthy life

447. Describe an exciting sport you like

448. Describe an interesting conversation you had with others

449. Describe an interesting TV program

450. Describe a film or a TV program that made you laugh

451. Describe an interesting website you often visit

452. Describe a website you often visit

453. Describe the differences your first mobile phone made to your life

454. Describe your favorite TV program or radio program

455. Describe your favorite house or apartment

456. Describe your ideal house or apartment

457. Describe the ideal house you would like to have

458. Describe a house or an apartment you would like to live in

459. Describe something or activity you do to stay healthy

460. Describe a trip that you went on by public transportation

461. Describe a time when you were shopping in a street market

462. Describe a party that you went to

463. Describe a sport that you have watched (on TV) before and you would like to try

464. Describe an experience of online shopping

465. Describe a problem you had while shopping online or in a store

466. Describe a line (or a few words) that you remember from a poem or song

467. Describe an art exhibition you recently saw

468. Describe a beautiful sky you enjoyed seeing

469. Describe a game show or a quiz program you watched on TV or online

470. Describe a performance you watched recently

471. Describe a sports program you enjoy watching

472. Describe a new development in the area where you live (e. g. shopping mall，park)

473. Describe a live sports match

474. Describe someone or something that made a lot of noise

家庭类

475. Describe a family (not your own) that you like

476. Describe a family celebration you attended

477. Describe a family member you spend most time with

478. Describe a family member you would like to spend most time with

479. Describe a family member you would like to work with in the future

480. Describe a happy family event in your childhood

481. Describe something you would like to do with one of your family members

482. Describe something you enjoy doing with an old person in your family

483. Describe a leisure activity you do with your family

484. Describe a family member you are proud of

抽象类

485. Describe a decision that took you a long time to make

486. Describe an important decision that you made

487. Describe an important decision you made with the help of others

488. Describe a good decision you made recently

489. Describe a difficult decision that you once made

490. Describe a dream you had

491. Describe a goal you want to achieve in the future

492. Describe a good service that a company or shop offers

493. Describe a good service you received

494. Describe a group work you took part in

495. Describe a piece of advice someone gave to you

496. Describe a piece of good news that you read from newspaper or magazine

497. Describe a piece of good news that you received from TV or Internet

498. Describe a piece of good news that you heard about someone you know well

499. Describe a piece of international news you have just recently heard

500. Describe a prize you won

501. Describe a prize you would like to win

502. Describe a traditional festival you have experienced or heard of

503. Describe an ambition you have not achieved yet

504. Describe an important conversation you had

505. Describe an interesting tradition in your country

506. Describe a tradition in your country
507. Describe a kind of weather you like
508. Describe an interesting talk or speech you heard recently
509. Describe an invention that has changed the world in a positive way
510. Describe an invention that is useful in your daily life
511. Describe an achievement that you are proud of
512. Describe a memorable story told by someone
513. Describe a period of history that you think was interesting
514. Describe a piece of technology you like (not computer-related)
515. Describe a piece of technology you own that you feel is difficult to use
516. Describe a competition (e.g. talent show) you would like to take part in
517. Describe a contest/competition you would like to participate in
518. Describe a recent development in your city or town
519. Describe something you want to do for a long time but you haven't done yet
520. Describe a risk you have taken which had a positive result
521. Describe a piece of advice you received on choosing your major or work
522. Describe your grandparent's job
523. Describe the most important message you have ever received
524. Describe a piece of news that local people are interested in
525. Describe a (jigsaw) puzzle
526. Describe a traditional celebration (a festival or ceremony) in your country that you enjoy
527. Describe a complaint that you made and you were satisfied with the result
528. Describe a rule that you don't like
529. Describe a natural talent you want to improve
530. Describe an argument two of your friends had
531. Describe a kind of weather that you like
532. Describe a disagreement you had with someone
533. Describe a historical period/moment you would like to learn more about

法律类

534. Describe a law about the environment you would like to see in the future
535. Describe a law about the environment
536. Describe a law or regulation about environmental protection
537. Describe a good law in your country

其他

538. Describe an interesting animal you have seen
539. Describe a wild animal you saw